Hypernomics

Hypernomics

Using Hidden Dimensions to Solve Unseen Problems

DOUG HOWARTH

WILEY

For general information on our other products and services or for technical support, please contact our Customer Care Department within the United States at (800) 762-2974, outside the United States at (317) 572-3993 or fax (317) 572-4002.

Wiley also publishes its books in a variety of electronic formats. Some content that appears in print may not be available in electronic formats. For more information about Wiley products, visit our web site at www.wiley.com.

Library of Congress Cataloging-in-Publication Data is Available:

ISBN 9781394208883 (Cloth)
ISBN 9781394208906 (ePDF)
ISBN 9781394208890 (ePub)

Cover Design: Wiley
Cover Image: © filo/Getty Images
Author Photo: Courtesy of the Author

SKY10062325_121223

Contents

Introduction

"Man's mind, stretched by a new idea, never goes back to its original dimensions."

Oliver Wendell Holmes, Jr.

Times were tough. Too many omelets to make. Not enough eggs. So, the woodcutter and his wife hatched a plan. We will abandon the kids deep in the woods, far from home; they schemed aloud, within earshot of the youngsters in the next room. With them, we starve. Without them, we eat. Once they're gone, we will be fine, the parents told themselves.

There was a way around that, the kids figured. They decided we'd get some white pebbles and drop them behind us as we walked into the woods. Then, after we are alone, we will follow them back in the moonlight. In this way, Hansel and Gretel made it back to their home.[1]

So, what are *you* to do when you are in uncharted territory? An economic territory, that is.

Do what Hansel and Gretel did.

Plot the dots.

If there were only one sentence to explain this book, that would be it.

Everything else follows from that.

Why Hansel and Gretel wanted to return to a place where they were unwelcome is anyone's guess. But notice what they did in the process. They laid out a trail of high-contrast dots (the bleached pebbles) that traced the way home. Going in another direction might lead them deeper into the woods or, worse yet, into the paths of mythical animals involved in other incredible fairytales (say, a talking Big Bad Wolf[2] since they are Grimm Brothers' characters). Instead, they constructed a plan.

Without the rocks, they had no point of reference. With them, they had a way home.

So, why would you plot the dots or, more precisely, the market dots? In part, you will do it for the same purpose as Hansel and Gretel—so you will not become lost. Beyond that, you will find many more reasons to plot the dots within the framework this book describes for the first time. H & G found their way home, sure. Did they find their *optimized* way home? They will never know.

1

You can.

In our observations about market dots, we are not talking about pebbles, rocks, or pieces of the Earth, though we will see many analogies to the Earth's geography. So precisely what kinds of dots are we addressing?

We will look at dots representing *value, demand,* and *cost.*

As used in this book, these dots typically relate to goods and services in markets. We'll find that when it comes to economic activity, buyers in markets collectively self-organize in ways we can discover, portray, analyze, and exploit using dots. Understanding this self-organization is crucial for buyers, sellers, and new market entrants. We'll also examine other realms in which approaches used here may prove helpful.

Importantly, we will find that doing this shows us the limits markets face, how buyers change their behaviors when prices and features change, and where the competition lies—and where it does not.

Because we need to know where the dots (read that as competitors) are and where they are not, in so doing, we'll be throwing away the hypothetical constructs of what we now call modern or Neoclassical economics in favor of the empirical approaches that Hypernomics employs uniformly.

We will prove that consumers ultimately determine both value and demand. In these systems, we always have left-hand or green dots for value and opposing right-hand or red dots for demand, each of equal height, representing different aspects of the same product in linked adjoining realms. We will want to hold them, remove them from the flat of a page, and turn them into spheres. The ones on the right match the ones on the left, and both have the same distance from the base. We have a pair for every product we buy, representing a dual state—with left and right spheres.

Dr. John Snow was one of the first researchers to plot the dots with significant effect. A cholera outbreak besieged the Soho district of London, United Kingdom, where he lived in 1854. Determined to find the source, Dr. Snow plotted the Soho deaths from cholera using dots, one dot to a person. He discovered their locus at the Broad (now Broadwick) Street water pump, which he urged authorities to turn off. They did. The epidemic subsided.

Some have used dots or lines to represent troop movements on the battlefield. Interestingly, battles and markets have many things in common. We will use combat analogies in our study of markets and their changes over time.

However, people have not yet felt much need to plot the dots for their markets.

That changes now, as this book introduces Hypernomics (or Multidimensional Economics [ME]), a discovery about how customers make buying decisions and how those actions work with the producers' costs to provide goods and services.

These market dots representing individual products have deep meaning, both by themselves and taken together. Once analyzed, they reveal the inner workings of every market.

Green or left-hand dots stand for values, the prices buyers are willing to pay for products based on their features. What you are ready to shell out for a given good or service may differ from what your neighbor will gladly pay or what I will. Given enough dots for values, market patterns emerge as lines, inclined planes, or curved surfaces. Those patterns will reveal how people, in general, value a product, what features they like, and which attributes they want more than others. Overpriced or underpriced new products cause lost profits. Worst cases lead to product failures or bankruptcies.

At the same time and on the other hand, we have customer demand. With our right-hand dots plotted, we can find demand limits as fuzzy lines that we must identify and the market reactions to them that we will discover we are obliged to know. Producers expecting to sell goods and services far beyond customer-determined demand limits will find sales lagging below goals.

When we compare the consumers' left-hand dots for value and the right-hand dots for demand to producers' costs, as blue dots, we can determine profitability for past projects and predict it for future ones. We can map future outcomes like we plan a camping trip and find the best spots with the fewest neighbors.

We will have lots of dots. We need to have a wide-open space to hold them all. For that, we will go to the South Pole. We will need Elvis, too. Not the King himself, mind you. Elvis left the building some time ago. Instead, we will retrieve his home, that two-room place where he was born in Tupelo, a white clapboard shotgun shack, its central wall intersection with one of its outer walls squarely planted over the South Pole. The house will keep us warm and help us plot our dots. We will find that the House of Elvis is analogous to a pair of essential constructs, collectively known as coordinate systems, which allow us to plot items of interest.

Note to self. And to you, too. Let's leave our negativity at home. There are no negative regions here. Hypernomics will not abide by them.

That said, be aware that flexibility is essential for you and the dots within this new type of market analysis. Dots move, and we will need to accommodate and anticipate that.

We'll find that market dots are as fundamental to economic analysis as subatomic particles are to physics or cells are to biology. Just as we can make molecules from disparate elements and build bodies with dividing cells, we can consider the entire global economy in one view—if we plot and analyze enough dots.

The notion of how to account for the position of dots began nearly 400 years ago with the French philosopher and mathematician René Descartes.

Various stories abound about how Descartes came about his Cartesian coordinate systems in the early 1600s. Perhaps the one told most often describes him lying in bed, looking up, watching a fly (a moveable dot!) creep across the ceiling, and wondering how to define its position. Another relates how he went into an abandoned oven and thought about the nature of a location. He came to a pair of new ways to describe a place with mathematical precision relative to a point on a plane or in space. Centered on an origin, with two or three lines at right angles to one another for his two-dimensional and three-dimensional systems, we cannot overstate the importance of these arrangements to modern mathematics.

By design, these systems necessarily entertained negative numbers. The notion of negative spaces is crucial in many instances. A bird flying with an airspeed of 20 miles per hour head-on into a 30-mile-per-hour wind moves negatively at 10 miles per hour relative to a fixed point on the ground. When loaded at sea, boats routinely find a portion of their hulls below the waterline, which Cartesian coordinate systems can describe as negative positions in space (often using the "waterline" as an axis).

By the time Descartes came up with his systems, scientists had long had the notion of front, back, left, right, up, and down to describe physical space. Therefore, his use of orthogonal axes made sense. Physicists, engineers, and mathematicians the world over loved it. No one seriously questions the utility of the Cartesian coordinate systems.

This book certainly does not.

But consider this: Are we, in all instances, bound to them? Are those schemes designed for the physical universe the end-all for economics?

Do we *require* negative dimensions?

Must we have right-angled axes?

It turns out that the answer to all of these questions is "no," as we will see throughout the following chapters.

Thus, this is a book about economic phenomena across multiple market dimensions. It bridges the fields of microeconomics and macroeconomics, and places them in a single collapsible and expandable worldview. It provides for the exhaustive study of any market or multiple or all markets simultaneously. We begin with four axes to describe any market and add three dimensions for each added market. This construct has no upper limit to the number of axes within it.

These observations about markets necessarily require novel ways to consider them. The most important of these new techniques in *Hypernomics: Using Hidden Dimensions to Solve Hidden Problems* (hereafter, *Hypernomics*) involves 1) the Law of Value and Demand, 2) Four-Dimensional

Coordinate System, 3) Five-Dimensional Coordinate System, and 4) N-Dimensional Coordinate System. This book addresses all of these concepts.

This book is the first of its kind at the time of its writing. That makes it dissimilar from others you have read about economics and may make this book appear very different from what you think you know. However, the phenomena described herein with these new constructs can trace their existence to the very first markets, which defines this book primarily as discovery rather than invention. It offers new views of transactions that date back to initial exchanges of goods and services between people, and trace through to modern times.

You, the reader, take part in them virtually every day.

Indeed, these trades of money for goods or services define markets. To many, market workings lie deeply embedded in mystery and are hard to discern. Myths abound. Solid facts are hard to find. This book's usefulness lies in its ability to separate economic facts from financial fiction and offer mathematically supportable ways to analyze markets empirically and determine the product features needed to enter given markets in an optimized fashion. Alternatively, given a product in a market, Hypernomics offers ways to enhance its profitability through price changes or feature modifications possibly.

So. . .what is Hypernomics? It is a new field of study, the name for which comes from:

Hyper-
> *pref.*
> *3. Existing in more than three dimensions: hyperspace.*
> *[Greek* huper–, *from* huper, *over, beyond;]*[3]

and

-nomy
> *suff.*
> *A system of laws governing or a body of knowledge about a specified field: aeronomy.*[4]

So, combining the suffix and the prefix, we get the singular noun that we call *Hypernomics:* "the study of forces in four or more dimensions."

Hypernomics unavoidably varies from standard representations that mimic the material world to do this. If you were to ask them, physicists would tell you that we live in a three-dimensional physical world. A line or axis describes movement forward and backward, one for right and left and another for up and down, with all axes at right angles or orthogonal.

If they consider it, time adds another dimension for physicists, a fourth. This three-dimensional framework works well for us in many respects. We can build buildings, boats, and aircraft or just about anything else with it and work out trajectories to distant objects. It allows us to solve a variety of mathematical problems.

While three-dimensional systems well describe physical properties, such arrangements do not do nearly as well with market economics. Physical dimensions bear little resemblance to economic dimensions. Concerning the empirical analysis of financial systems, as we will see through this book, a reasonably detailed analysis of any given market begins with four dimensions. Adding time gives us the fifth dimension. A deeper analysis reveals that other factors still influence demand, value, cost, and critical constraints on these dimensions. While not exhaustive, this book shows many such elements and their effects.

To date, most books on economics have used two dimensions to describe economic behavior. Changes over time have often been added as a third dimension in such analyses, though these studies typically have remained confined to straight and curved lines on a single plane. While usually contained in theoretical constructs, these approaches provide knowledge about various critical economic issues.

On the other hand, there are many questions in economics for which two and three-dimensional systems do not offer nearly enough flexibility or insight into the elements forcing or constraining their solutions, optimized or otherwise determined. This book directs itself to practical solutions to these real-world conditions. As these issues are diverse, cross the entire breadth of the world economy, and change over time, the study herein cannot possibly incorporate all the conditions that arise from such analysis. It amounts to a primer on the subject, a first cut. That stated, it offers new and valuable empirical ways to analyze markets to place products with justifiable reasons for success.

We will begin our study in two dimensions, as do many other texts. Then, we will expand our analysis to include three, four, five, and eventually n dimensions. While the limits of this text necessarily force us into two-dimensional representations of multiple dimensions, we will find that we can easily create a seven-dimensional model with a three-dimensional printer, creating physical market models that we can hold in our hands. We will do this not for show or academic exercise, but because this type of study reveals several important classes of analysis not attainable with other frameworks.

You may not have entertained such notions previously. That said, no matter what your background in business, economics, or mathematics is, you have everything at your disposal needed to become fluent with the most salient elements of Hypernomics. There are two significant reasons for this.

First, while this book offers different perspectives, it uses everyday objects you are familiar with to depict them. The most complicated visual frameworks you will encounter look like an extendable mirror, oddly shaped pie, or vertical Rolodex. These structures are the basis of the new coordinate system at the core of *Hypernomics*. You have undoubtedly seen bed sheets. Imagining sheets suspended over floors is also handy, as they represent the responses from buyers and suppliers alike. Finally, when it comes to visualization, the last distinct element you will need is the ability to imagine lines, which can take on many shapes. We must examine several types of them to represent economic forces adequately.

Second, and more familiarly, this book describes something you already intuitively know—your economic behavior and that of your friends, family, and everyone else. Hypernomics does not address some arcane concepts, such as String Theory, that you do not see yourself affecting in any discernible fashion. Among other elements, it addresses buyers' influence on the prices of goods and services provided to them in markets. As the book repeatedly emphasizes in various ways, markets are not hypothetical institutions you read about in books, magazines, or newspapers. In their most basic sense, markets consist of two groups: sellers and buyers. Have you ever purchased some vegetables? Bought electronics? Subscribed to a wireless service? You likely have made all these purchases at some time in your life. In every case, you helped form the market for the products in question. . .as a buyer. We will see how you valued the products you purchased and how others in the same markets made their value estimations. Subsequent purchases support sustainable prices in a process known as Value Estimating.

Understanding the worth of products, as revealed empirically through analysis of the markets themselves, is the key to understanding the Law of Value and Demand. The Law of Supply and Demand, about which you may have passing or even detailed knowledge, is, in fact, no "law" at all, as the Law of Value and Demand reveals. This is not to say that more than ample or limited supplies do not affect prices, which they empirically do. Instead, the Law of Value and Demand points out that outside of single-feature commodities (as, say, pure gold or silver or crude oil of a given grade), the would-be upward-sloping supply curves, as shown in many economics books in support of the Law of Supply and Demand, simply do not exist. Many markets have wide ranges of products with varying prices and quantities sold. Because of this, there are no sustainable market equilibriums in which supply curves and demand curves intersect at a single point to derive the quantities sold and price of goods for these markets, as Neo-Classical Economists would have you believe.

Instead, markets, like your body, manage to keep working through sustainable disequilibria. You can walk if your muscle power can overcome

Earth's gravity. Ships move forward if they have more thrust than drag. Helicopters rise skyward when they produce more lift than their weight. In much the same fashion, markets continue to function when producers sell goods or services for more than their costs and if, at the same time, they satisfy their consumers' value propositions consistent with their demand limits.

While long-standing point solutions for equilibriums for entire markets do not exist, there are special classes of vertical lines for individual products known as Profit Lines. Such lines describe per-unit profits of given goods or services and two or more of their features, costs, prices, and, in another dimension, their quantities sold.

The determination of Profit Lines turns out to be helpful.

Not having this information leaves market analysis, product formulation, and revenue projections to guesswork, which can be financially dangerous. We will entertain a few instances where such investigations went wanting and show how the producers of the products in question suffered gravely because of it. Sometimes, simple errors cost hundreds of millions to billions of dollars. Indeed, those producers would have instead kept those dollars in their pockets. Hypernomics shows how this is possible.

Even with the best applications of Hypernomics, it is quite possible to miss the most favorable positions in market spaces. You can follow a map and still get off course. However, using it allows you to visualize your destination. With a map in hand and eyes open to see what changes along the way, you have a better chance of getting there.

This dramatic break from conventional thinking often forces a particular organization on this book. In many chapters, a short section addresses the Neoclassical (or modern) Economics view of a specific topic to state the mainstream thinking on the subject to date very briefly. Immediately following this section is the Hypernomics viewpoint on the same subject. While the latter area will necessarily have to entertain some analytic geometry to get specific points across, separate endnotes address these topics more thoroughly, with more detailed mathematics supporting such analyses. Readers pressed for time who want to understand Hypernomics can forgo the details in those endnotes as the text within each chapter introduces the subject. Those who want to dive deeper into the workings of the economy and these new structures to describe them will likely find those endnotes helpful. They allow readers to recreate the results or extrapolate the topic at greater length. Vignettes sprinkled throughout the book show Hypernomics in action.

But enough talking about what we are going to see. Let's look at it.

Let's put some dots under the microscope.

CHAPTER 1

A Brief History of Position and Direction

"The day science begins to study non-physical phenomena, it will make more progress in one decade than in all the previous centuries of existence."

Nikola Tesla

ANCIENT MAPS

"Here are Dragons" (*HC SVNT DRACONES* in the original Latin). These are the words of warning on the Lenox Globe (c. 1510) near the eastern coast of Asia. Such admonitions were common during the early Renaissance, as cartographers laced uncharted regions with hippos, lions, and sea monsters on their maps to scare away explorers. The unknown was terrifying. It still is.

Not knowing a safe way to get to the clean water on the Serengeti can get you killed. Every cave dweller knew that. What they needed to know was where the bad routes lay. Survival, then as now, depended on learning how to get from here to there in one piece.

You do not want to die of thirst. Yet, you do not want to have to guess about how to get to a river in the safest fashion, either. If you are on an isolated hike, something as simple as a badly sprained ankle can be fatal. You may need to deal with the good paths, the obstacles, the predators, the people along the way against whom you compete, and those with whom you conduct commerce—all of them to stay alive. What to do? Where to go? How to do it?

Humans have many capabilities brought on by millions of years of evolution. Our ancestors demonstrated our faculty for abstraction in the Serengeti, where researchers found some of the first stone tools, and animal remains together, suggestive of early hominin mutual support dating back roughly 2 million years ago. As members from that prehistoric campsite walked together across the often-uneven Olduvai Gorge, they must have seen the dangers of the terrain and the predators. Marches like those going on over the millennia may have forced the hikers to speak for the first time. The first cliff avoided, the lion attack thwarted, or an enemy fought off due to the first vocalized warning must have been quite a heady moment. Language was here to stay. The more information early humans could convey to one another, the better. Clearly, in our digital age, this trend continues.

Proto-languages appeared between 600,000 and 2.3 million years ago, with formal language developing only about 100,000 years ago. Written language, by contrast, only goes back about 5,500 years. In between, people discovered something often equally important. They found the art of map making.

Anthropologists have discovered that maps existed at least 6,000 years ago and may reach back 25,000 years, with the earliest recorded map-like representation of the terrain around Pavlov in the Czech Republic.

Imagine that your tribe has a rudimentary sense of this mapping technology (and none of your modern conveniences) as you live back in the Stone-Age Serengeti. Suppose your slightly older brother had drawn a diagram in the dirt showing the best way to get to the water. Maybe you would not have comprehended the sketch just a few years earlier, but now, with your growing cranial capacity and enhanced imagination, you do. You can understand its meaning. You see what to avoid and where to go. Now instead of having to dodge black mambas as they lunge at you out of their hole in the outcropping beside a ledge, you have a drawing that shows where they live. Where are the lions' dens? What parts of the river should you avoid because the black rhinos and crocodiles like to frequent them? To which location did the warring tribe move? A well-drawn map could show you all of that and more.

Of course, not everyone is out to get you. Maps can show you directions from one place to another and help you determine what you might find when you get there. Once again, suppose you were back in Olduvai Gorge with your brother and the rest of your tribe. You know you are good at making stone hand axes, but you cannot easily access figs. Meeting people at what might have been the first version of a marketplace would allow you to exchange one for another. You have to know where to find the market. It has a position. How do you get there? What are the directions to it?

The earliest maps were local by nature, describing as they did the surroundings near the cartographers who created them, and virtually all of the mapmakers drew their representations of the nearby geography as if from a bird's-eye view, as in Figure 1.1.

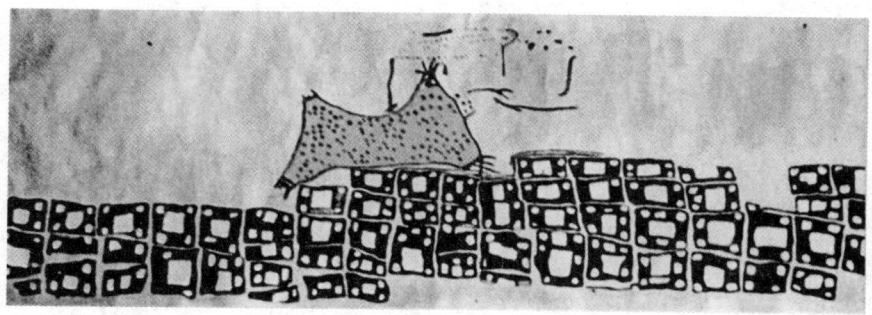

FIGURE 1.1 Perhaps the earliest authenticated map in the world is this one depicting a town in west-central Turkey, hard against an erupting volcano. It dates to about 6,000 BCE.[1]

Anaximander's Map of the World

FIGURE 1.2 Anaximander's world map, c. 570 BCE.[2]

While mapmaking graduated to regional and worldwide scales, the tradition of representing the countryside as if we are looking down on them from the sky continues. As we will discover in Hypernomics, however, thoroughly entertained economic landscapes require different types of imagery.

There was a long transition from local to global maps. Credit for inventing the first map of the known world goes to Anaximander of Miletus,

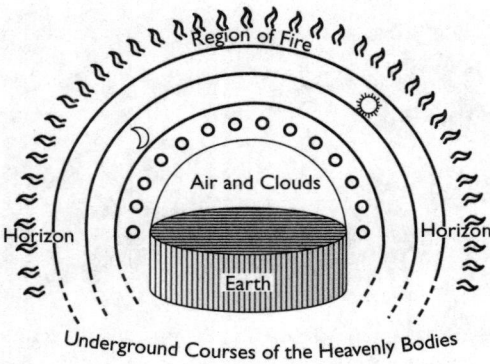

FIGURE 1.3 Side view of Anaximander's world-view, c. 570 BCE.[3]

around 570 BCE. Anaximander imagined the world as cylindrical and drum-shaped, and, when viewed from above, it consisted of Europe, Libya, and Asia surrounded by a circular ocean.

The idea that a ring of ocean circled the known dry land dates back to Homer, though he never recorded it.[4] This map, shown in Figures 1.2 and 1.3, may seem crude by modern standards. However, it offered its users some information they never had before in a single document: its worldview offered physical relationships between landmasses and seas and oceans, thus highlighting physical borders for all to see. It spelled out the relative positions of Europe, the Black Sea, Asia, and the Nile River and indicated the perceived sizes of all its landmasses and oceans. It, of course, lacks many of the features we have come to expect in modern maps. It has poorly defined coastlines; its proportions are inaccurate; the map shows rivers running from one sea to another. Moreover, the Earth's shape is more like a sphere than a drum.

Importantly, though, it offers a view of the world. Just because it is not nearly as accurate in its view of what we now call modern maps does not mean it was not extremely important in its time. As the biologist Richard Dawkins points out, "Vision that is 5 percent as good as yours or mine is very much worth having in comparison with no vision at all. So is 1 percent vision better than total blindness. And 6 percent is better than 5, 7 percent better than 6, and so on up the gradual continuous series."[5] With Anaximander's map, people knew the relative positions of Greece to Italy and Greece to Egypt and Turkey, the main rivals of that era along the Mediterranean. Knowing competitors' positions is always vital.

GEOGRAPHY BEGINS

Centuries later, Eratosthenes (275–195 BCE), in addition to being the first person to use the word *geography* as he invented the field, devised meridians, or north to south lines, and "parallels," imaginary east to west lines, which divided the Earth into sectors. We see his map in Figure 1.4. Eratosthenes spent a significant effort figuring out the distance between his home in Alexandria, Egypt, and the ancient Egyptian city of Swenet (now known as Aswan), which he believed to lie on the Tropic of Cancer. Using the distance between the two towns and a gnomon that he placed in Alexandria at noon at the summer solstice, he worked out the circumference of the Earth. He may have been accurate to within 1% of the actual figure. His earth grid system allowed people to calculate their position globally for the first time. Every point on the planet would forever have its place designated by its latitude and longitude.

MATH AND POSITION PROBLEMS

Mathematics took quite a bit longer to work out an analogous coordinate system. In 1637, working independently, René Descartes and Pierre de Fermat came up with the ideas that formed the bases for the Cartesian coordinate systems.

From Descartes' standpoint, the story (or myth) of its discovery was that he was lying in bed and observed a fly enter his room. Wondering how he could portray its position as it crawled across a wall, he envisioned the two-dimensional system. He came up with the three-dimensional design as it flew about the room. When other mathematicians enhanced these fledgling systems, they became the two-dimensional and three-dimensional Cartesian coordinate systems displayed in Figures 1.5 and 1.6, respectively. These systems allowed the development of calculus by Sir Isaac Newton and Gottlieb Leibnitz, who each separately derived this new branch of mathematics. Newton started his work in about 1666, but published nothing about it until 1693 and only gave his complete account of it in 1704. Meanwhile, Leibnitz offered his full description of the subject in 1684. The legendary dispute over who should have credit for the discovery of calculus has ended as both men have had their contributions recognized.

John von Neumann said, "The calculus was the first achievement of modern mathematics, and it is difficult to overestimate its importance. I think it defines more unequivocally than anything else the inception of

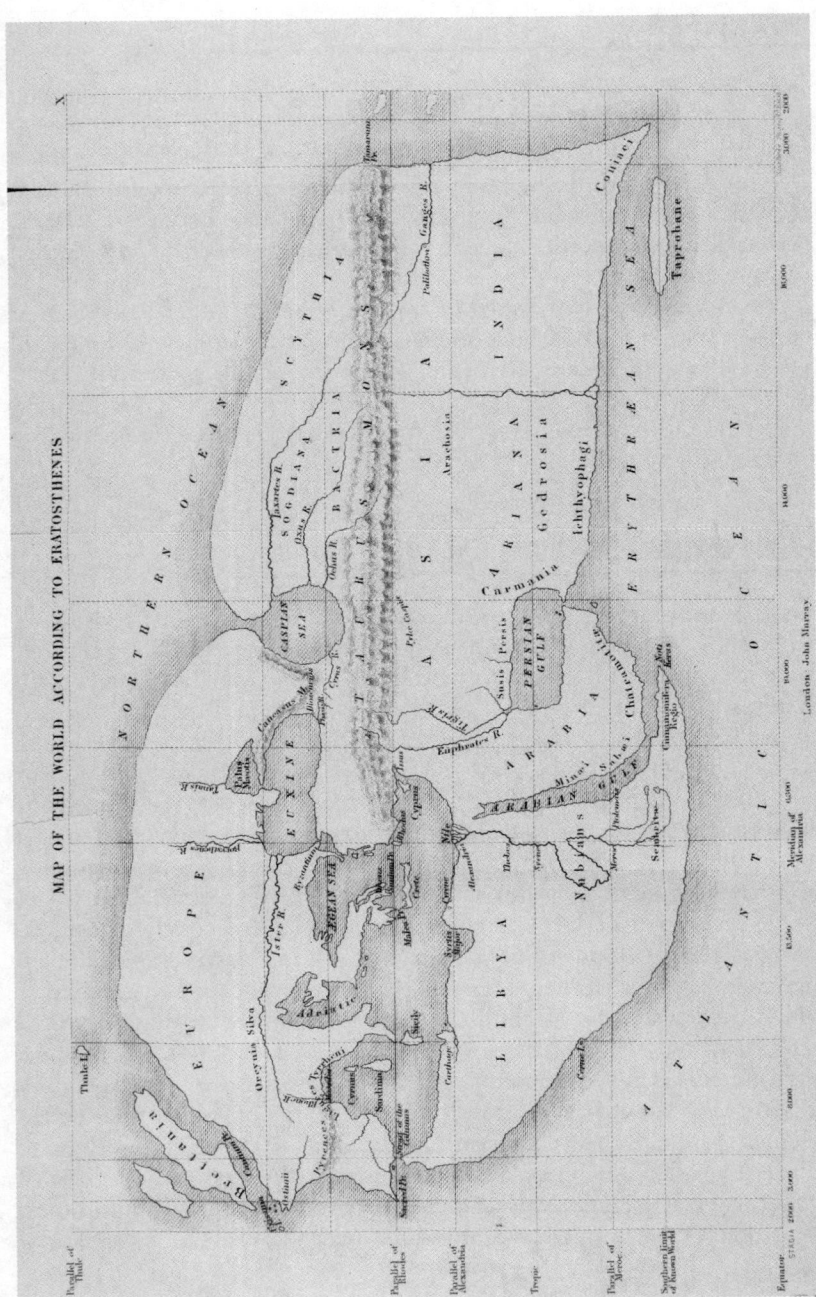

MAP OF THE WORLD ACCORDING TO ERATOSTHENES

FIGURE 1.4 Here is a world map by Eratosthenes, c. 194 BCE. Note the use of parallels and meridians, an invention by Eratosthenes and a first in mapmaking.[6]

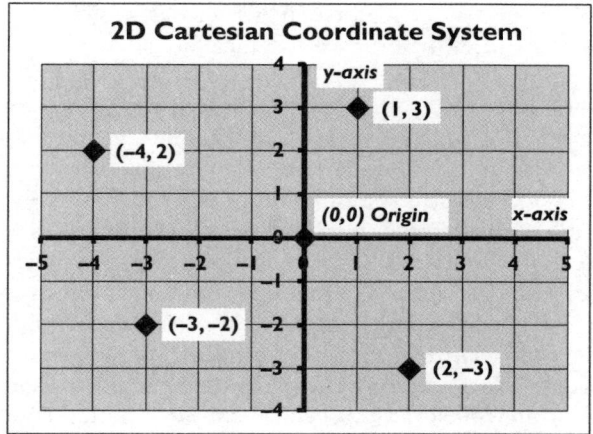

FIGURE 1.5 The 2D Cartesian coordinate system.[7]

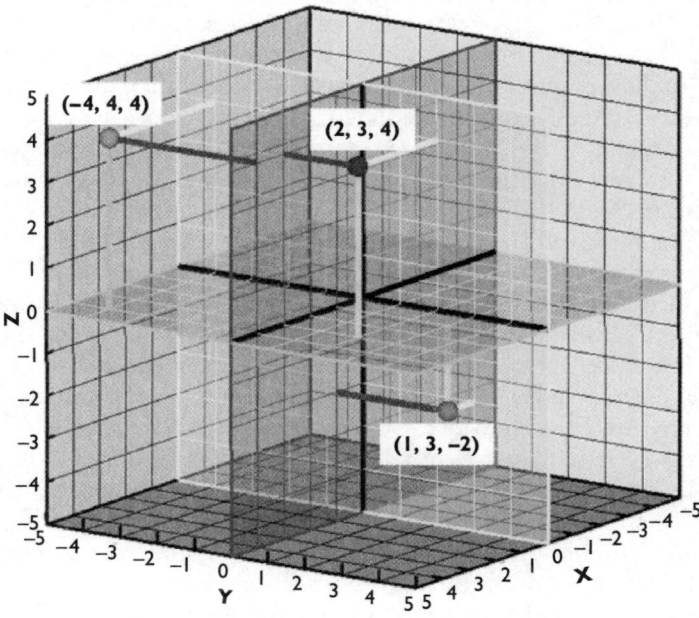

FIGURE 1.6 The 3D Cartesian coordinate system.[8]

modern mathematics, and the system of mathematical analysis, which is its logical development, still constitutes the greatest technical advance in exact thinking."[9]

While "exact thinking" is not always possible in using the principles from Hypernomics, given that it studies the statistics and analytic geometries of consumer and producer behaviors, the drive to be *more exact* is always a goal. As we will discover later, exactness is a function of our accuracy (how far away from our target are we?) and precision (how broad are our errors?). We shall strive to improve both. Goods and services face competing products with a wide variety of features. It is not enough to design and build a product and see "what the market will bear." Many companies do that. Many products fail. But what if we could *map competitors' positions* and *determine customers' directions* about product features in advance? If we could do that, we could minimize competition while offering clients what they want, do not have, and can afford. This may seem impossible, but it is really at the heart of this book—and it turns out that we can do just that. However, we first need to know positions and directions in an economic space to enable that.

As sailors have long known, having a position is not the same as knowing your place. Understanding one's location and heading on the ocean is incredibly crucial. While determining latitude was relatively easy on the sea centuries ago, finding longitude was not. Oceans do not offer the stable, immovable surfaces that dry land affords, and calculations of east-west locations were often fraught with significant errors. Given that the Earth rotates 360° per day or 15° per hour (in mean solar time), time and longitude have a direct relationship. With the prime meridian (0° west longitude) in Greenwich, United Kingdom, and Denver, Colorado, at 105° west longitude, we know that if it is noon in Greenwich, it is 5:00 a.m. in Denver. We know this not only concerning the time within each city's time zone but also, more significantly, in the sense that the sun will be at its highest point in the sky on any given day in Denver seven hours after that happens in Greenwich. Because of this phenomenon, knowing one's longitude with the requisite exactitude to navigate effectively and avoid known obstacles is possible *if* one has a chronometer with sufficiently high precision. In the early 1700s, however, sea-faring timepieces could not regularly offer the accuracy needed to avoid disaster.

After leaving Gibraltar on September 29, 1707, less than a month later, on October 22 (November 2 on the new calendar), some of the 21 ships returning to Portsmouth, England, led by Commander-in-Chief of the British Fleets Sir Cloudesley Shovell, found themselves badly off course. Believing they were nearly 100 nautical miles south-southeast of where they were, four ships crashed into the low rocks off the Isles of Scilly and sank.

At least 1,400 and perhaps over 2,000 marines, sailors, and officers died in the disaster.

In the aftermath of this catastrophe, finding that errors in navigation were the root cause of the event, the British government passed the Longitude Act in 1714, which established the Board of Longitude and offered large cash prizes to anyone who could accurately determine longitude at sea. John Harris, an English carpenter turned clockmaker, largely solved this problem with his series of timepieces developed over four-plus decades. King George III tested one of the later versions in 1772 and found it accurate to within one-third of a second per day. At sea level, one minute of angle along the equator or a meridian is approximately equal to one nautical mile, which is exactly 1,852 meters or about 6,076 feet by international agreement. With 60 seconds per minute, each second is about 101 feet. With John Harris's chronometer to King George III, a third of a second error translates to about 34 feet per day. Had that instrument been available to Sir Cloudesley Shovell's navigators and properly used, the east-west course error over the 23 days since they began their voyage and crashed into the rocks would have been about 780 feet, not the error measured in dozens of miles that they had.

Note that the position problem for the Scilly misadventure was not only one of mistaken longitude but one of errant latitude as well. The badly miscalculated estimate of their north-south position may have been due to human error that added to the miscalculation in predicted longitude and prevented ships from finding safe passage through the English Channel. History shows that that combination on the high seas was deadly.

By contrast, when the latest product goes bust in the market, people seldom die over it. Fortunes dedicated to its development may be forever lost, and companies funding such products are placed under deep financial stress. They wonder what went wrong. Mariners discovered they had to know their positions and headings and compare them to their charts to make it safely to their destinations. Mathematicians found they could describe instantaneous points in space, direction, speed, and acceleration for various objects. At the same time, companies have long speculated: What must we do to become more profitable? What position and direction should we take?

At the same time King George III wandered about London with John Harris's chronograph, a Scottish philosopher wondered about economics. In 1776, after 10 years of working on it, Adam Smith published *An Inquiry into the Nature and Causes of the Wealth of Nations* (usually shortened to *The Wealth of Nations*). This was the first deep look into the subject, and because of that, many modern scholars hail Adam Smith as the "father of modern economics."

As the field was wide open as he invented it, he focused his study on what most now call *macroeconomic* behaviors. This field addresses the structure and behavior of a national, regional, or world economy. This contrasts with *microeconomics*, which studies the component elements of national economies, including firms, households, and consumers.

While Smith addressed many topics, we shall concentrate on one of his most enduring points. This is his notion of "an invisible hand," or, more broadly and less figuratively, the enlightened self-interest of producers to give the public what it needs.

Smith described that idea in this way:

> *As every individual, therefore, endeavours as much as he can, both to employ his capital in the support of domestic industry, and so to direct that industry that its produce maybe of the greatest value; every individual necessarily labours to render the annual revenue of the society as great as he can. He generally, indeed, neither intends to promote the public interest, nor knows how much he is promoting it. By preferring the support of domestic to that of foreign industry, he intends only his own security; and by directing that industry in such a manner as its produce may be of the greatest value, he intends only his own gain; and he is in this, as in many other cases, led by an invisible hand to promote an end which was no part of his intention. Nor is it always the worse for the society that it was no part of it. By pursuing his own interest, he frequently promotes that of the society more effectually than when he really intends to promote it.[10] . . . . It is not from the benevolence of the butcher, the brewer, or the baker, that we expect our dinner but from their regard to their own interest. We address ourselves, not to their humanity but to their self-love, and never talk to them of our own necessities but of their advantages.[11]*

That there are forces afoot that allow producers to maximize their gain and promote positive outcomes for their customers is a firmly held tenet in this book. In this regard, Hypernomics aligns itself with *The Wealth of Nations*. As we march further into the work at hand, however, we will discover those producers *must* promote their customers' interest in particular ways. Those ways will vary from market to market but always involve specific, *visible* product points relative to Value Space and Demand. Businesses can succeed to the fullest extent possible through the deliberate satisfaction of their clients. With this tenet, this book is diametrically opposed to *The Wealth of Nations*.

It was hard to understand until Hypernomics's observation that "visible hands" work throughout the economy. Consumers place values and limits on goods, which are readily discernible. The economic forces at work were not fully apparent to Smith, given his era's lack of data and mathematical modeling techniques. In modern times, however, we can make manifest "visible hands" within and across markets with enough research and mathematics. Correctly displayed, they allow us to see what had been previously unseen.

A previously invisible atmospheric occurrence became apparent after the 1883 eruption of the Krakatoa volcano. Observers noted that ejected ash went high into the atmosphere and flew in a fast, thin meandering river of air running west to east.[12] Initially called the "Krakatoa easterlies,"[13] we now call these phenomena the jet streams, as depicted in Figure 1.7. These air currents range in altitude from 23,000 to 52,000 feet, are one to three miles thick, up to hundreds of miles wide, and may run in length for thousands of miles. Once discovered, pilots from World War II flying from the United States to the United Kingdom could use these air columns to their advantage. They are powerful enough to add 100 miles per hour or more of ground speed from high-flying aircraft flying west to east or remove an equivalent amount for vehicles moving east to west. Predicting jet stream movements and strength is vital in modern aviation and weather forecasting. Knowing that jet streams are forceful, movable, and real are reasons to study them if your livelihood depends on them, even if you cannot always see them.

Adam Smith understood that fundamental forces are at work in the economy and created a landmark book to describe them. We now call his brand of study classical economics. While he addressed the idea of economic position little, if at all, he understood the notion of economic direction from the beginning. He noted, "[W]hen cultivation is extended over the greater part of the country...[then t]here is then more bread than butcher's meat. The competition changes its direction, and the price of butcher's meat becomes greater than the price of bread."[14] Mathematical explanations of the economy's position and direction were not yet apparent in Smith's era. Had they been, Smith likely would have employed those devices.

The ability to describe position and direction mathematically took a significant leap forward with the advent of regression analysis. Invented by Adrien-Marie Legendre in 1805[15] and refined by Carl Friedrich Gauss in 1809[16] and 1821,[17] regression analysis allows forecasters to find trends in data. Legendre and Gauss were tracking celestial bodies and needed a way to predict where those objects would be, based on where they had been. To do that, they had to invent and refine a process known as least squares regression.

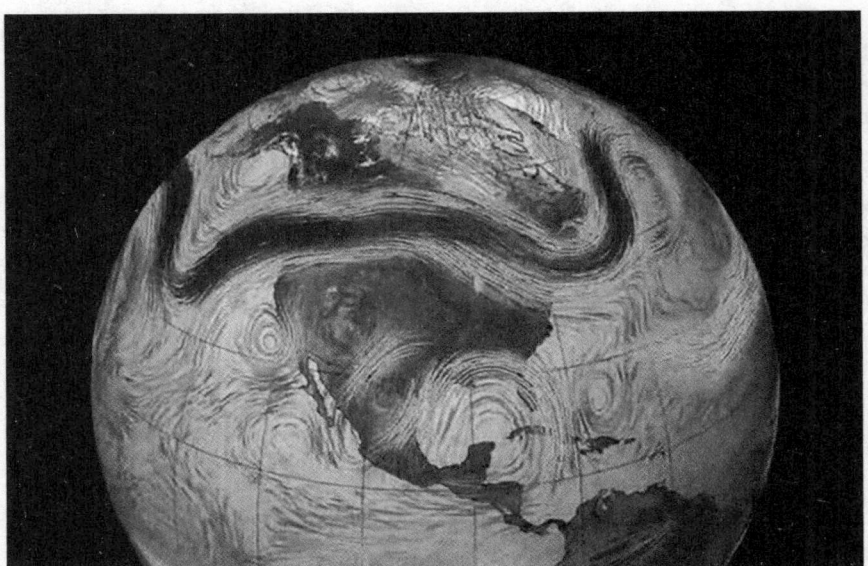

FIGURE 1.7 Usually invisible but always real: there are prevailing wind currents across the globe; the fastest of these are the jet streams capable of speeds of 200 miles per hour, which were unknown until 1883.
Note: NASA/Goddard Space Flight Center, 24 January 2012
This file is in the public domain in the United States because it was solely created by NASA. NASA copyright policy states that "NASA material is not protected by copyright **unless noted**".
Source: https://en.wikipedia.org/wiki/File:Aerial_Superhighway.ogv

Regression analysis considers the position of the points in a data set and finds the mathematical direction through them.

As shown in Figure 1.8, given a series of independent variables (in this case, engine size in cubic centimeters) and dependent variables (All-Terrain Vehicle or ATV prices) depicted as a series of ordered pairs (every dot on the figure represents the engine displacement as the horizontal component and price as the vertical element of a single ATV model), regression analysis finds the line of best fit through the data.[19] If that line satisfies specific established criteria, as does the one in Figure 1.8, we say it is statistically significant, meaning we can use it for predictions.[20]

Decades later, Alfred Marshall, with his 1890 book *Principles of Economics,* founded the field we now call neoclassical economics. Because of that, many recognize him as the father of modern economics (thus taking it from Smith). Along with Keynesian economics (which addresses macroeconomics), neoclassical economics (primarily concerned with microeconomics) dominates the mainstream study of the field today. As a practical matter,

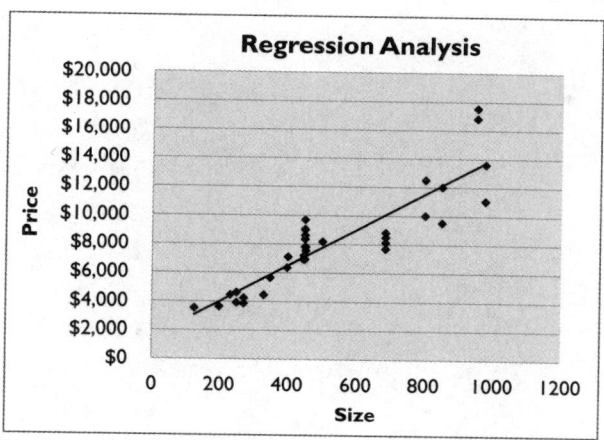

FIGURE 1.8 Making the invisible visible: regression analysis finds data trends that permit statistically significant predictions and forecasts.[18]

when most commentators talk about mainstream economics, they usually mean neoclassical economics for microeconomics and some mix of neoclassical and Keynesian economics for macroeconomics. (Some economists, Marshall included, believed that economics should take up philosophical questions in addition to those dealing purely with the math of markets. In his preface, Marshall argued, "Ethical forces are among those of which the economist has to take account.)"[21]

Hypernomics prefers to leave issues of fairness to the markets themselves, as it shows how buyers sort out their ways and means within and between markets, ultimately establishing value responses, demand curves, and prices. While many prefer beef to bombers, quantifiable markets exist for both when we do the analysis. In this respect, this book has no opinions, only observations and outcomes. It does think that losing money is a bad idea, however. It believes that diligent research produces less loss and more profit.

In *Principles*, Marshall laid out one of his most enduring ideas that neoclassical economics holds to this day, the equilibrium (or Law) of Demand and Supply, as shown in Figure 1.9 (which Marshall denoted).

In it, we have a downward sloping (from left to right) demand curve D.D.', which is indicative of people being willing to buy more of anything (in the horizontal direction, which modern neoclassical economists now denote as Q) if the price drops (along the vertical axis, which economists designate P). Simultaneously, we have an upward sloping (from left to right) supply curve S.S.'. Marshall and neoclassical economists find equilibrium at Point A, where the supply curve intersects the demand curve.

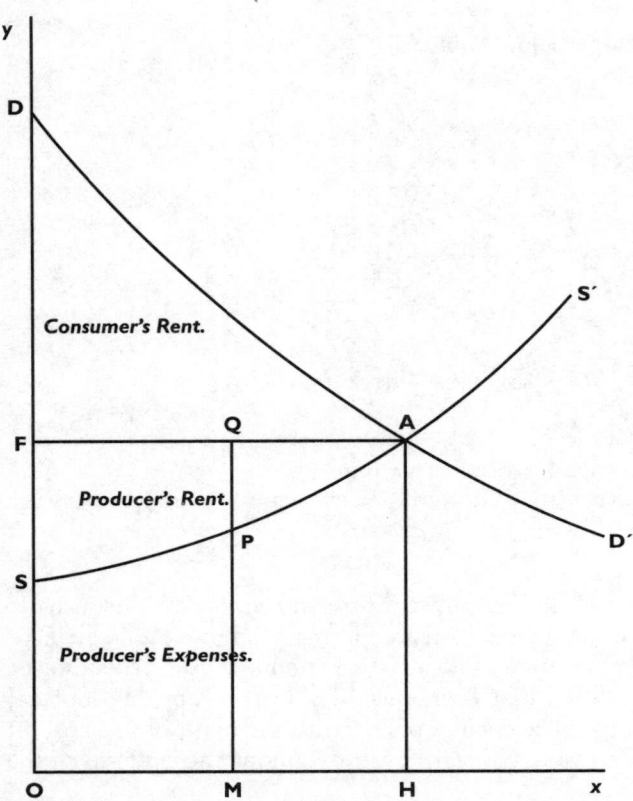

FIGURE 1.9 Alfred Marshall popularized the idea of supply and demand curves intersecting at a single sustainable equilibrium point with this diagram.[22]

This has been a primary modeling tool for economists for over 125 years at the time of this writing. The rationality of the model fits our expectations. Concerning demand, it makes sense that people buy less as the price increases and more when it falls. On the supply side, Figure 1.8 reveals, in one interpretation, that producers would like to make more products if they can sell them for a higher price. Who wouldn't, we wonder. In Marshall's words, the intersection of the two curves is a "typical case of stable equilibrium."[23]

Since this approach appeals to and develops through logic, we should take particular notice. Even though Legendre and Gauss offered ways to discover trends in data decades earlier, Marshall did not attempt to gather observations concerning demand or supply. We have none of Marshall's market positions (as ordered pairs in Figure 1.8) from which we can accurately determine direction. Given that demand deals with quantity and price, he could have gathered data on quantities sold, and prices received for the beef market. Had he done that, he could have proven that demand has a downward slope.

Hypernomics takes no issue with downward-sloping demand curves as the book proposes and then proves their existence, slopes, and intercepts using the techniques that Legendre and Gauss offered us. It is not enough, however, to "strike a line" representing demand and then propose that it has mathematical meaning. As we will observe, significance comes from statistical studies wrought from carefully constructed databases.

On the other hand, upward-sloping supply curves, thought by Marshall and others as ubiquitous, are much more disquieting. Think about what curves such as these mean. Since supply curves reflect producers' outlays, with quantity on the horizontal axis and dollars on the vertical axis, a rising supply curve means that costs increase as quantities increase. In the case of automobiles, since labor is the most significant cost component, if curves like this reflected reality, this would mean that workers, on average, take more time to accomplish tasks the more they perform them. Yet, study after study shows the opposite—they indicate that workers become *more* proficient with additional quantities produced. Costs *fall* over time. Exceptions may exist for the total expenses required to gather and deliver some refined elements (such as the purest silver, gold, and platinum, for example). However, when we combine material and labor expenses for virtually every other type of market, *costs decrease with added quantities.*

Thus, the notion of an upward-sloping supply curve is incorrect for most markets.

Because of this, the perception that stable equilibria form at the intersection points of supply and demand curves is also without merit. Much enamored with thermodynamics, some economists believe that economies work like fluid systems. Add hot red dye to the cool green dye and produce a lukewarm yellow tint. Both the resultant temperature and color are the inevitable results of equilibrium effects. Markets are similar to such systems, they believe. What holds for these systems should hold for the markets as well, they argue.

Once we plot competitors' positions and examine markets' directions provided to us by their customers, however, we discover something entirely different. The neoclassical view is unsupportable and unsupported. Markets do not resemble containers of miscible fluids.

Markets look like maps.

More precisely, markets look like battlefield maps.

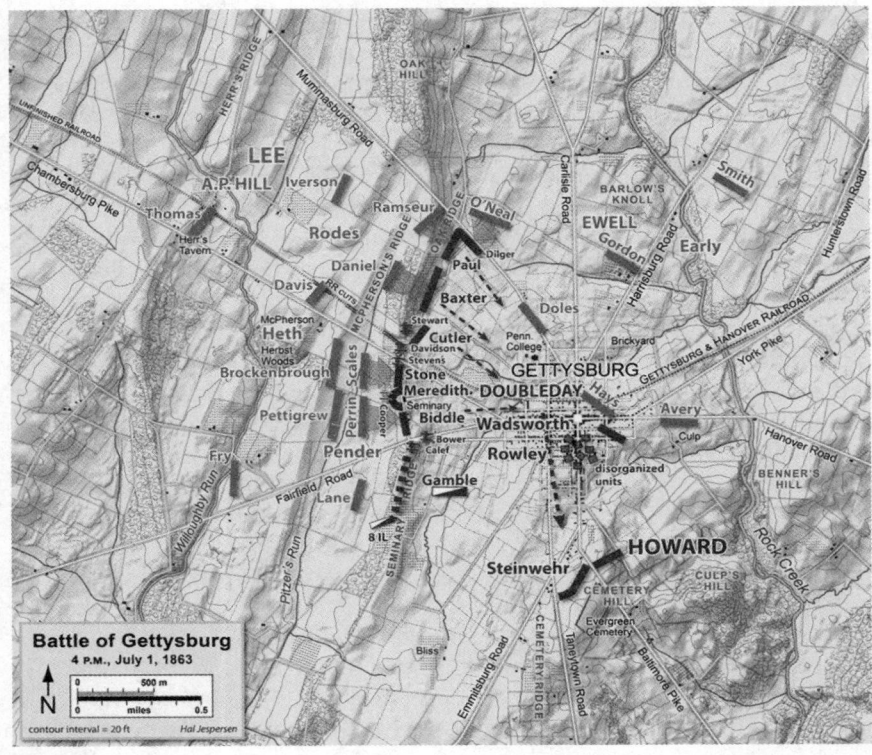

FIGURE 1.10   Confederates east, west, and north, Union in the center.[24]

In war, opposing forces stake out locations. As they line up for battle, their positions reflect their latitudes, longitudes, and altitudes. Armies like to fight from the highlands if possible. From Day 1 of the Battle of Gettysburg, Union and Confederate forces jockeyed for the position (as shown in Figure 1.10), looking for high ground to get to it and any other advantages that the landscape offered them.

Products have multiple features, which reveal their absolute locations on market maps and relative positions relative to their competitors (Figure 1.11). In many markets, however, each firm faces more than one opponent. In the 2013 market for Sport All-Terrain Vehicles (ATVs), eight producers offered various ATV combinations of engine and suspension packages. Some regions in this part of the larger market were highly contested—consider the region between 440 and 450 ccs on the horizontal axis and 17 to 22 inches of total suspension travel on the vertical. In this area, four manufacturers crammed in six models. While other features not pictured here enter into the customers' buying decisions, this region suffered from overcrowding. In

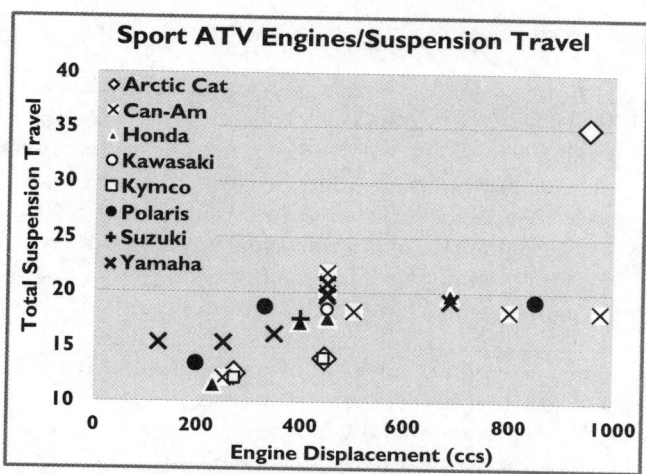

FIGURE 1.11 ATVs have many features; here, we look at two.[25]

a war, people die over disputed territory. In markets, products not valued as highly as their costs disappear. In any market region, customers collectively determine market splits to the producers, as they reward or penalize product features according to their preferences, which we must measure.

Customers care about many features[26] and shop in many markets. While demand curves are crucial, we will soon discover that the product value hinges on not only the quantity purchased but also whatever attributes the customers decide that they want and for which they are willing to pay. However, a critical difference between markets and battlefields is that there are multiple ways for multiple parties to win in the former. Winning in the market means selling products for more than they cost their producers to make them.

Given its conditions, optimizing in a market might mean extracting its maximum possible profit. Occasionally, favorable conditions can occur due to luck or being first in a new and promising market. Alternatively, such outcomes can come from hard work and good research with the proper tools. The latter method improves the chances of success.

A primary observation made possible by mapping the markets in such fashion as Figure 1.11 is that while producers could choose to go head-to-head with competitors and offer virtually the same products, perhaps at lower prices, to attract customers, they could instead decide to avoid their rivals to the fullest extent possible from the beginning. Instead of offering another ATV with 450 ccs of engine displacement and 18 inches of shock travel, producers can decide to make a vehicle that falls into the open market expanse with larger engines and more suspension travel. No one offers an ATV with suspension travel between 22 and 35 inches in this market segment. If models sell at either end of this range, what might happen for configurations in between?

Note that Figure 1.11 offers no insight into the features that ATV buyers likely find helpful. With this view, we have yet to learn how much they like larger engines or better suspensions. Furthermore, there is no mention of the number of seats, wheel options, or possible options such as fuel injection or power steering as they impact vehicle value. Just as importantly, with Figure 1.10, as we examine engine size and suspension travel as our axes, we cannot relate to customer demand, which has quantity and price as axes.

We observe that marrying ourselves to unrelated two-dimensional views limits our insight.

This, in turn, mandates expanding our view of market forces. We will employ some new methods and three new coordinate systems. We call this new approach Hypernomics, or Multidimensional Economics, or ME, for short.

Since Descartes brought the world three dimensions, our next logical step is to move on to four dimensions. Let us see what insights such systems provide us.

SUMMARY

As evinced through maps, position and direction have been necessary to humankind since prehistoric times. Knowing how to get from one place safely to another is a prime concern for everyone. Over 2,200 years ago, Eratosthenes devised the grid system that we use today, where latitude represents position relative to the north and south, and longitude depicts it east to west. Over 1,800 years later, Descartes invented his two- and three-dimensional plotting systems. Combined with Newton and Leibnitz's calculus, those systems allow mathematicians and physicists to depict position and direction. Work by Legendre and Gauss on the ordinary least squares regression method gave analysts the capacity to predict direction given historical positions. Adam Smith coined the term *the invisible hand* to characterize the economy, but had he thought to plot some of the information before him in a meaningful way, he may have revealed the "visible hands" first discussed in this book here centuries earlier. Preferring deduction and induction to observation, Alfred Marshall ignored ordinary least squares regression as he derived the Law of Supply and Demand. While downward-sloping demand curves greatly appeal to reason, upward-sloping supply curves do not. The often-held view that markets represent thermodynamic systems does not hold up under inspection. Markets instead look more like particular types of maps—those depicting battles. Current mapping techniques do not allow us to display all the information we want in one view. Hypernomics offers help in this regard with three new coordinate systems.

VIGNETTE: RESTAURANT MATH

"I was at this restaurant. The sign said, 'Breakfast Anytime.' So, I ordered French Toast in the Renaissance."

Steven Wright

Forget about ordering off the menu; first, you must get a seat.

It was never a slam dunk to get into our preferred local eatery. It was still more complicated once COVID-19 forced all patrons outside with social distancing. We began to fidget as we sat, waiting for some seats to open for us for the third weekend in a row. What to do? In an era where restrictions abounded, sometimes it was hard to see the options.

As it happened, we knew the owner and every boss in the place. I pulled our most-beloved manager aside and asked her if she would be willing to rearrange the furniture and make more money. I explained that a few large tables crowded out several smaller ones. Why not go from your arrangement (which was A) to a new one (which became B)? I asked. If you track the revenue changes, you'll be pleasantly surprised.

As shown in Figure 1.12, she did just that. Revenue went up by over 25% in two months. Unlike A, Setup B recognizes they face a demand curve, with more parties of one or two people than groups of five or more.

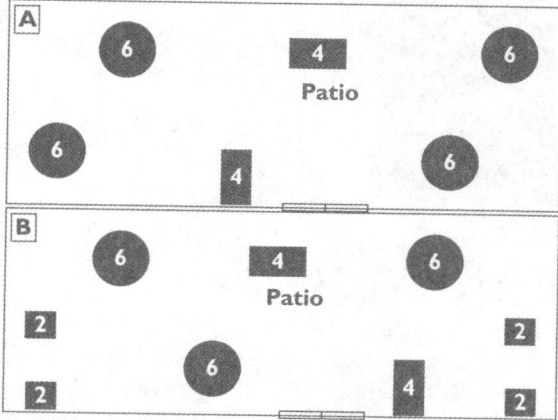

FIGURE 1.12 In May 2020, the COVID-19 pandemic forced our favorite eat-in and take-out restaurant to only seat people on its patio, configured as A. The problem with A was that many of the restaurant's parties consisted of one or two people. The patio filled quickly during peak periods, with many occupied tables mostly empty. To accommodate the small groups and free up the tables with more seats for larger parties, I suggested B. By July 2020, revenues increased by over 25%.[27]

So, the suggestion worked. But why?

The short answer is pattern recognition.

Over years of going there, one could see that there were consistently more parties of two than four or six at this eatery. Ideally, the restaurant might have kept records of party sizes by the day and time they came in, and we could appeal to that; but such accounts were unavailable here. Failing that, we might want to find more global data and see if that offers insight.

It turns out that broader data does give us a better picture of restaurant visits. According to a March 3, 2020, report from NPD.com, "Last year solo diners represented 35% of restaurant visits whereas parties of two represented 27% of visits; parties of three, 14%; parties of four, 12%; and parties of 5 or more, 13%."[28]

When we take that data, we can find a pattern we can observe in Figure 1.13. Significantly, the restaurant in question was over twice as likely to have a party of two versus one of four. Recognizing that fact enabled the establishment to grow its revenues in a down market.

Hypernomics is the study of finding patterns and putting them to work for us. We'll always look for patterns we can discover and employ.

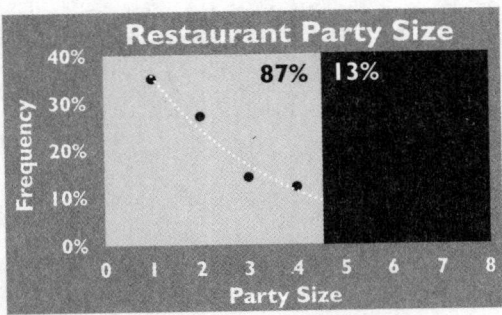

FIGURE 1.13   Restaurant visits.[29]

CHAPTER 2

Four-Dimensional Systems

"Space is big. You just won't believe how vastly, hugely, mind-bogglingly big it is. I mean, you may think it's a long way down the road to the chemist's, but that's just peanuts to space."

Douglas Adams

DOT PLOTS BEGIN

As we discovered, maps have played an important part in history. They let us know the limits we face, the competitors we will encounter, and where we might find the nearest markets. Hypernomics sees maps as a crucial and growing field worthy of deep interest and analysis. We will find that economic maps form the backbone of this new discipline. Interestingly, one of the most outstanding achievements in science, and the creation of the field of epidemiology, came about through a particular type of cartography known as "dot-mapping."

In late August and early September 1854, the Soho district of London faced a massive cholera outbreak. Over 500 people died within two weeks. A resident, Dr. John Snow, did not subscribe to the then-current miasma theory, which held that noxious "bad air" caused disease. Snow determined he would find the source of the problem and end it if he could. He plotted the cholera cases, one square dot representing one fatality due to the disease, as shown in Figure 2.1. He found "that nearly all of the deaths had taken place within a short distance" of a pump on Broad (now Broadwick) Street. Authorities turned it off once Snow made them aware of the problem. Cholera deaths, which had slowed with people leaving, dropped steeply; this launched the science of epidemiology.

Dr. John Snow made some hugely important conclusions, with observations reduced to a series of dots. It makes us wonder what we might do relative to markets if we could make sense of some observations similarly.

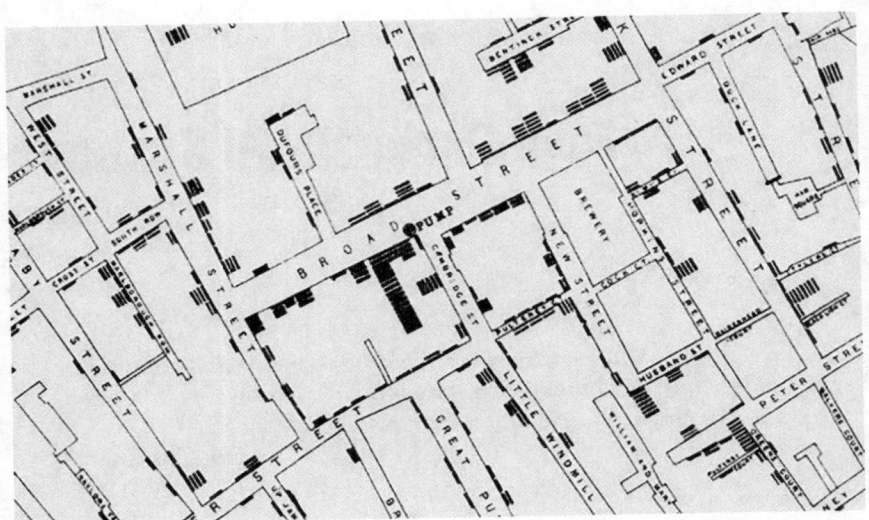

FIGURE 2.1 Dr. John Snow created this "dot-map" of the cholera cases in Soho, London, England, in September 1854. This map pointed him to the Broad Street pump as a contamination source. Once notified by Snow, officials turned off the pump, and the epidemic subsided.[1,2]

We touched briefly on the observation that since products have features, it would be helpful to describe market reactions to those features in specific ways. Having a hypothesis about market reactions is useful. The world has such a theory.

"X" MARKS THE SPOT

Paul Samuelson, considered by many the father of modern economics and the 1970 winner of the Nobel Memorial Prize in Economic Sciences, had definite thoughts about price determination. As he put it, the law of supply and demand meant that "the equilibrium price, i.e., the only price that can last. . .must be at this intersection point of supply and demand curves."[3] In so doing, Samuelson confirmed what Marshall had posited decades earlier.

You will find that every introductory text in economics has this paradigm in it, in one form or another, but that the relationships in those books portrayed by this method are uniformly hypothetical. Where do we find the law of supply and demand in the real world?

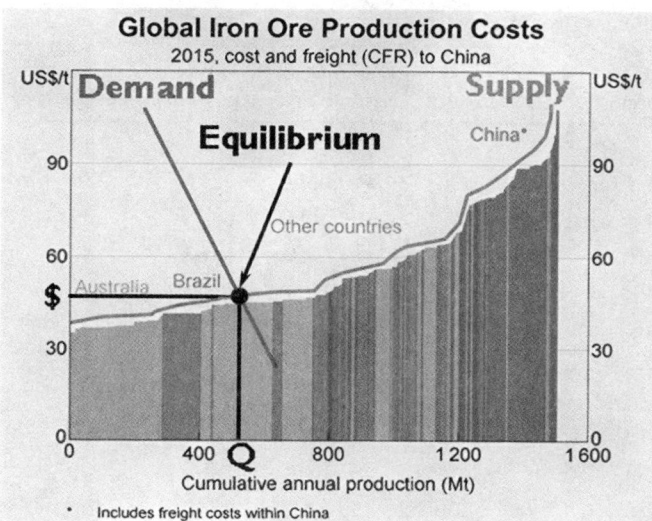

FIGURE 2.2   Iron ore market equilibrium.[4]

As Figure 2.2 reveals, we find a solid example of this phenomenon in the market for iron, where costs progressively rise from mine to mine. If we add a profit margin to the extraction costs, the excavations collectively form an upward-sloping supply curve, crucial to the law of supply and demand. With a single down-sloping demand curve, observe that the two lines intersect at a single equilibrium point, where supply equals demand. Collectively, they form a singular "x," marking the site like many treasure maps.

But iron is used in many products—how would we explain how those markets work?

MOST MARKETS DON'T ADDRESS COMMODITIES

Take the market for electric cars—each car uses iron, and there are several models for sale. How could we explain the lack of equilibrium? Submitted for our consideration is a part of the economy that has been emerging for the last 125 years: the market for electric automobiles, shown in Table 2.1 for 2011.

TABLE 2.1   The world mass-produced electric car market in 2011.[5-20]

Manufacturer	Model	Est. 2011 Sales Qty	Est. 5 Yr Vehicle Price	Horse-power	City Range miles
Commuter Cars	Tango T600	80	$108,000	805	120
Tesla	Roadster	500	$108,000	275	288
Think Global	Think City	300	$38,000	46	99
Mitsubishi	i-MiEV	5,000	$33,891	63	82
Smart	ED	550	$28,750	74	87
Nissan	Leaf	12,000	$35,340	110	75
Chevrolet	Spark EV	100	$27,495	130	82
Ford	Focus Electric	20	$39,995	143	76
Honda	Fit EV	100	$36,625	134	100
Wheego	Whip	15	$32,995	60	100
Bolloré	Bluecar	500	$31,416	67	160
BYD Auto	e6	300	$35,000	215	122
Renault	Fluence Z.E.	700	$36,307	94	115

When the first electric car, the Flocken Elektrowagen, appeared in 1888,[21] it did not catch on initially. Over a century later, when modern mass-produced electric cars began to appear, they were not in wide use early on. In fact, by 2011, the world produced only a little more than 20,000 electric cars per year, as Table 2.1 reveals. This compares to an annual world market of about 80 million full-sized cars and commercial vehicles.[22] However, given improving battery technologies and rising fuel costs of the day, the market for electric vehicles is on the rise and may continue growing in the near future. This market seems to be as good as any other as a starting point.

As we look at Table 2.1, a seemingly mundane fact should not escape our notice—*all of its numeric values are positive.* Sales quantities, prices, horsepower, and range all have positive values. None of them may have negative values (it is possible to have no sales, but in no event will sales be less than zero). While we may want less of some features of electric cars (such as less time to charge fully, lower battery replacement fees, and prices), we observe and understand that *we will never encounter negative values relative to product features.*

The history of mathematics is chock-full of many huge discoveries and inventions. One of the most important of them was the category of negative numbers. We use them for a variety of reasons and in a variety of places.

Businesses and economics need to use negative numbers to find and document those instances in which people, companies, or governments have spent more than they have. We need a way to account for negative financial situations just as much as we need positive numbers to account for profitable or surplus conditions.

CARTESIAN SYSTEMS AND NEGATIVITY

In our brief examination of René Descartes, we found that he produced a pair of coordinate systems that allowed us to plot various problems facing engineers and scientists. As those systems relate to economic matters, however, we might want to step back from these systems to take note of the tremendous amount of space the negative regions command compared to the areas that only support positive numbers. For example, in Figure 2.3, observe that three of the four regions in the two-dimensional Cartesian coordinate system, all shaded, support negative numbers. Quadrant II has the ordered pair (-4, 2), with the horizontal x value negative; quadrant III holds the point (-3, -2), with both x values negative, while quadrant IV holds (2, -3), with the vertical value y negative. Only in quadrant I do we find a region in which all numbers are positive, one of which is the ordered pair (1, 3).

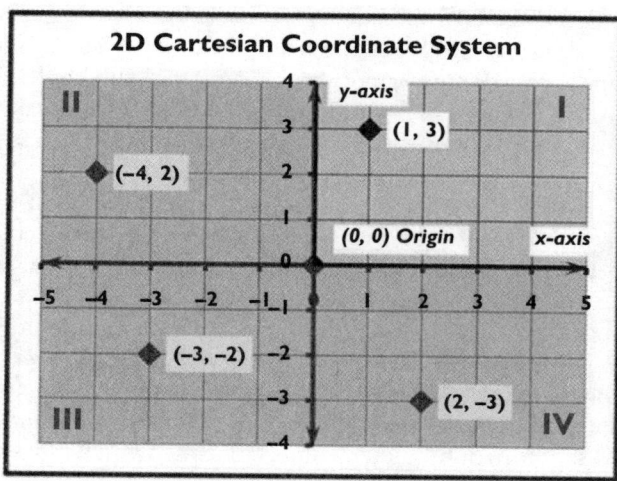

FIGURE 2.3   Three of the four regions in the two-dimensional Cartesian coordinate system support negative numbers.[24]

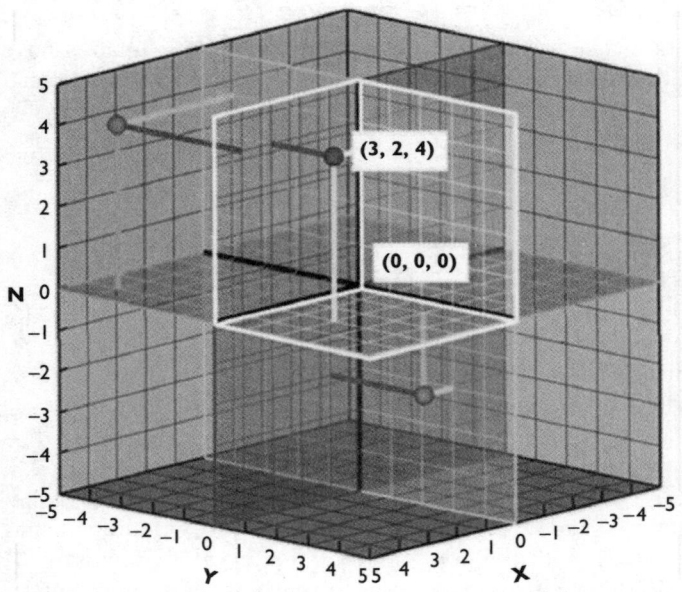

FIGURE 2.4 Seven of the eight regions in the three-dimensional Cartesian coordinate system support negative numbers.[25]

Cartesian three-dimensional space swells with support for negative numbers. As the shaded areas in Figure 2.4 reveal, seven of the eight regions that make up entertain negative numbers. The only part of the system that holds only positive numbers is the uppermost and nearest one (highlighted by thick lines) in Figure 2.3, where the x (horizontal), y (horizontal), and z (vertical) components are all positive (and which holds the ordered triple 3,2,4).

While Cartesian systems allow for a great deal of negativity, most of the graphical displays for classical economics rely solely on the first quadrant of the two-dimensional Cartesian coordinate system, as shown in Figure 2.5.

There is a good reason for this. Many current studies of economic forces focus on the relationship between supply and demand, as we will study in upcoming chapters. Demand relates positive numbers in quantity to positive numbers of dollars. Analysis of Gross Domestic Product, or GDP, typically uses the horizontal axis to represent time, which always marches forward, and money as the vertical axis. In contrast, an analysis of savings might place those figures on a vertical axis relating to income on a horizontal axis.

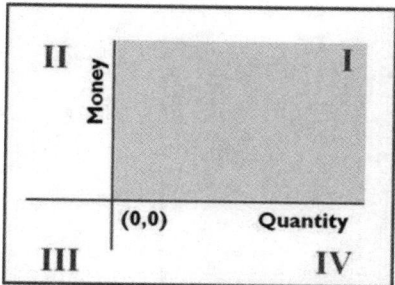

FIGURE 2.5 To date, most representations of economic activity take place in quadrant I of the two-dimensional Cartesian coordinate system.[26]

TABLE 2.2 Sample business case where operation starts with a loss then breaks even and goes on to make a profit.[27]

Month	Cost	Revenue	Profit (+)/ Loss (-)
0	$ 0.00	$ 0.00	$0.00
1	$ 5.00	$ 3.00	−$2.00
2	$ 7.07	$ 5.41	−$1.66
3	$ 8.66	$ 7.63	−$1.03
4	$10.00	$ 9.75	−$0.25
5	$11.18	$11.78	$0.60
6	$12.25	$13.76	$1.51
7	$13.23	$15.68	$2.45
8	$14.14	$17.57	$3.43
9	$15.00	$19.42	$4.42
10	$15.81	$21.24	$5.43
11	$16.58	$23.03	$6.45
12	$17.32	$24.80	$7.48

Since this method is both tried and apparently true, one might wonder if it is the only way to portray economic forces at work. We will find that other methods are available for these displays through a little more research.

Consider Table 2.2, where a sample company has a cost, revenue, and profit stream.

For example, there are instances in business analysis, as displayed in Figure 2.6, where it may make sense to use quadrants 1 and 4 of the

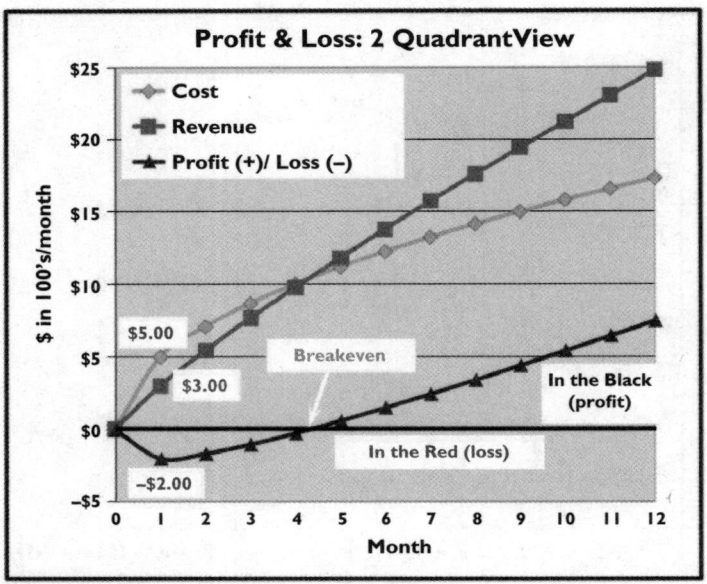

FIGURE 2.6   Sample business case where operation starts with a loss then breaks even and goes on to make a profit using Cartesian quadrants I and IV.[28]

two-dimensional Cartesian system. Table 2.2 shows the cost and revenue of a business over 12 months. In Figure 2.5, the line with square points portrays revenue, while the one with diamonds depicts costs. By subtracting costs from revenues, we can determine profits or losses graphically using the line with triangles. The company loses money when it lies below the horizontal intercept (i.e., a loss line). Notice, too, that we use the fourth quadrant of the two-dimensional Cartesian coordinate system in this view of the problem.

If we find it a more convenient method (as we will in later chapters), we should avoid working in quadrant IV and keep the entirety of our work in quadrant I. We can do this by the method shown in Figure 2.7.

Here, we have dropped quadrant IV of the Cartesian system and just focused on quadrant I. We keep track of profits and losses by noting that when costs exceed revenues, we are in a loss position, which we denote using dotted lines. Conversely, when revenues exceed expenditures, we make profits, which we indicate with solid vertical bars. Also, in Figure 2.7, we note that if we are making money, we say we are "in the black" (that term, and its counter, "in the red," spring from traditional bookkeeping methods, in which firms post profits in black ink, and losses in red).

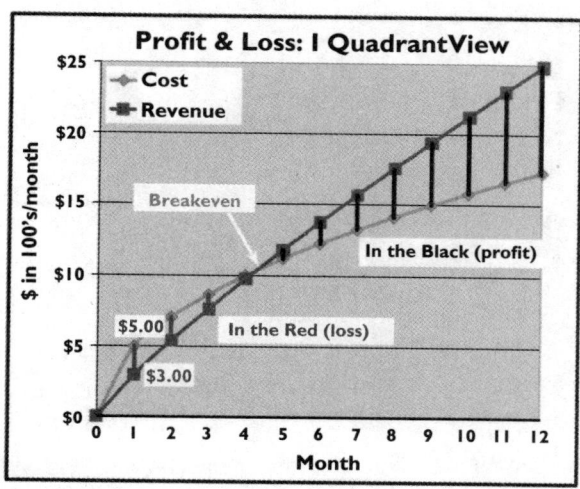

FIGURE 2.7 Sample business case where operation starts with a loss, then breaks even and goes on to make a profit using Cartesian quadrant I only.[29]

So, why did we go through how we use two- and three-dimensional systems before jumping right into the four-dimensional constructs? This is to refresh our memories about where we have been mathematically and show us what we need to do in our study of economics and the tools we have to go about it. The origins of plotting systems are hugely important, as we need both a starting point and a point of reference. Both the Cartesian systems have to have their origins to make sense of the regions in which they work. Our four-dimensional systems must have origins as well.

With a bit of manipulation, we discovered we could move from a concept requiring two of the four quadrants in two-dimensional Cartesian space (2.6) to one that only needs one (2.7), using the same data but displaying it differently. Our purpose is to have the tools to find the best places to enter new markets and determine their best product features. As it turns out, we will need extra dimensions to give ourselves the wherewithal to do that. Even more surprisingly, we will discover that we have been using these dimensions as consumers throughout our adult lives.

We will find that the data we need is available if we only go out and get it. To display that information, we will need a new way to view it. It will prove helpful to have a physical representation for our new coordinate system, as it may seem unduly abstract without it, at least at first.

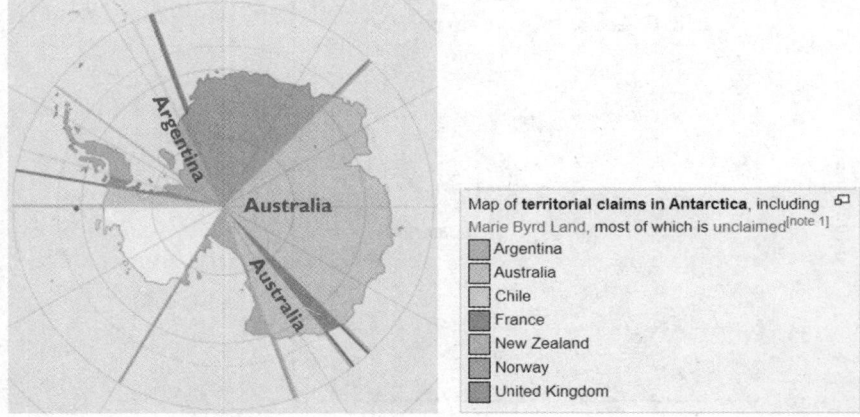

FIGURE 2.8   A political map of Antarctica. Note that all claims meet at the South Pole, and some overlap on another.[30]

GEOGRAPHY IS NEVER NEGATIVE

We start by going south—all the way south. Specifically, we will begin by going to the South Pole. Figuratively speaking, of course. We have a map of Antarctica in Figure 2.8.

An American scientific research facility called the Amundsen–Scott South Pole Station lies between the East and West Antarctica Ice Sheets at the confluence of the north-to-south meridians. The South Pole Station (Figure 2.8) shows the new research facility (brown buildings), the territorial claims in Antarctica by several nations, and the actual geographic South Pole, 90° south latitude, shown as a small circle. In Figure 2.8, we see the South Pole close up, as a direct vertical stake in the ice between the American flag on the left and a sign to the right commemorating the separate discoveries of the site by Norwegian adventurer Roald Amundsen and British explorer Robert F. Scott.

While the South Pole Station facilities are elevated like the structure in Figure 2.9, this building seems oddly out of place. And it is. That is because Figure 2.10 is the birth house of Elvis Presley, a simple two-room structure located in Tupelo, Mississippi. That is a long way from 90° south. For our purposes, however, we will often like to envision moving the house of Elvis to the South Pole, as we find that two-room constructs such as this one often make it easier to visualize four-dimensional systems.

We also want to be in Antarctica figuratively for several other reasons. As Figure 2.7 shows us, several nations have claimed various parts of the

FIGURE 2.9 The marker for the South Pole had a candy cane stripe and a ball on top of it for a time. The United States Amundsen-Scott South Pole Station is in the background; in between are the flags of the original 12 nations that signed the Antarctic Treaty.[31]

FIGURE 2.10 The birth house of Elvis Presley in Tupelo, Mississippi.[32]

FIGURE 2.11   American expatriate Sheila lives in Australia.[33]

continent, and the sovereignty over some areas is in dispute (Argentina, Chile, and the United Kingdom all lay claim to the Antarctic Peninsula). One nation, France, has just a tiny sliver of the land that the Australian claim bounds on two sides. Meanwhile, Australia's part exceeds over one-fourth of the 360° arc that extends outward from the South Pole. The southern terminus for all nations is the South Pole, making the whole arrangement look like an enormous pie with some interesting and valuable geometries. We will find that we can make analogies of these South Pole geometries to the math needed for plotting in more than four dimensions.

Consider twins Sheila and Cristina in Figures 2.11 and 2.12, respectively.

Imagine that the twins grew up studying in a guesthouse that mimics the house of Elvis, much like the one in Figure 2.13, where Sheila's room is marked "S" and Cristina's is marked "C" (and no, they don't have to use an outhouse as Elvis did, they just went to the main house).

Sheila was greatly enamored with geography, so she recreated paper-mâché topographies like Figure 2.14, which portrays the High Tatras Mountains that run through Poland and Slovakia. She would sometimes add spheres (often in green) to make it easier for her to find the local peaks.

On the other hand, her twin Cristina liked two-dimensional maps like the one in Figure 2.15. In her youth, Cristina developed a passion for travel.

FIGURE 2.12 American expatriate Cristina lives in Argentina.[34]

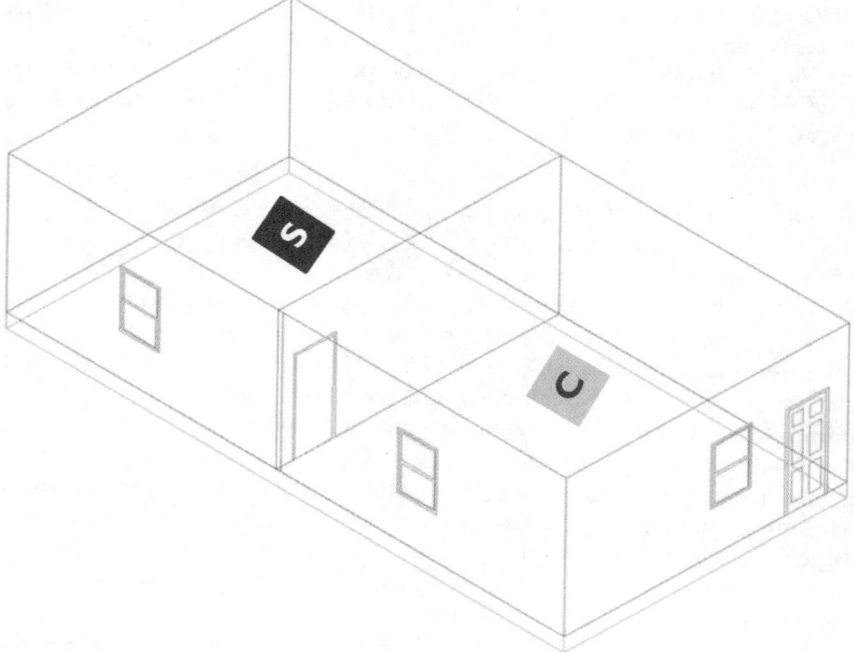

FIGURE 2.13 Line drawing of Cristina's and Sheila's guesthouse.[35]

FIGURE 2.14   Paper-mâché model of the Tatra Mountains recreated by Sheila.[35] Even as a child, Sheila liked to make paper-mâché topographies, often covering much of the floor of her room with her work. She would put green spheres on the peaks in her maps so that she could easily find them. When she grew up, Sheila became a geologist and moved to Australia to map its mines.[36]

She became enamored of push-pin maps and always had one on her wall (the far wall in C, the one without a window, and the one not common to her sister's room) as in Figure 2.15, which shows breweries in Spain and Andorra. She wanted to do something in the field of transportation, which would enable her to pursue a career and be free to travel. Because of that, she moved to Argentina and became an analyst for the automobile market. Always curious about new markets and very aware that the market for electric cars was growing, she is intent on studying how the vast lithium supplies nearby can help her company.

As the girls were growing up, a typical layout in the guesthouse looked very much like Figure 2.16. Sheila, ever the cartographer, would place her paper-mâché map on the floor and jam one corner of it into a matching part of the room. Her map, of course, addressed all three physical directions. She measured longitude from side to side; she concerned herself with latitude from front to back. With the mountains she constructed and the spheres

FIGURE 2.15   Map of breweries in Andorra and Spain by Cristina.[37]

she affixed atop them, she characterized elevation as she formed her three-dimensional map.

Meanwhile, Cristina tacked her floor-to-ceiling maps on a wall of her room such that the maps virtually touched one another at the corner of the floor, with only the width of the wall between them. Her map gave latitude as a typical up-and-down direction and longitude as the side-to-side component of position. Together, the girls could tell you anything you wanted to know about the detailed maps they studied. Importantly, they might acquaint you with a few facts that may seem trivial but are quite the opposite.

You see, the twins have studied analytic geometry in detail and the work of René Descartes in particular. They have difficulty coming to grips with Cartesian systems as they compare them to the relationship of various points in the physical world. Their issue centers around negativity.

The girls are invariably optimistic people. They have a smile for everyone they meet. They love their jobs, parents, and occasionally annoying family dog. Even their blood types are B-positive.

But ask them about negativity, and they get, well. . .negative.

For example, if you asked Sheila which countries you would find the High Tatras, she would give the standard answer that they cover parts of southern Poland and northern Slovakia. She might point you to the border of the two countries along a ridge in the mountain and point out the important peaks on which she has placed her omnipresent spheres. That much

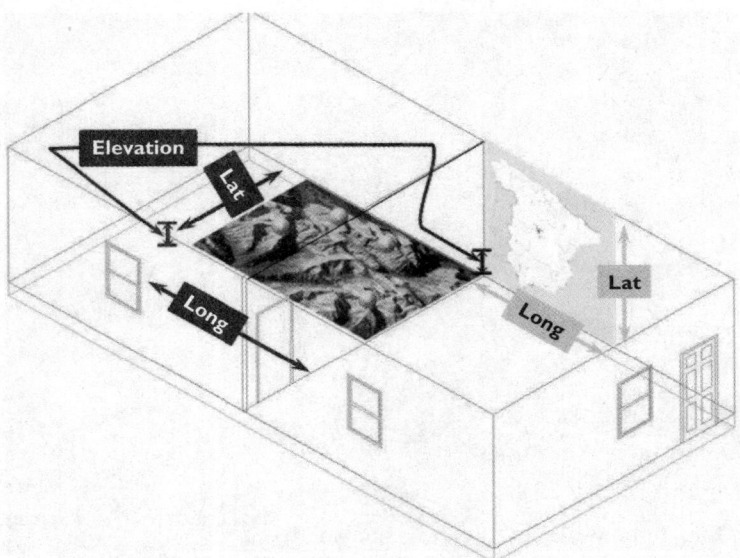

FIGURE 2.16 As children, the twins decorated their rooms in different ways. On the left, Sheila would place her topographies on the floor. In so doing, she accounted for all three physical dimensions: North-South (with Latitude), East-West (with Longitude), and up-down (with Elevation). On the right, Cristina's maps addressed only two of the material dimensions, North-South (as Latitude) and East-West (as Longitude). The girls were in separate but adjoining realms in their rooms, sharing a common wall. Distinct but adjacent zones are critical in the theory and application of Hypernomics.[38]

might be exciting but not out of the ordinary. Those are straightforward answers from a well-informed researcher. However, Sheila might let you in on her insight: Going south into Slovakia from Poland does not mean that you are in a negative Slovakia space. And vice versa.

Cristina could regale you with information about Spain and Andorra in much the same way that Sheila did, directing you to cities, rivers, and landmarks. In the same instant that Sheila thought about going from Poland to Slovakia, Cristina realized that crossing the border into Andorra was not a negative space for Spain.

Moreover, they both realized that the way they each had aligned their maps with the house's long side seemed to suggest that it ran east to west. After all, Sheila's three-dimensional map has a longitude parallel to the house's long axis, and so does Cristina's two-dimensional map. Many homes in city grid arrangements across the planet line up with the parallels of latitude. If the house were so aligned, the maps would be in harmony with the world.

What if they were not?

That is, what if the southern edge of their guesthouse was *not* exactly parallel to a parallel latitude? What does that say about the accuracy of their three-dimensional and two-dimensional maps?

You already know the answer—*it says nothing at all.*

The meaning of those maps is locked within its keys—each one tells you which way is north, how many parts of an inch equates to 100 miles, and what the colors mean in the mountain ranges. Here is the more important thing the twins recognize: *the dimensions of those maps and the house are independent of their positions relative to physical space.*

Figure 2.17 shows us that from the corner where their maps met in Figure 2.16, going along the line where the far wall meets the floor within Cristina's room, there is a *Cristina room length*. At the same time, we can say that there is a *Cristina room height* associated with this space. On the opposite side of the house, we have *Sheila's room height,* which describes the distance from the floor to the ceiling (which likely matches *Cristina's room height*), along with *Sheila's room length* in apparent direct opposition to the like figure for her sister.

Since both sisters share a common wall, we can take notice that *Sheila's room width* gives us the distance of this shared structure. Given these uniformly positive measurements, each twin noted that going from her room to the other was an exercise dealing entirely with nonnegative numbers. As

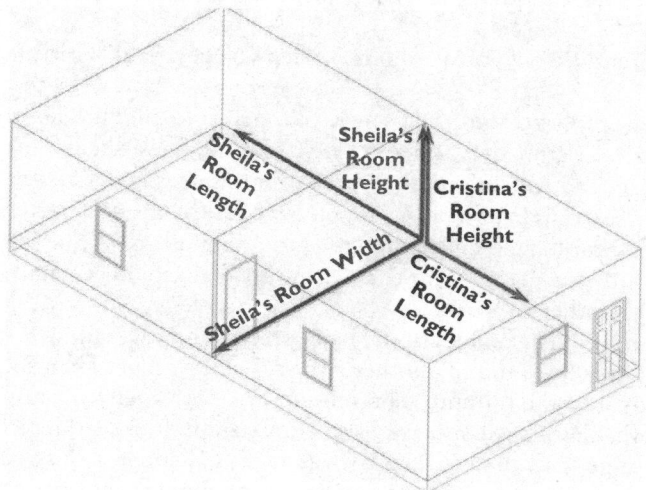

FIGURE 2.17 Looking at the twins' rooms from a different perspective.[39]

Sheila walked through the common door, she entered Cristina space, which she could have described with the appropriate length, width, and height. What Sheila did not have to do in that instant was concern herself with "negative Sheila space," as that concept is meaningless in Cristina space. The same, of course, would go for Cristina when she wandered into her sister's room.

The twins, now grown, would think about their childhood home often. It was a large part of their upbringing. Sometimes when they talked on the phone, they imagined working next door to each other again. Their career paths made that seemingly impossible, however.

When she left the guesthouse for good to go off into the world, Sheila became a geologist working for mining companies in Australia, making three-dimensional maps of their properties, using many techniques she began to pick up as a child.

Cristina always liked to travel; getting there was a big part of the adventure. Deciding to combine her hobby with her vocation, she moved to Argentina and began working in the automobile industry, focusing on the growing electric car market. She became very interested in Table 2.1 and wondered if there was a way to portray its meaning in a new way that was useful, novel, and not obvious. Then she saw the map in Figure 2.18, and it hit her.

"Come to Antarctica. The South Pole. Immediately," she called to her sister in Australia in the dead of night there, forgetting the time difference. "I need to experiment!"

Sheila fumbled with the phone groggily. "Antarctica! Now? Are you crazy?"

"No, it will be great! I'll tell you all about it when you get here!" Cristina shouted excitedly.

So, off they went, only to find themselves plopped into the middle of Figures 2.18 and 2.19. Cristina drew lines in the snow that show Sheila how the claims of Australia and Argentina meet at the South Pole. Then, Cristina showed Sheila that Australia has over a 90° pie section (or a one-quarter, right-angle slice) of Antarctica, enough to make a representation of Sheila's room, as we found in Figure 2.13. With these geographical references made clear, one twin put the other to work.

In Figure 2.18, in her sister's direction, Sheila placed one stick along the ground to represent horsepower and another to stand in for range. Then she pushed one vertically into the ground, representing price or dollars. Finally, homage to her youth, she placed spheres atop transparent sticks to depict their horsepower, range, and price. Similarly, the identical spheres showed latitude, longitude, and elevation in the three-dimensional maps she created as a kid. This map is the same in principle as those, less only the mountains that held up the spheres.

FIGURE 2.18 Sheila places spheres atop transparent sticks marking the horsepower, range, and price points for electric cars from Table 2.1.[40]

FIGURE 2.19 Cristina places spheres atop transparent sticks marking the quantity and price points for electric cars from Table 2.1.[41]

Working in Figure 2.19, Cristina concerned herself with the electric car quantities on the horizontal axis and prices on the vertical axis, acting like she was working against a wall. Placing spheres atop transparent sticks reminded her of the push-pin maps she made as a kid, as the spheres represented their horizontal and vertical components.

FIGURE 2.20 The twins step back from their parts of the puzzle and notice a common thread.[42]

When they stepped back from their work, they realized something remarkable.

To see their vision more vividly, they clear their maps of all the spheres and supporting transparent sticks, leaving only the axes behind in Figure 2.20. They observe that the axes there are virtually identical to those they had in Figure 2.16, that diagram of their childhood home. However, there is a significant difference (Figure 2.21). In the old guesthouse, the girls were separated by the width of the common wall, and each twin could treat the height of their room as if it were different from the other. Each side of the collective data map uses currency (USD or $) as a vertical axis. The prices used in Sheila's zone (regarding range and horsepower) are identical to those in Cristina's. This means they can move their respective maps such that their common vertical axis originates out of the South Pole, as in Figure 2.22. There, where all of the sticks meet, where the South Pole emerges from the ice, is a place that we will consider the center of our economic universe.

When we overlay the twins' four-dimensional system atop the three-dimensional Cartesian system, we get Figure 2.23.

Extracting their four-dimensional arrangement, the new view appears as Figure 2.24.

In Figure 2.24, we can see the house of Elvis has evolved into our new coordinate system. We observe how it relates to the three-dimensional Cartesian system familiar to us for centuries. Figure 2.24 gives us the two-room

FIGURE 2.21   The twins realize they've discovered a four-dimensional system.[43]

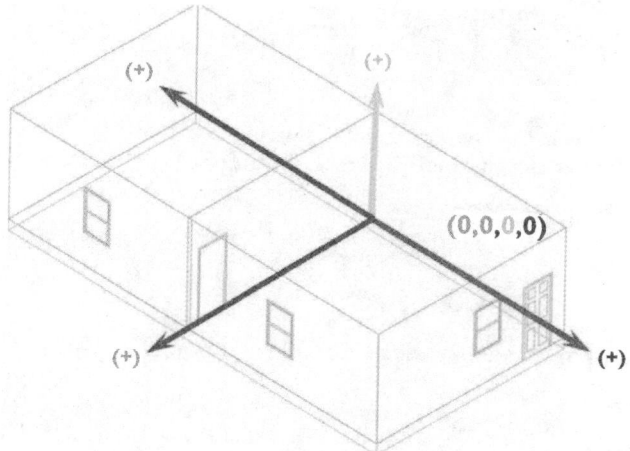

FIGURE 2.22   The twins' four-dimensional system looks like their rooms as kids, except that four axes emanate from where the common wall meets the floor, with all the axes being positive.[44]

structure critical to understanding four-dimensional structures. It looks like the house of Elvis because it is the house of Elvis. Peeling away its façade in Figure 2.13 reveals a scheme very much like what we saw in our depiction of the twins' rooms in Figure 2.17. In this case, three thick lines meet the origin, the center of our economic universe. Here, we have four dimensions, three

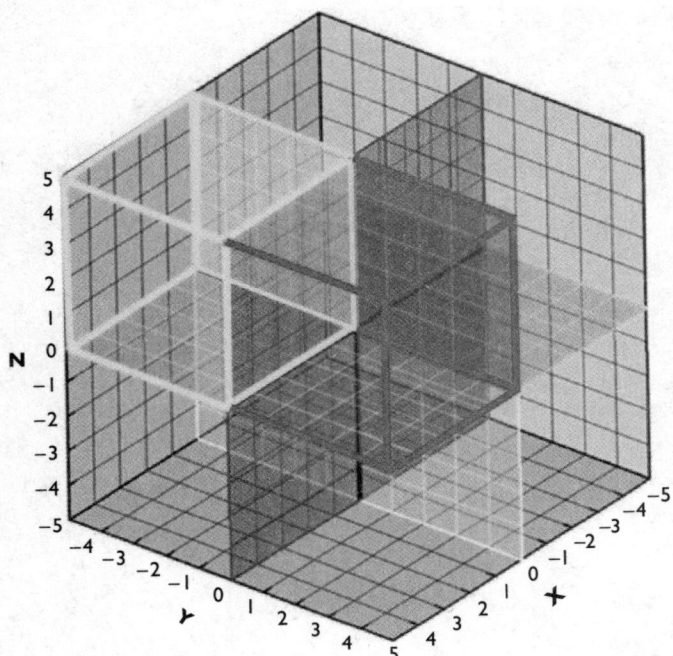

FIGURE 2.23 The two rooms in this figure resemble this high-lighted portion of the three-dimensional Cartesian coordinate system.[45]

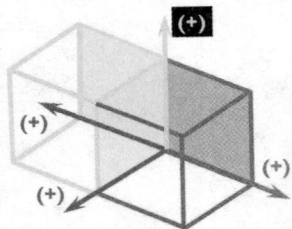

FIGURE 2.24 Hypernomics uses a left-hand Value Space matched to a right-hand Demand Plane.[46]

horizontal and one vertical, all beginning at (0,0,0,0), representing the starting point for an environment of ordered quads. Observe that as we begin at the origin and move horizontally along the back wall in the left-hand room along the heavy line, we are moving away from the origin in a positive way, meaning that that axis only entertains nonnegative numbers. The same is true for its horizontal counterpart on the back wall of the front room—which moves away from the origin in ever-increasing positive increments. The line between them (on the floor of the dividing wall) also moves away from the common starting point, albeit in a different direction, always away from zero in a positive sense. Finally, the vertical axis is locally vertical and at right angles from the other axes, and it, too, considers no negatives.

If we note that we have a two-dimensional Demand Plane on the right of this arrangement, abutting a three-dimensional Value Space on the left, we derive the line drawing in Figure 2.24. It is, in essence, a line drawing in keeping with Figures 2.20 and 2.21, reminding us that it entertains nothing in the way of negative numbers. We could place Figure 2.24 over what appears to be a corresponding three-dimensional Cartesian system in Figure 2.23, but here we instantly recognize the differences. Figures 2.22 and 2.24 have no negative numbers, but an upper left section of the Cartesian system in Figure 2.23 does. Our left-hand area is different from his. Thus, we now make a break from Descartes (Figure 2.25).

With Table 2.3, we consider a smaller subset of Table 2.1.

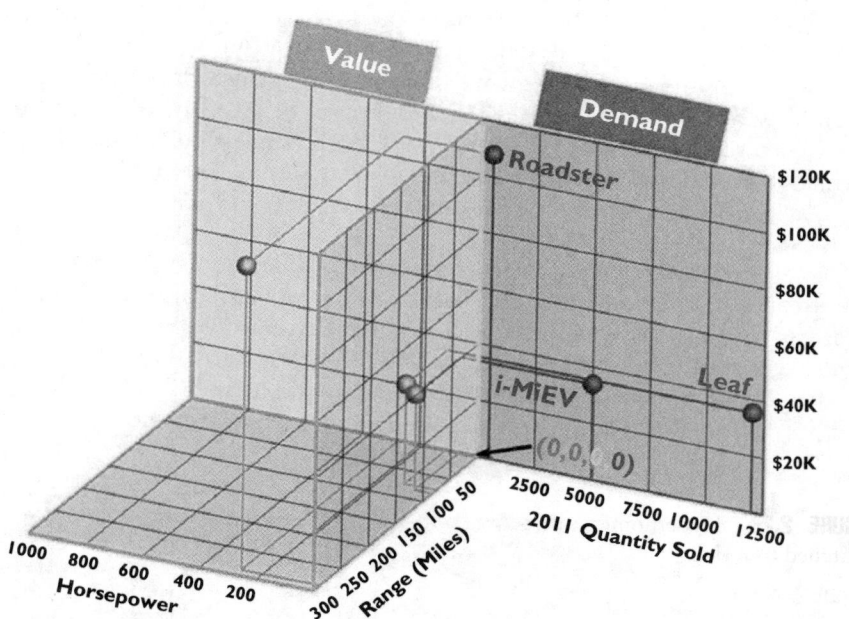

FIGURE 2.25   This is the four-dimensional system that governs all economic activity, less simple commodities.[48]

TABLE 2.3   This table is a subset of Table 2.1.[47]

Manufacturer	Model	HP	Range	Price	Qty
Tesla	Roadster	275	288	$108,000	500
Mitsubishi	i-MiEV	63	82	$33,900	5,000
Nissan	Leaf	110	75	$35,300	12,000

PLOTTING IN FOUR DIMENSIONS

Figure 2.25 shows how our four-dimensional system handles the data that the twins worked at the South Pole. On the left, with the two horizontal axes, we have *Value Space*. This region addresses features that customers value, including horsepower and range for electric cars. At the top of the table, the Tesla Roadster has 275 horsepower. If we go along the horizontal horsepower axis, we will see that the uppermost sphere reflects that value, along with the range of the car, also on a horizontal axis, which is 288 miles. Together, they relate to a price of $108,000, which we find along the vertical axis. On the right-hand *Demand Plane,* the Roadster sold 500 vehicles in 2011, and the price identical to the one we found in Value Space is reflected on this Demand Plane. Similarly, we reproduce the value of the Mitsubishi i-MiEV, with its 63 horsepower and 82-mile range along their respective axes, both relating to its price of $33,900; at the same time, its matching Demand Plane shows that price and the quantity sold of 5,000. The Nissan Leaf, at the time the most popular of all-electric cars in terms of sales, has its relevant numbers displayed similarly.

In every case in a four-dimensional system, we must use ordered quads, representing the values in the following order: (Valued Feature A, Valued Feature B, Price, and Quantity). These systems have an origin of (0,0,0,0). Thus, we denote the Tesla Roadster as (275, 288, $108,000, 500), the ordered quad associated with it. In Figure 2.25, it simultaneously has a location in Value Space (the uppermost sphere) and on the Demand Plane (the

FIGURE 2.26   This ancient ruler captures distance in one direction.[49]

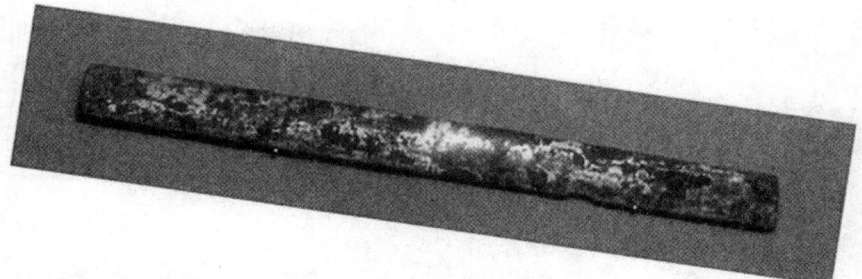

FIGURE 2.27   A ruler retains its meaning in any direction.[50]

highest sphere on the right). It thus exists, as do all products in all markets, *as Hypernomics works across Multiple Dimensions.*

By this means, Value Space relates to the (sometimes green) left-hand side (as seen from the perspective that we currently have) of our market structure. In contrast, the (sometimes red) right-hand side (again, when viewed from this angle) portrays the Demand Plane, with both of them sharing a common price (or currency) axis. When we use color, we use green for Value Space to indicate that Values for products can continue progressing as producers add desired product features. Opposed to Value Space is the Demand Plane, which, by convention, when in color, we always depicted in red. The significance of using red for Demand is that we often define Demand in terms of its limits, which eventually puts a stop to buying. Finally, if color is available to us, we use gold as the color for the central or price (or currency) axis, as we can relate all purchases to the amount of gold they require.

Perhaps the easiest way to imagine a nonnegative system is with a ruler, as in Figure 2.27. A ruler only has positive dimensions.

A ruler's information is not lost as we reposition it in space, as we remind ourselves in Figure 2.28.

We can build physical four-dimensional models using a 3D printer that we can hold in one hand, as demonstrated in Figure 2.29.

Just like the ruler keeps its data as it moves through space, 4D systems have like properties, as we see in Figure 2.30.

How can we have a four-dimensional system in a three-dimensional world? you might ask. The answer lies in the *type* of dimensions that we will use here. Though four-dimensional economic systems are *analogous* to Cartesian systems, they are *not* identical. The physical dimensions described in the coordinate systems by Descartes address "fundamental measurements of a physical quantity."[51] Mathematical dimensions are "any of the least number of independent coordinates required to uniquely specify a point in space."[52]

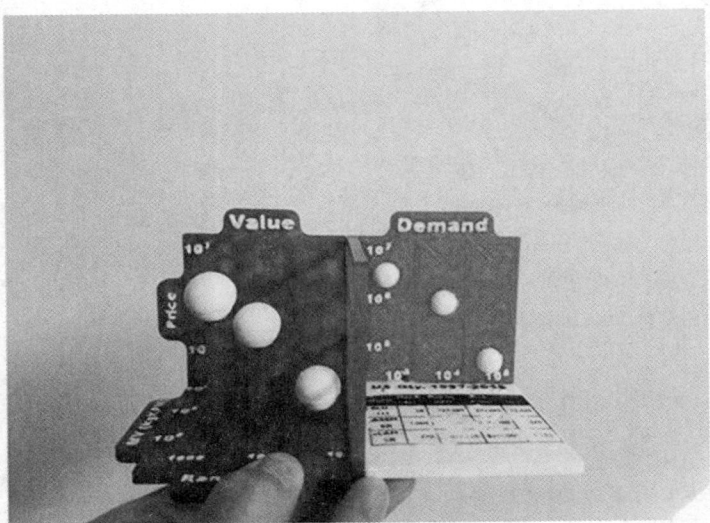

FIGURE 2.28 A physical four-dimensional system—each point in the left-hand Value Space has a match on the right-hand Demand Plane.[53]

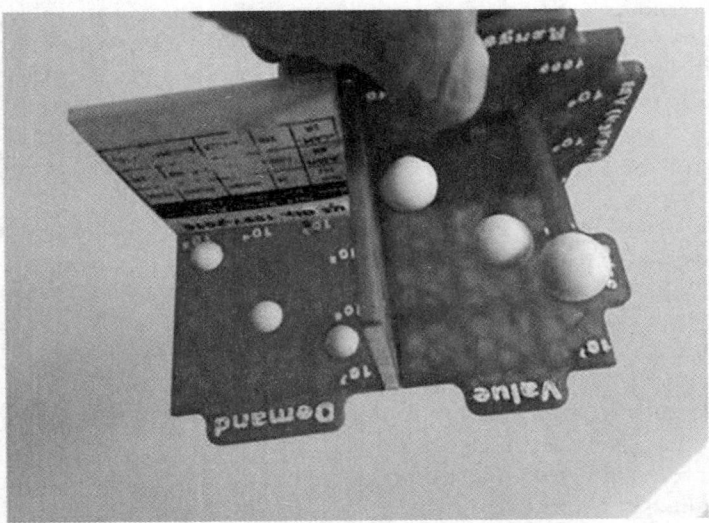

FIGURE 2.29 Four-dimensional market systems retain their information even if rotated.[54]

FIGURE 2.30   The actions of the twin forces are embodied in every one of us taken together.[55]

Thus, physical dimensions describe up or down, left or right, and forward or backward. By contrast, mathematical dimensions, as used for four-dimensional economic systems, depict the extent to the origin of two valued features, currency, and quantity. The seemingly unusual element of this essential concept is that the four-dimensional points in *Hypernomics* have a duality—they exist in Value Space and the Demand Plane *at the same time.*

We will find the analogy to geography and its attendant spatial locations crucial to our understanding of *Hypernomics*. If we stand at the South Pole and move into the Australian claim, we are not in "negative Argentina space." The same goes if we venture into Argentina's territory. We may have left the Australian space to get there, but we did not encounter a negative dimension. *Hypernomics* addresses negative numbers, but it never entertains negative dimensions.

Furthermore, *Hypernomics* observes that every buyer performs these types of analyses whenever they buy any product. It is as if our brains have a partition right in the middle (which, of course, they do), and that we must balance our demand on the one side with our value assessments on the other, as we are working with *Hypernomics of value and demand*. Indeed, as the woman straddling the Prime Meridian in Greenwich, United Kingdom, shows us in Figure 2.30, on the one hand (in this case, the right one, in the Eastern hemisphere), she makes a value assessment, the price for which she indicates by the height of right hand, in which she holds a ball. At the same time, in her left hand, she has a ball at the same height (in the Western hemisphere), indicative of that price playing in her decision regarding how many items to buy as part of her demand consideration. Her extended arms reflect the dual state she balances, with a sphere representing value in her right hand and an orb representing demand in her left.

This woman's exact decision mechanisms in buying her electric car will serve her when she buys a package of ground beef or when her daughter makes her first candy purchase.

SUMMARY

Dot-mapping helped establish modern epidemiology. Hypernomics also depends on this technique. Most contemporary economic works used only the first quadrant of the two-dimensional Cartesian coordinate system, usually limiting analyses to a single input variable with a single output variable. However, data in the real world reveals that consumers balance the competing forces of value (how they determine the worth of products) and demand (the means that they have to buy those products and how they react to changes in price). A four-dimensional system forgoes negative regions, allowing us to capture these market forces more completely. We need four dimensions (Valued Feature A, Valued Feature B, Price, Quantity), which we plot about an origin denoted (0,0,0,0) as ordered quadruples or quads. With this construct, we imagine a center of the economic universe, which we place at the South Pole to aid our imagination. The analogy to geography reminds us that while Value Attribute Axis 1 appears to be going in the opposite direction from the Quantity Axis and may appear negative, in economic space, as with geographic space, there need not be any negative regions. Movement into the Australian claim in Antarctica is not a "negative Argentinean" space. All purchase decisions necessarily address a value proposition on the one hand and a demand consideration on the other, with the price for both always the same.

CHAPTER 3

Five-Dimensional Systems

"How did it get so late so soon? It's night before it's afternoon. December is here before it's June. My goodness, how the time has flewn. How did it get so late so soon?"

Dr. Seuss

PHYSICAL CHANGES OVER TIME

Things change. Every day, the Earth is a little farther along in its orbit. Every hour, it wheels around 15 degrees about its axis. The Sun and the entire Solar System move relative to the center of the Milky Way Galaxy, which is also moving. Despite these many complexities, celestial mechanics often offer predictable methods for tracking heavenly bodies.

Occasionally, astronomers discover a previously unseen mass zipping across the sky as a point of light. Knowing the size, speed, and orbit of such things is helpful. Here in the United States, we have people who study such things for a living.

The National Aeronautics and Space Administration (NASA) searches for and identifies Near Earth Objects (NEOs), having discovered over 30,000 they have cataloged, transforming our understanding of our neck of the universe.[1] They identified a unique body in space in 2002, as shown in Figure 3.1.

What is it? Where is it going? When does it get close to us? Astronomers initially could not resolve any of these questions about the Near Earth Object J002E3, pictured in the circle over time. Market analysts must analyze like questions about position, direction, speed, and proximity.

When it was first discovered, astronomers initially thought it was an asteroid, which was unusual since the only large mass orbiting the Earth was the moon. Other objects typically eject our orbit due to the variances in gravity between the Earth, Moon, and the Sun. After performing spectral

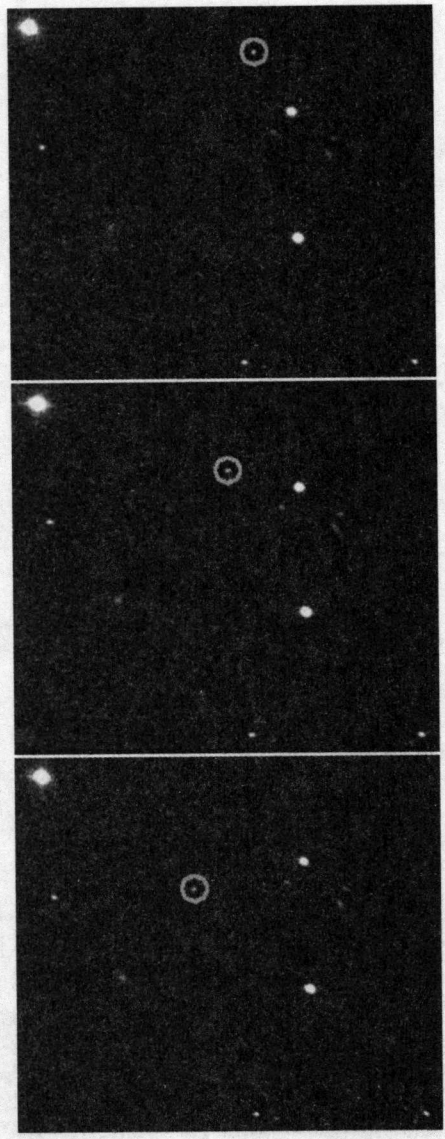

FIGURE 3.1 Unique body in space.[2, 3]

analysis on the object and finding it had titanium dioxide in the paint often used in rockets, researchers came to believe that it was the third stage of the *Apollo 12 Saturn V* rocket, which launched on November 14, 1969. What's more, they now think it went into an odd cycle whereby it alternates between orbiting the Earth six times before it goes into a Heliocentric orbit, only to come back our way. It might return in the mid-2040s. Objects of this size typically burn up in the Earth's atmosphere, but given the sometimes steeper orbit of J002E3, it may be able to come to Earth in one or more large pieces.

If a giant asteroid were spotted and headed to a spot where it would eventually crash into Earth, we would want to take steps to avoid that collision. Competing for space in space can be a deadly affair. About 66 million years ago, all of the dinosaurs and most other species on the planet found this out the hard way when a 10-kilometer-wide asteroid crashed into Earth just off the Yucatan peninsula. Now, modern technology may be able to guide the next would-be colliding giant asteroid with the Earth out of our path. In 2022, the brilliant minds at NASA conducted an experiment in which their "Double Asteroid Redirection Test (DART) investigation team show[ed that] the spacecraft's kinetic impact with its target asteroid, Dimorphos, successfully altered the asteroid's orbit. This mark[ed] humanity's first time purposely changing the motion of a celestial object and the first full-scale demonstration of asteroid deflection technology."[4] The key to successfully engaging this technology in the future is acquiring and analyzing exhaustive knowledge about large masses coming our way, as our survival depends on it. And it is the same in battle as it is in defensive astronomy.

In a war, the ultimate objective is often to acquire a specific piece of territory or a hunk of land. To gain that ground, opposing forces often go head-to-head over extended periods. Plotting the movement of massing, contesting factions during hostile engagements is battlefield mapping, as shown in Figure 3.2, which depicts troop movements during the first day of the Battle of Gettysburg during the American Civil War.

In some respects, the maps for the Battle of Gettysburg in Figures 3.2 to 3.4 resemble those for the newly discovered Near-Earth Object in Figure 3.1. In Figure 3.1, the background stars' positions remain relatively unchanged as we move from the upper to the middle and then the lower frame. The stars are effectively in the exact locations in the third frame as in the first.

While the armies started warring generally north of Gettysburg on July 1, the first frame of this time lapse mapping in Figure 3.2, by July 3, the third and final frame in Figure 3.4, they are all south of it. Note that the town of Gettysburg stays put as a point of reference. The various creeks and roads did not move either, nor did Cemetery Hill, where some of the bloodiest actions occurred.

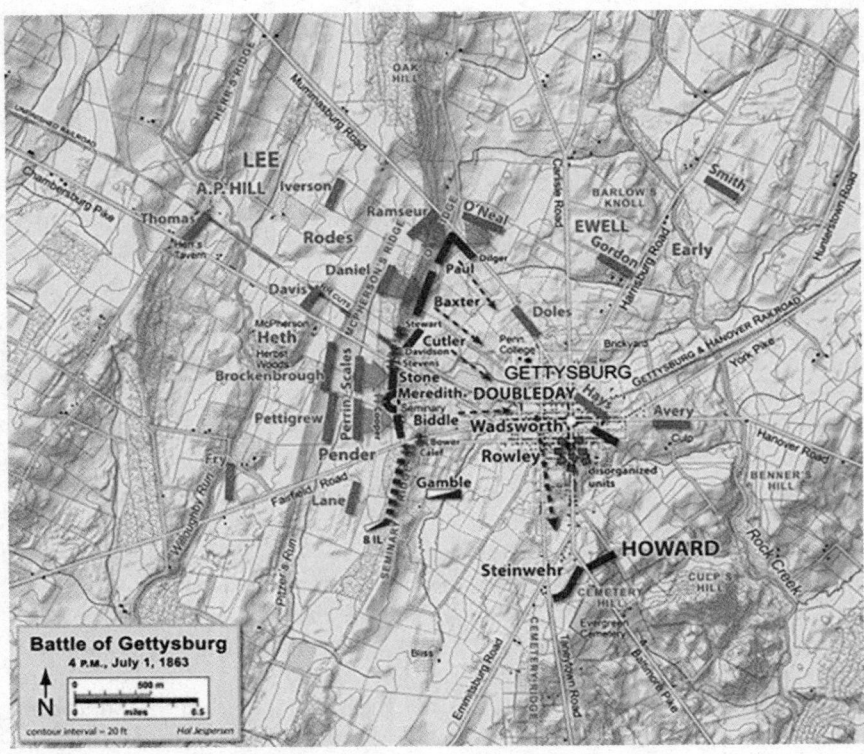

FIGURE 3.2   The Battle of Gettysburg, Day 1.[5]

The pictures in Figure 3.1 are two-dimensional representations of that object's three-dimensional positions. Besides its inclination and right ascension, NASA also calculated its distance from Earth, heading, and speed with the time-lapse shots against the immovable backdrop of stars.

The battlefield maps for Gettysburg are also two-dimensional depictions of three-dimensional spaces. Shading on the map indicates altitude, with Cemetery Hill higher than its surroundings, giving us a three-dimensional feel to the maps. Comparing the positions from day to day, knowing the distances involved allows us to calculate the average speed of each large group, and arrows on the map show us the course for each army.

The Battle of Gettysburg took place over three days and involved 160,000 soldiers. In a battlefield scenario with a high number of combatants, it is not practical to track every single soldier. It is better to map the

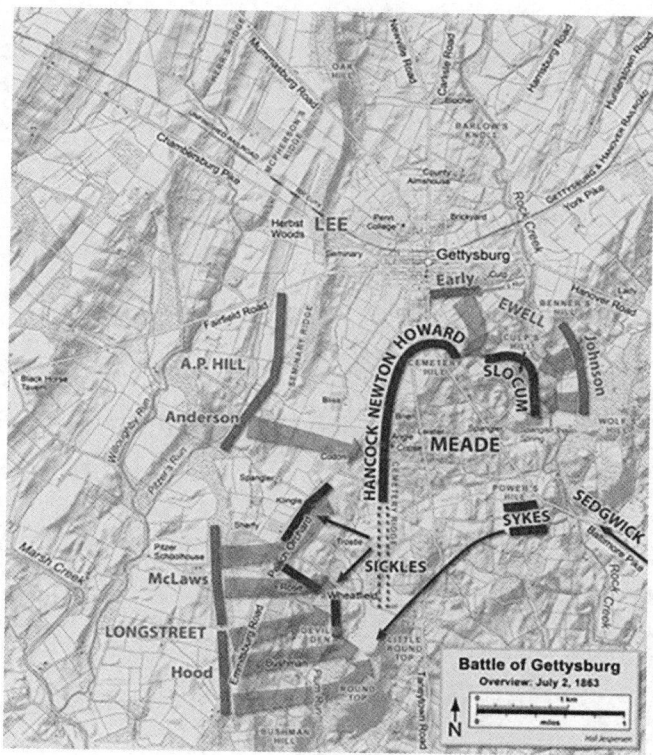

FIGURE 3.3 The Battle of Gettysburg, Day 2.[6]

movements of entire corps or divisions, both subsets of their entire armies, each representing large aggregations of individual soldiers.

By contrast, when we study Near Earth Objects, we necessarily examine each singular entity, as any sufficiently large one could pose a problem for the planet.

We describe battlefields and NEOs in three dimensions, as latitude, longitude, and altitude for the former, declination, right ascension, and Earth distance for the latter.

How do market positions change over time compared to Near Earth Objects or warring armies?

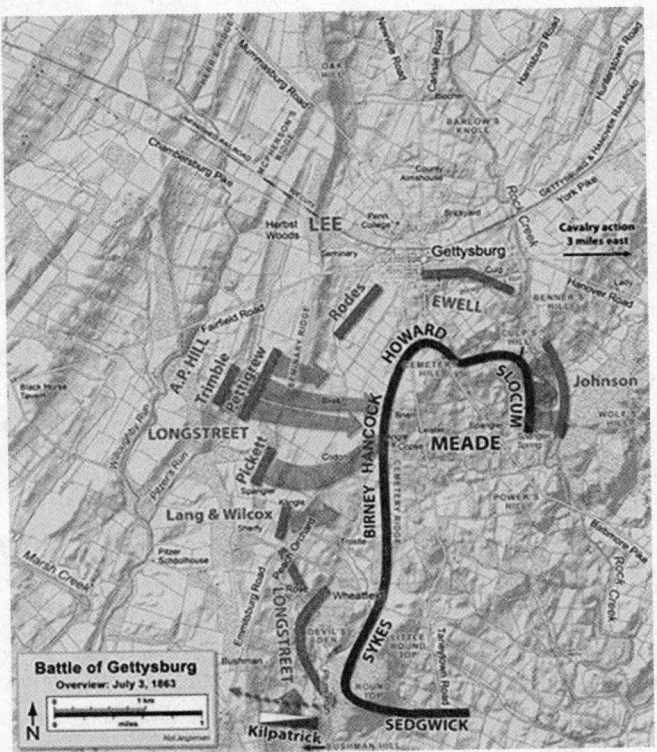

FIGURE 3.4   The Battle of Gettysburg, Day 3.[7]

ECONOMIC CHANGES OVER TIME

In Chapter 2, we saw how a single market needed four dimensions to characterize it at a particular instant. Thus, it follows that adding time to the analysis adds another dimension, for a total of five. For any market, its five-dimensional position requires plotting 1) Value Attribute 1, 2) Value Attribute 2, 3) Price, 4) Quantity, and 5) Time. Table 3.1 gives us an example of these requirements.

As time goes on, markets transform. The market for electric cars during the early 2010s offers us an excellent example. Some of its models dropped out in just three years, and many more came in. Note the sales figures from 2011 to 2013. What do they indicate about electric car demand?

Table 3.1 offers us some history that we can use to compare market positions over time.

TABLE 3.1 Requirements for four-dimensional markets.[8]

Manufacturer	Model	1st Prod Year	Last Prod Year	2011 Sales Qty	2012 Sales Qty	2013 Sales Qty	5 Year Price	H/P	City Range miles
Commuter Cars	Tango T600	2005	N/A	80	90	100	$108,000	805	120
Tesla	Roadster	2008	2012	500	250	0	$108,000	275	288
Think Global	Think City	2008	2012	300	150	0	$38,000	46	99
Mitsubishi	i-MiEV	2009	N/A	5000	8000	11000	$33,891	63	82
Smart	Ed	2009	N/A	550	1200	2100	$28,750	74	87
Nissan	Leaf	2010	N/A	12000	25000	50000	$35,340	110	75
Chevrolet	Spark EV	2011	N/A	100	800	1560	$27,495	130	82
Ford	Focus Electric	2011	N/A	20	685	2100	$39,995	143	76
Honda	Fit EV	2011	N/A	100	300	700	$36,625	134	100
Wheego	Whip	2011	N/A	15	30	40	$32,995	60	100
Bolloré	Bluecar	2011	N/A	500	1000	1600	$31,416	67	160
BYD Auto	e6	2011	N/A	300	800	1700	$35,000	215	122
Renault	Fluence Z.E.	2011	N/A	700	1200	2000	$36,307	94	115
Renault	Zoe	2012	N/A	0	2000	6900	$33,490	87	130
Tesla	Model S	2012	N/A	0	1200	10000	$57,400	302	208
Tesla	Model S Signature	2012	N/A	0	700	6000	$95,400	362	265
Tesla	Model S Signature Performance	2012	N/A	0	600	5000	$105,400	416	265
Toyota	RAV4 EV	2012	N/A	0	500	1400	$49,800	154	103
Roewe	E50	2012	N/A	0	500	1000	$37,589	63	110
Fiat	500e	2013	N/A	0	0	1100	$32,500	111	100

When we plot their movements, we find that markets (which we could describe as several companies offering multiple goods and services of the same general category with many more customers buying those products) have elements of celestial bodies and warring armies. New products spring up in markets as we discover new objects in the sky or as new combatants enter a battle. Table 3.1 reveals 13 models in the electric car market in 2011. In 2012, six more models joined the picture (Renault Zoe; Tesla Model S, Model S Signature, and Model S Signature Performance; Toyota RAV4 EV; and Roewe E50).

In that same year, two models in the market for several years were in it for the last time (Tesla Roadster and the Think Global Think City). A year later, there was one new entrant (the Fiat 500e), and the other 2012 market contestants stayed in for another year in 2013.

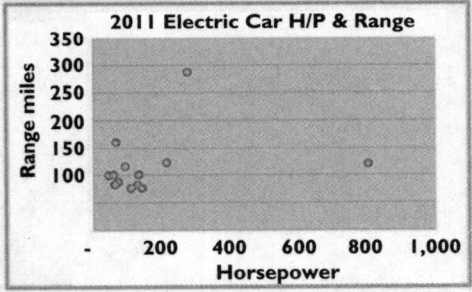

FIGURE 3.5 The horsepower and range combinations for the 2011 electric car market entrants, where each dot represents one model.[9]

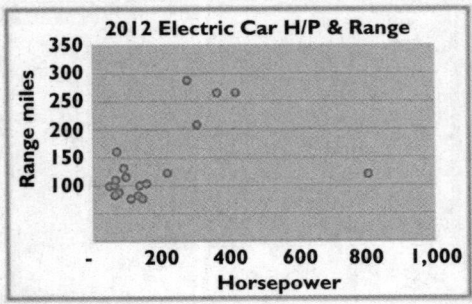

FIGURE 3.6 In 2012, some horsepower and range pairs on offer for the electric car market changed.[10]

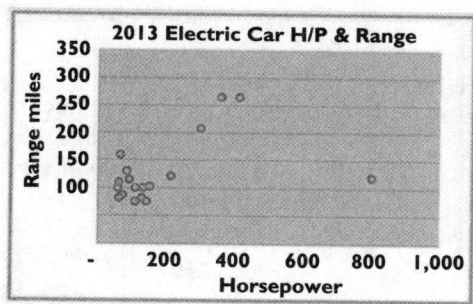

FIGURE 3.7 In 2013, more horsepower and range combinations modifications became available in the electric car market.[11]

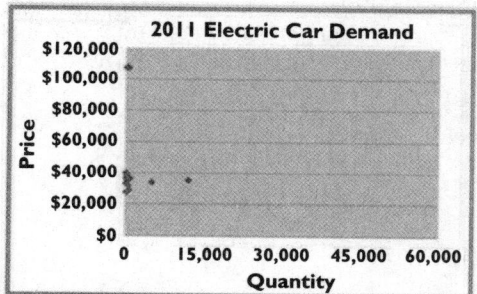

FIGURE 3.8 This diagram captures the quantity sold and prices for the 2011 electric car market.[13] Every point here has a match in Figure 3.5.

In the example presented in Table 3.1, the features of each model, their horsepower and range, did not change from year to year. By contrast, the quantities sold did change, often quite a bit. Figures 3.5 through 3.10 allow us to see these market changes over time.

In its left-hand column, we know the horsepower (on the horizontal axis) and range (on the vertical axis) portrayed by a series of dots over time. Each dot represents one model. In 2011, we had the 13 points that began our study. The following year saw our new entrants. The last year, 2013, offers a slightly different picture than the two preceding years as a pair of vehicles fell out of the market and one model entered it. Market entrants and withdrawals are analogous to the maps we have of Near Earth Objects. Just as new NEOs come into view, we find markets entertaining fresh models all the time. Occasionally, just as the NEO Comet Schumacher-Levy 9 disappeared as it smashed into Jupiter in 1994, products in markets vanish.

Sometimes, when a model (such as Think City) leaves a market, it takes its company (Think Global) along with it.[12]

When a company removes one product, they replace it with others. Table 3.1 and Figure 3.3 indicate that Tesla released its Roadster model in favor of three variations of its Model S. The burgeoning sales of the Model S confirm the move as favorable to the company. As you might imagine, we can plot Demand over time like we did for horsepower and range.

While a few models experienced decreasing sales from 2011 to 2013, most increased substantially. That means the Demand in the market grew during this period.

Armed forces cluster large numbers of troops into battle groups. We see representations of the movements of such groups in Figure 3.2. Each line symbolizes an extensive collection of soldiers and approximates the position of each unit.

We can also create the same depictions for demand, as shown in Figure 3.11. Using a process called demand aggregation (much more on this in Chapter 5), we can work out the aggregate demand line (as of units sold

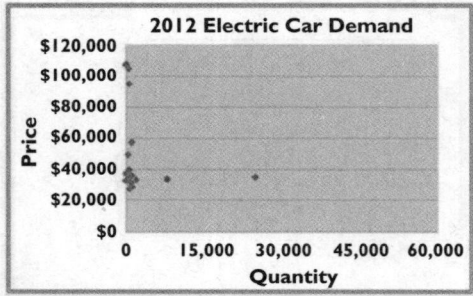

FIGURE 3.9   By 2012, Demand in the electric car market moved.[14]

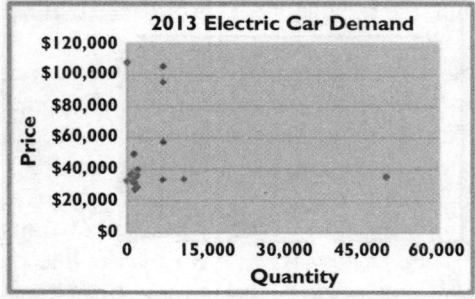

FIGURE 3.10   The year 2013 saw more changes in the Demand for electric vehicles.[15]

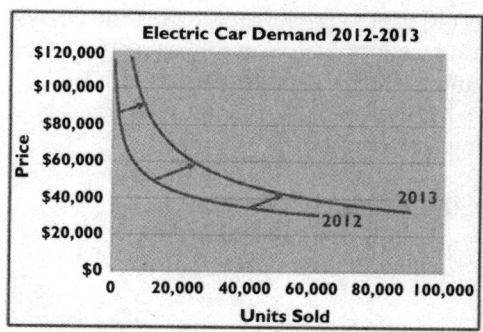

FIGURE 3.11 Markets have movements that mimic the massed formations of armies.[16]

versus price) for any point in time. These statistically significant lines for 2012 and 2013 indicate that demand is "shifting to the right," meaning it is growing, with more money pouring into this market.[17] Observe the similarity of the shifts in demand in Figure 3.7 to those of the armies in battle in Figures 3.2 to 3.4.

When celestial bodies crash into one another, or armies engage in a battle, the outcomes can be gruesome. Regarding extraterrestrial masses and warring factions, we invariably want to know their size, positions, and headings. Not knowing their directions is fraught with danger. A single picture will not reveal this to us. We gain some helpful knowledge about their movements only with several such maps over time.

While Jupiter or the Sun may affect the course of an asteroid or a comet before its next pass near Earth, we might only know that once we plot their paths in advance. The courses of such objects, of course, are primarily determined by gravity and chance. Any mass in space that is sufficiently large and close enough to any other will redirect its route. Celestial bodies governed by Newton's Laws of Motion always have a direction but never an intention.

Armies at war, by contrast, do have intentions, and while still beholden to the same Laws of Motion, can radically change directions on command. Theories about objectives during war abound, but the singular goal central to most, if not all, is that by the end of the conflict, the parties to a battle want to win. Victory in a military sense may seem relatively clean-cut, but history is replete with cases where the definition of winning became ambiguous. When the Greek king Pyrrhus of Epirus suffered massive losses in twice defeating the Romans during the Pyrrhic War, Dionysus reported that after the latter battle, Pyrrhus said, "One more such victory would utterly undo him."[18]

In markets, multiple companies competing for the same or nearly identical market positions can leave them with thin or nonexistent profits, or worse, as they fight for customers. If producers engage in detailed mapping in advance, they can plan to land their products in their markets' open spaces. Markets move over time, and we can plot them in Figure 3.12, in which we depict position as ordered quintuples consisting of (Valued Feature A, Valued Feature B, Price, Quantity, and Time).

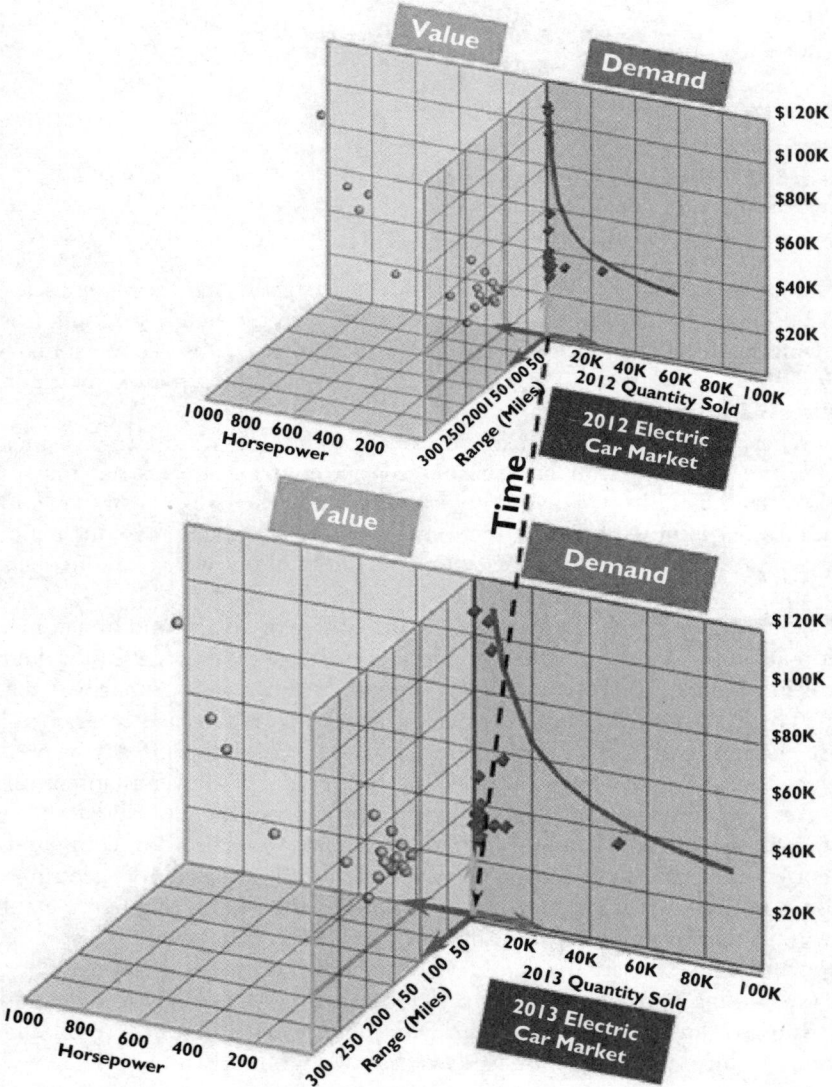

FIGURE 3.12 When we add time to four-dimensional models, we get five-dimensional models.[19]

As a byproduct of plotting all competitors' positions and how customers react to them, market mapping will also show the boundaries that the buyers display. Markets will reject products with features that do not exceed their market's minimum requirements. Likewise, they will not support goods or services that exceed the thresholds of what they can collectively absorb. There is little sense in going "head-to-head" or "off the map" when making new products. We will address the issues of product placement, market boundaries, and competitive distance in more detail in Chapter 9's study of "Aiming, Leading, and Missing."

Before we get there, however, we might adequately wonder about the forces that support prices in the first place. It is that concept, the idea of product value, to which we will turn next.

SUMMARY

Change comes over time. It happens with celestial bodies and warring armies. It also happens to markets. Market movements have some aspects of the maps astronomers create for Near Earth Objects, as previously unseen products enter or leave markets all the time, just as comets and NEOs enter and leave our field of vision. In other ways, market movements resemble the movements of armies, with large aggregations (as products in markets or troops in a battle) moving as long, broad lines. The quantities purchased of various models in markets vary as well. Market maps show where the competitors lie, what open spaces exist between them, and the customer limits regarding the minimum features offered and the maximum amount their combined numbers can buy.

CHAPTER 4

Value

"I conceive that the great part of the miseries of mankind are brought upon them by false estimates they have made of the value of things."

Benjamin Franklin

HUMAN TRAITS

This book aims to enhance our predictions about human economic behavior. Since these actions cover millions of markets, billions of buyers, and trillions of transactions, this may seem a monumental undertaking. People see markets in unique ways. Some clients bought their first mobile phone in the 1980s; others just made their first purchase, and some will never own one. The prices customers are willing to pay for goods and services are reflected in their eagerness or reluctance to enter a market. Enthusiasts bought the first mass-produced, flat-screen televisions for thousands of dollars with only 720 lines of resolution and with less than 40 inches across on their diagonal measures. Now customers can buy a much larger set with more resolution for far less than they paid for an inferior product over a decade ago.

Different people see things differently. The same people see things differently over time.

Since economics only has meaning with people, it makes sense to examine people more closely to see if we have ways to make sense of the human condition and appeal to what we already know about ourselves. We will find patterns in humanity that we intuitively knew, but perhaps had not reflected on graphically.

Imagine you are a preschool teacher, and today you are attending a large convention of your fellow educators. While you teach little tykes every school day, one thing you know as you open the door—you will not see any of your students, or anyone else's, in attendance there.

What does this mean concerning something we could measure about the people you will encounter? Clearly, with your students out of the mix, the average height in your room is different than it is on your regular school day. If you were so inclined, you could prove this by finding the heights of the women and men at the conference and then parsing those observations into frequency bins, as shown in Figures 4.1 and 4.2, respectively.

Three things are immediately apparent when you do this. First, there are limits to the heights of adults as both women and men have lower and upper bounds to their heights as a group. There are no 10-foot men. We find no 9-foot women. Second, while some women are taller than some men, the average height for women is less than that of men. Finally, your sense of the complete normality of the distribution strikes you. You took a random sample. It seems to match your observations to date. Nothing looks out of the ordinary. You have a group representing a cross-section of the area in which you live. Nothing stands out. If you had your preschoolers in the mix, you would note that they have their groupings of heights well below what they will attain when they become adults.

However, if some National Basketball Association All-Stars rolled into the room, they would stand out as they formed their distribution, as shown in Figure 4.3.

Figures 4.1 to 4.3 remind us that human heights fluctuate within limits. Knowing details about a specific group of people gives us more profound insights into their heights.

If we got enough random adult male heights, we could build graphs like those in Figures 4.4 and 4.5. In Figure 4.4, we see a bell-shaped curve take form if we accumulate enough observations and smooth them. In Figure 4.5, we continuously add the data as we go along, creating an S-shaped

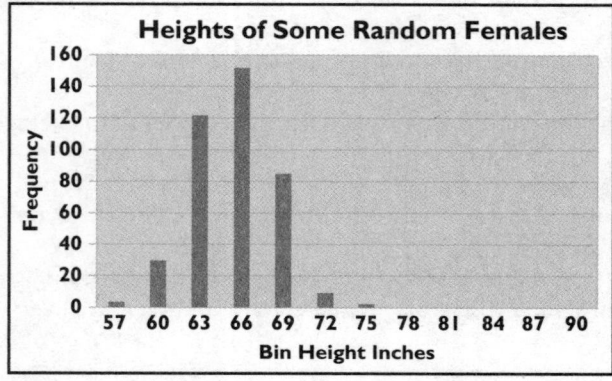

FIGURE 4.1   Women have a distribution of heights.[1,2]

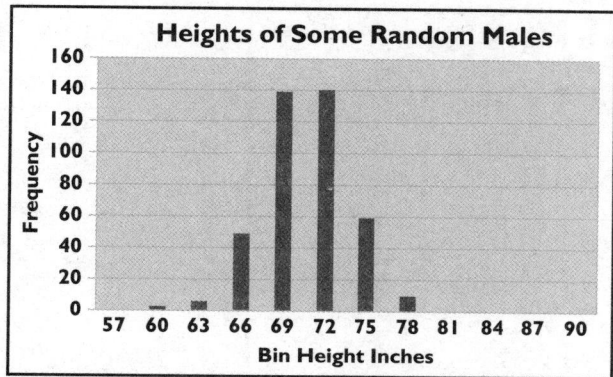

FIGURE 4.2 Men's heights tend to be taller than women's.[3, 4]

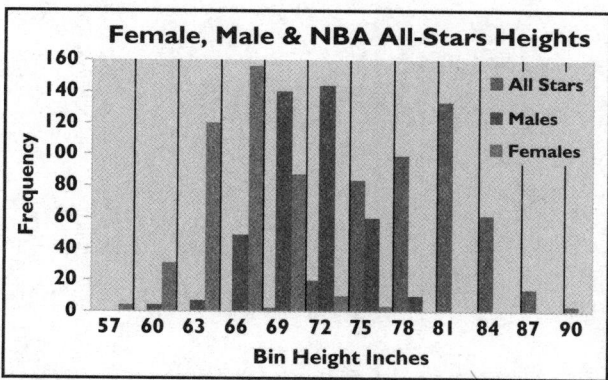

FIGURE 4.3 NBA players' heights tend to be taller than women and men in the wider population.[5, 6]

cumulative distribution. The peak of the curve represents the average or mean of the observations, while the vertical lines on either side of the mean are the standard deviations away from the mean; standard deviations are numbers used to express how far away from the expected value (mean, or average) the observations in a group lie. Lower standard deviations mean that most of the values in a set are close to the average, while higher standard deviations mean the values have wider spreads. It happens that the standard deviation for female heights is lower than it is for males, meaning that if you didn't know anything about the next random person that you met, chances are that if she were a woman, she would be closer to the norm

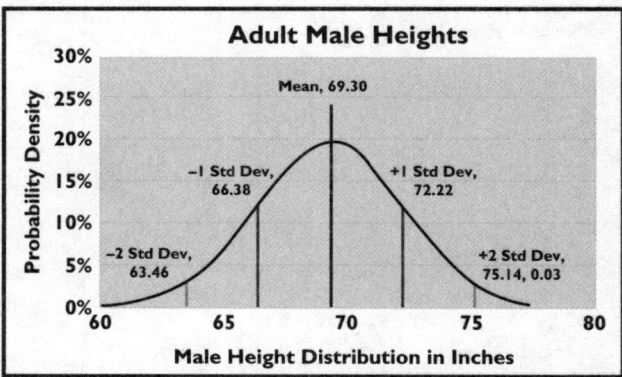

FIGURE 4.4 Human heights follow a normal distribution, which creates this bell-shaped curve.[8]

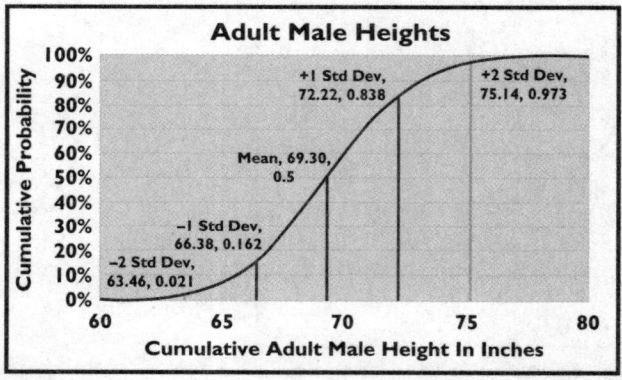

FIGURE 4.5 Adding the incremental values of the Figure 4.4 curve forms an *S*-shaped cumulative density curve in this figure.[9]

and that the next man would be little further off the mean. And you thought that was just your intuition.

Since these distributions work well for human physical characteristics, we wonder if they would do the same for human market interactions.

It turns out that they do. Our upcoming exploration of value will show us how.

WHAT DOES VALUE MEAN IN HYPERNOMICS?

You have probably noticed the wide variety of meanings the word *value* can carry. There is the value of an education, the values of your parents, and the value of one nation's currency against that of another country.

Perhaps the most common usage of the word *value* relates to the amount of money a good or service commands. Often implicit in such a notion is some measure of fairness in the amount paid for a product. Something is an excellent value if the price falls far below what a reasonable person or several rational people expect. Conversely, if another product's price were deemed unfairly high, reluctant buyers of that good or service may say that they did not receive good or even fair value or may suffer buyer's remorse.

Hypernomics *is very interested in economic value*. Economic value, or value for short, as used here, has a specific meaning that differs slightly from those previously mentioned.

Value: The value of a good or service is the amount of money buyers are willing to pay for it based on its attributes.

Economic values across markets are the collective wisdom of everyone. Every buyer in every market influences values. When we simultaneously consider all the buyers' actions, we observe shared views about what products are worth.

What is it that we value in products? What features do we want? What attributes are worth the money we pay for them? Many things may come to mind and form a long list. While the following list of valued attributes is extensive, it is not exhaustive. Note that all of the following features lend themselves to definitive accounting using universally recognizable units of measure:

Valued Attributes Include (But Are Not Limited To)

Capacity: The ability to hold or accommodate something or someone has value. The number of passenger seats is a capacity attribute for cars, buses, or trains. In computers, memory, measured in gigabytes or terabytes, offers a measure of capacity. Appliances such as microwave ovens, refrigerators, and washing machines have capacities measured in cubic feet.

Speed: Trains that travel over 180 miles per hour save time compared to trains that travel one-third as fast. Internet connections moving data at eight megabits per second are worth more than connections going less than 1/100th that speed. Getting there quicker conveys more value to consumers.

Comfort: Aircraft that offer cabins well over six feet tall are more comfortable than planes with only four-foot tall cabins. Houses of 4,000 square feet are more valuable than 3,000-square-foot homes in the same neighborhood. More room offers more comfort. Added comfort translates into extra value.

Range or Endurance: Cellular phones that can last 48 hours between charges are more valuable than similar units that last 12 hours on a charge. Aircraft that can fly 5,000 miles without refueling are worth more than those that can only go half that far before stopping for fuel.

Durability: Television sets that can operate for 20,000 hours are more valuable than otherwise identical sets that can only guarantee a 2,000-hour lifespan. Car models that run for 250,000 miles are more valuable than similar cars with much shorter usable lives. Knowing the product you just bought will last a long time has a definite value.

Power: Cars with greater horsepower fetch more money than models with smaller engines. Stereos with powerful amplifiers command more dollars than those with less powerful amplifiers.

Portability and Flexibility: Wallet-sized cell phones and portable entertainment centers represent a tremendous gain in digital media portability over brick-sized devices popular decades earlier. Devices that can transport many large digital files in small containers are more valuable than bulky alternatives. Vehicles that manage rough off-road conditions have more value than ordinary passenger cars that cannot easily handle that terrain.

Safety and Health: Automobiles that offer "run-flat" tires provide protection not found in cars without that feature. Boats with two or more engines provide more security than those with a single engine. Medications that can control blood pressure with little or no side effects are more valuable than pills with severe side effects.

Reliability: Phone services that work 99.9% of the time are worth more than those that work 95% of the time. Automobiles that break down infrequently are more valuable than cars that often break down.

Operating Cost and Resale Value: Machines that require less fuel and maintenance are more valuable than machines with high operating costs. Consumers spend more money to buy products if they have higher resale values than their competitors.

Indeed, you could come up with several other broad categories of valued attributes that are easily quantifiable or find more examples in each of the preceding groupings. The goal here is not to name everything that might add to the attractiveness of products, but to show that many characteristics with which you are already familiar determine value.

DETERMINING VALUE

Some things are easier to measure than others. You can calculate your height in inches, weight in pounds, and age in years. It is easy to convert parameters such as height, weight, and age into universally recognized units of measurement.

Using Utility Theory, Jeremy Bentham measured happiness using utilities, or utils, as the basis of a felicific calculus. Bentham argued that better methods of distributing stocks of happiness offered the maximum benefit to society.[10]

Happiness, as it stands alone as a descriptor of the well-being of consumers, is a little too fuzzy for Hypernomics. Happiness is hard to hold down. In Bentham's world, many utils making their way to you should make you content. But what if you are manic-depressive? No amount of utils might ever make you happy.[11]

But what if we try to measure happiness instead of measuring satisfaction? That is to say, what if we could observe and eventually predict satisfaction with goods and services based on consumers' valuation of their attributes? What could we do with that knowledge? How might we go about acquiring it?

Some people are never happy. However, they can attain satisfaction. Since consumers are the buyers in markets, we need to study their past behaviors to predict their future actions and measure their satisfaction. If they exchange money for goods or services, they explicitly demonstrate that the value of those products meets or exceeds the cash that they offered for them.

Let's examine a consumer known for especially high standards.

Mick Jagger once famously complained in a song:

I can't get no satisfaction,
I can't get no satisfaction.
'Cause I try and I try and I try and I try.
I can't get no, I can't get no.[12]

We can then agree that the lead singer for The Rolling Stones is an uncommonly tricky individual to please. However, we all have something in common with him. Mick Jagger, like the rest of us, buys things. Mick makes purchases. Some of them are pretty large. Frequently on tour, Mr. Jagger has to go from place to place in a hurry, and he would like to get there in style. What better way was there than the Aston Martin DB6? Thus, when Mick Jagger bought a brand-new Aston Martin DB6 in 1966 (which he crashed soon after),[13] we can state with confidence that he satisfied his Value-Price Threshold subject to his budget constraints. Yes, it cost a lot of money, an estimated £25,000 in 1966 or roughly $646,000 in 2023 currency.[14, 15]

> **Value-Price Threshold:** This is the point at which a buyer's product value meets or exceeds its price, as evidenced by a purchase. This point varies from buyer to buyer.

Mick Jagger understands, as we all do, that products are worth more to us when they have more of what we want in them. We may depict this in a general way, as shown in Figure 4.6, in which the graph indicates that as we receive more of the features we like in a product, the value of that product goes up. This applies to any product or service. For electric cars, for example, we might reason that more horsepower should be a feature for which we would be willing to pay more, or perhaps range.

In some situations, when we get less of something we do not want, as Figure 4.7 depicts, our value also increases. An example is consumers paying more to buy cars with lower overall operating costs and those requiring

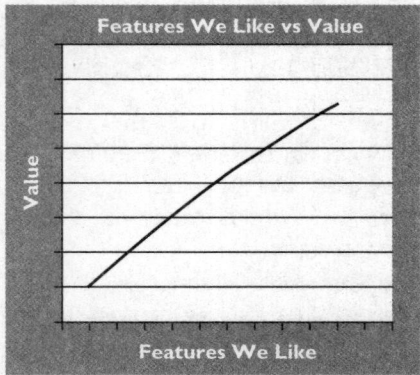

FIGURE 4.6   People willingly pay more for features they like if they can afford them.[16]

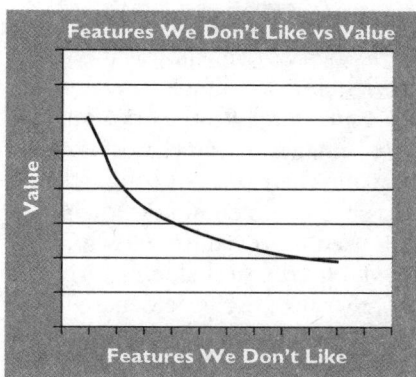

FIGURE 4.7 If they have the money to pay for it, buyers will pay more for fewer features they dislike.[17]

less attention. Once customers purchase electric cars, they enjoy much lower energy costs and get back the time it took waiting to fill up their previous vehicles with gas.

Producers, those companies and individuals that provide goods and services to consumers, are generally free to choose the attributes or features they incorporate into their products.[18] Since value depends on the features suppliers put into their products, their choices dictate sustainable value to consumers. Another, more formal way of stating this is that value in a good or service is a function of its attributes or features consumers want.

Because producers are free to pick any combination of attributes they want to put into products, those attributes are independent variables.[19] Product value, in turn, depends on product attributes, so value is a dependent variable.[20] But what is the nature of the dependency? How can we describe it?

At this point, we have examined the market for electric cars and have a familiarity with it that we would like to exploit. We will want to make some sense of what makes this market function. What makes prices move? How will we go about figuring that out?

THE MARKET AS LABORATORY

Suppose you were an astrophysicist and noticed that each of a small number of galaxies studied had a supermassive black hole at its center. Given a growing number of like observations, you might hypothesize that every galaxy has a supermassive black hole at its center. Moreover, suppose you were either Professor Andrea Ghez or Professor Reinhard Genzel. In that case, you might spend years of your life making some unassailable observations and compiling statistics confirming your local version of this hypothesis, namely, that there is a supermassive black hole at the center of our galaxy, the Milky Way.

Working independently from the Keck telescope in Hawaii and the European Southern Observatory in Chile, respectively, Professors Ghez and Genzel each made measurements of infrared images of stars in orbit about the estimated center of the galaxy. They made their cases through closely observed changes in star triangulation and speed.[21] In coming to their conclusions, Professors Ghez and Genzel each used a procedure known as the *scientific method,* in which they formulated, tested, retested, and verified a hypothesis. Due to their compelling work, there is now little debate in the astrophysics community that there is a supermassive black hole at the center of the Milky Way galaxy.

A generally agreed upon procedure by which to formulate and test hypotheses, we can summarize the scientific method as follows:[22]

Scientific Method
1. Define the question.
2. Gather information (observations).
3. Form a hypothesis.
4. Experiment and collect data.
5. Analyze data.
6. Interpret data and draw conclusions for starting points for new hypotheses.
7. Publish results.
8. Retest.

The physics and chemistry fields typically lead the world using the scientific method. Here, we will simply be following their lead. The work performed by Professors Ghez and Genzel is particularly enlightening.

In employing the scientific method, they asked themselves: Is there a supermassive black hole at the center of the Milky Way Galaxy? They gathered some vital information about supermassive black holes. They discovered that every time researchers made detailed observations of galaxies, they found supermassive black holes at their centers. They then each formed the same hypothesis: There is a supermassive black hole at the center of the Milky Way Galaxy. This called for an experiment to see if they could reject that assumption. If a black hole did reside at the galaxy's center, given its super-dense mass, it would cause stars near it to speed up and orbit around it. By analyzing the acceleration of nearby stars and their centers of rotation, Professors Ghez, Genzel, and their respective teams could prove the existence of a supermassive black hole at the center of our galaxy and triangulate its position. They each published their findings, which found some immediate resistance. When colleagues began assailing their work, they found more evidence supporting their theory and published that. Their work helped set in motion even more studies about supermassive black holes. Researchers have since discovered dozens of black holes at the centers of galaxies. Protests against their theory have largely disappeared.

If we follow the scientific method for economics, we must begin by defining a question(s). The following should interest us:

1. **Define questions:** Can value analysis predict sustainable product prices? In the case at hand, can value analysis predict the values, as sustainable prices, of electric cars?

    This information would be helpful to know. Suppose we have dreamed up a new electric car model. Can we make money with it? If our price is higher than our cost, we can make a profit. If the predicted price that the market will bear is lower than our cost, we may need to reconsider our offering.

    The electric car market is well suited enough for value prediction. As we have seen, it has a limited and discrete number of models in production. Their information is easily retrievable, as most manufacturers post their sale prices and product features on their websites. This makes it a good candidate market for the next phase of the scientific method.

2. **Gather information:** The electric car market in 2013, as shown in Table 4.1, is the result of some data gathering.

    The number of entrants grew from 2011, and sales quantities increased for some market leaders. An updated market version to a later year would still have more competitors. A broader set of observations might consist of additional columns, as we would gather data on virtually anything we think might add value. Our default claim we want to test is the *null hypothesis*, which in this case would be that neither horsepower nor range, our independent variables, affect the price, which is our dependent variable.

3. **Form hypothesis:** A glance at Table 4.1 reveals that vehicles with more horsepower command more money. Our new hypothesis is that added horsepower may increase the value of electric cars. At this point, we want to test our hypothesis and see the results.

4. **Perform experiments and gather data from them:** In this case, we will find the line of best fit through the data and see if we can make any sense of Table 4.1.

    In Figure 4.8, we find this line and discover that it has predictive ability, which, stated another way, indicates that added horsepower increases value in a statistically sound fashion. While this result is significant, it is not perfect—a perfect correlation would have all the dots mapped along the line. We wonder if we can do better.

TABLE 4.1 The 2013 electric car market changed from 2011.[23–40] We need to make sense of it.

Manufacturer	Model	HP	Range miles	2013 Sales Qty	5-Year Vehicle Price
Commuter Cars	Tango T600	805	120	100	$108,000
Mitsubishi	i-MiEV	63	82	11000	$ 33,891
Smart	ED	74	87	2100	$ 28,750
Nissan	Leaf	110	75	50000	$ 35,340
Chevrolet	Spark EV	130	82	1560	$ 27,495
Ford	Focus Electric	143	76	2100	$ 39,995
Honda	Fit EV	134	100	700	$ 36,625
Wheego	Whip	60	100	40	$ 32,995
Bolloré	Bluecar	67	160	1600	$ 31,416
BYD Auto	e6	215	122	1700	$ 35,000
Renault	Fluence Z.E.	94	115	2000	$ 36,307
Renault	Zoe	87	130	6900	$ 33,490
Tesla	Model S	302	208	7000	$ 57,400
Tesla	Model S Sig	362	265	7000	$ 95,400
Tesla	Model S Sig Perf	416	265	7000	$105,400
Toyota	RAV4 EV	154	103	1400	$ 49,800
Roewe	E50	63	110	1000	$ 37,589
Fiat	500e	111	100	1100	$ 32,500

5. **Analyze data:** It is often not enough to acquire *some* relationship within the data. We need to explore the relationships in the data and improve them to the fullest extent possible. While our result in Figure 4.8 is good, we would like to find better price predictors. If we pay particular attention to the database in Table 4.1, we notice that we have gathered another feature that we think might affect the price—range. This observation leads us to our next phase.

6. **Interpret data and draw conclusions that serve as starting points for new hypotheses:** Given that horsepower did well in predicting electric car prices but not well enough, we may want to try to use other independent variables to forecast prices. In this case, we only have range. When we test the relationship between range and price, we get Figure 4.9.

The analysis indicates that range affects the price, but is less well correlated with horsepower. Since both features worked independently to predict

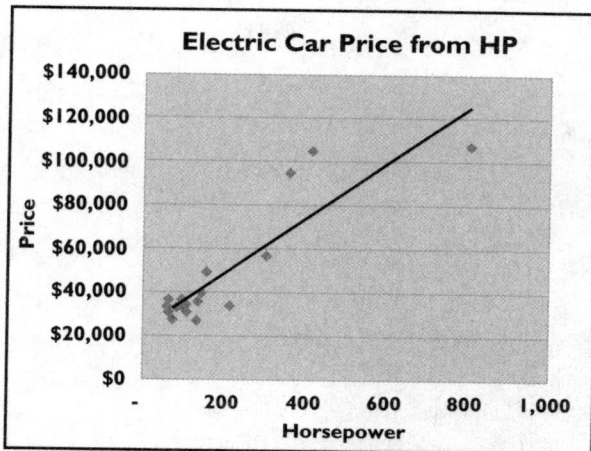

FIGURE 4.8 Horsepower adds value to electric cars.[41] This trend is helpful but not perfect.

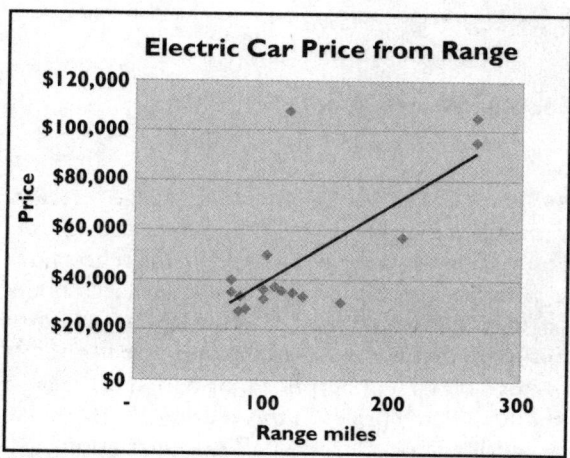

FIGURE 4.9 Plotting electric car prices from range by itself is statistically significant, but less so than using horsepower alone.[42]

price, we wonder what might happen when we combine them, as shown in Figure 4.10

Note that the slanted plane in Figure 4.10 considers the contribution of both horsepower and range to the predicted values (sustainable prices) of the

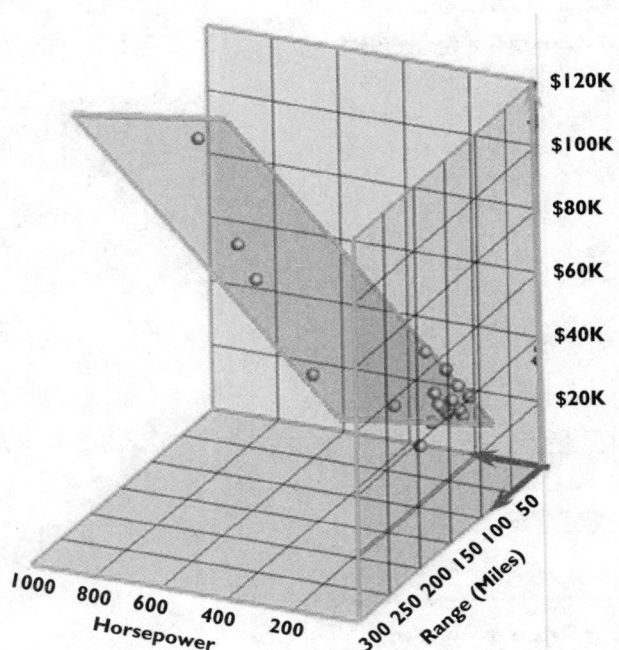

FIGURE 4.10   Using two variables, or features, to describe price offers a better answer here.[43]

models, and that the plane goes up as both horsepower and range increase. Observe that most of the spheres are closer to the plane than those same models were to their respective lines in Figures 4.8 and 4.9. This reflects our improved prediction. Those spheres higher than this angled surface (again, points representing models) may be overpriced, or other forces at work push the prices for those vehicles higher. We may say the opposite for points below the prediction plane—they may be underpriced, or perhaps, we have not considered everything that drives the prices in this market.

However, we know that we have not addressed all price variations yet, as Figure 4.11 shows.

A perfectly correlated result would have all points on the diagonal line. In practice, perfect correlations seldom appear, but as a practical matter, when it comes to Value estimation, with an adjusted R^2 of just over 90%, we likely have more work we could do to improve our predictions.

Surprisingly, you already have an intuitive idea about how added features would work, as shown in Figure 4.12, which addresses freight delivery by United Parcel Service (UPS). In shipping domestically via UPS from Los Angeles, the distance traveled and the size of our freight packages have a lot

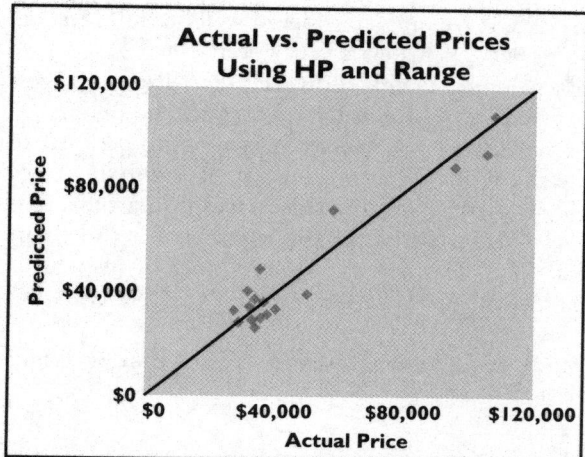

FIGURE 4.11 Here, we compare actual prices on the horizontal axis with predicted prices (with our equation, not shown) on the vertical axis.[44] Note that there are many cases where the actual prices do not exactly match the predicted values.

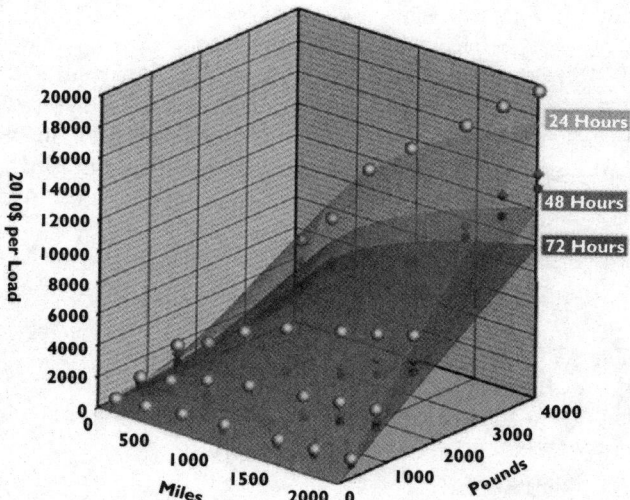

FIGURE 4.12 Prices for freight delivery are a function of at least three variables—load weight (or dimensions), distance traveled, and time from pickup to delivery.[45–48]

to do with the value of the load. If we only considered weight and distance, we would get a correlation of 92.7%, which is very good.

Every time you go to a shipping facility, however, they ask you about at least one other option—when would you like your package delivered? Time is valuable. If something is essential, you will pay more to get it there in a hurry. In Figure 4.12, we find dots of increasing heights signifying rates for 72-, 48-, and 24-hour deliveries, separating themselves into groups represented by the progressively higher surfaces. The equation for these surfaces has an adjusted R^2 of 97.6%, which explains more than two-thirds of the remaining variation from the mean than our two-variable equation did at 92.7%.

We will use this concept of prediction for values so often that we ought to name it, which we do here.

Value Estimating Relationship: Value Estimating Relationships, or VERs, are collective estimates buyers in markets make about the value of products offered based on their attributes or features.

We are driving at economic aiming, akin to taking target practice at a shooting range, as shown in Figure 4.13.

Marksmanship addresses accuracy, which is a measure of how close we are to our target, as well as precision, how repeatable we find our results to be. One can have low accuracy but be highly precise, as Figure 4.13 displays the leftmost target. On the other hand, a sharpshooter could simultaneously be very accurate and imprecise, as Figure 4.13's center panel shows us. In riflery, our goal is always to be accurate and precise, as in the rightmost

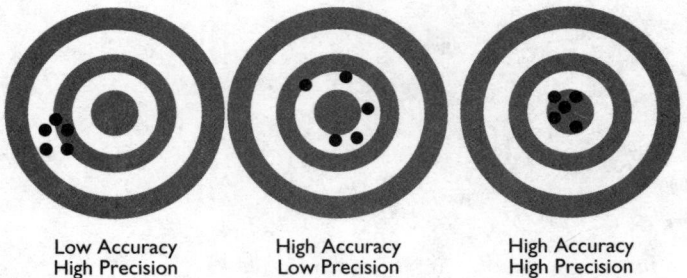

Low Accuracy   High Accuracy   High Accuracy
High Precision   Low Precision   High Precision

FIGURE 4.13   In shooting sports, accuracy is how close a measured value (a shot) is to the actual (target) value. How close the measured values are to one another indicates precision.[49]

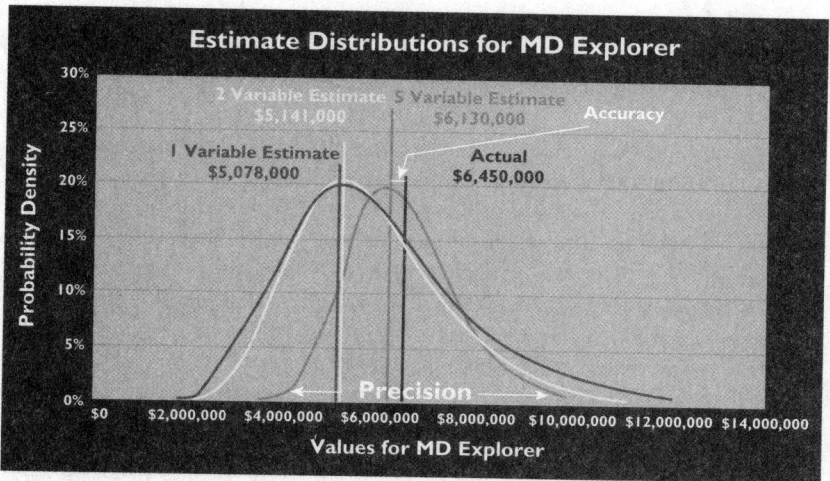

FIGURE 4.14 In this helicopter value analysis example, going from 1 to 5 variables improved accuracy (was 21% off, is 5% off) and precision (Standard Deviation was $4.85 million, is $1.32 million).[50, 51]

panel in Figure 4.13. In estimating product values as supportable prices, we strive for the same thing.

Figure 4.14 depicts estimated distributions for a helicopter model called the MD Explorer.

Each of these skewed bell-shaped curves shows their predicted values for that helicopter as the peaks of those curves (through which go the vertical lines, with their associated labeled estimates), as well as the errors in those estimates (as the lateral extents of the reaches of those curves, as determined by their standard deviations). In this case, a one-variable estimate for this particular helicopter type missed a fair amount (21% away from the mean value and with a standard deviation of $4.85 million). However, as we added a second, third, fourth, and eventually a fifth feature to the analysis, our average estimate became more accurate (now only 5% off) and precise (its standard error is a little more than a quarter of what it had been). While adding extra valued attributes is time-consuming and does not always result in improvements, we often benefit from the enhanced scrutiny as our predictions become more exact.

You might ask why all the bother with this value analysis in the first place. Precisely what is at stake here? In the case of the helicopters, if we are wildly inaccurate with our value estimate of a given model, we might wonder about at least two things: 1) Have we missed one or more essential features contributing to model value, and 2) Has the manufacturer correctly priced their model? Adding other variables for regression analysis is something that we can do if only we gather that information. Now, we can move to the next step in the scientific method.

7. **Publish results:** We have some statistically significant effects, so we might choose to publish now. Once we publish, other groups may take an interest in our analysis, or we might want to rethink what we have done. This pushes us to the last step in the scientific method.
8. **Retest:** Other groups may want to confirm or deny our results, and may choose to retest the data to see if they get the same results. Our initial research may be incomplete even if others get the same effect. Retesting the data often reveals relationships that have yet to be seen in previous analytic efforts. Additionally, markets change over time. Updated analyses often provide different results.

Correctly pricing items for sale is the function of the producer. If studies reveal that the value estimating equations are accurate and precise, and some prices still vary from the predictions, those producers may consider revising their prices.

How big of an impact might a producer have on his bottom line if he or she were to price products incorrectly? Let us consider the case of ground beef in the United States in January 2012, as revealed in Table 4.2 and Figure 4.15.

Note in that figure that there are five 100-pound package options, which producers sell at the wholesale level. Those wholesale items vary in the packages' percentage of lean ground beef. In addition to the wholesale boxes, there are several retail packages ranging in size from one pound to five and a half pounds.

If we take all of the data from Table 4.2, we can plot it as a series of spheres in Figure 4.15. When we do that, we notice a pattern in the data. That pattern has a mathematical description much like the one we found for electric cars, except that this pattern is not flat but curved.

Note that at the wholesale end of the chart (where the package size equals 100 pounds, closest to the front of the diagram, all of the spheres (which again represent 100-pound packages for sale) are on the curved surface—except one. Note that one sphere, marked "Actual Price $2.06/pound" runs below the surface. If, instead, that sphere was centered on the surface, the price would have been $2.40/pound. While $0.34 per pound may not seem like much when you consider that about 293,000,000 pounds of ground beef sold at that grade and price in the previous year, you discover that the wholesale manufacturers likely could have realized up to an additional $100 million had they added that difference to their sales price.

TABLE 4.2 Ground beef database, January 2012.[52–54]

Price per lb	Percent Lean	Package Size (lbs)
$0.99	50%	100.00
$1.83	73%	100.00
$2.04	81%	100.00
$2.06	90%	100.00
$2.55	93%	100.00
$2.97	73%	2.25
$2.50	73%	5.00
$4.25	93%	5.50
$3.86	90%	2.25
$3.86	85%	2.25
$3.98	85%	1.00
$3.00	80%	5.00
$4.48	93%	1.00
$4.00	85%	4.00
$3.28	80%	1.00
$3.98	85%	1.00
$4.28	85%	1.33
$3.16	80%	3.00
$4.98	96%	1.00
$4.35	93%	2.25

Beef, of course, is not a new product. What kind of effects might we observe in new products priced out of line with the rest of the market?

Let us consider a problem similar to the one that faces Mick Jagger when he buys a new car. What values do customers place on the features of a business or private aircraft? In the early 2000s, this information was crucial for a new entrant into this market: the Eclipse 500 produced by Eclipse Aviation.

This company, a newcomer to aviation manufacturing, sought to take the expertise its president had gained in the software industry and translate that into success in the civil aircraft market.

With the same type of analysis that we used for the ground beef and helicopter markets, we can work out the value of such a plane.

As shown in Figure 4.16, the 2002 price for the Eclipse 500, much less than $1 million, was so far below the estimated value of just over $3 million that the aircraft manufacturer had less than one chance in a thousand that they got the price right. By analogy, it was as if you had bought a new automobile

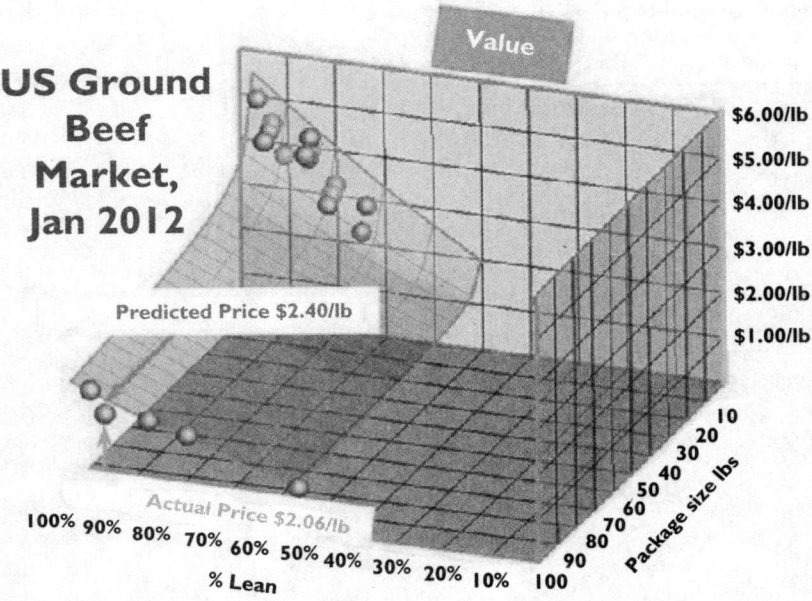

FIGURE 4.15 Value in ground beef is a function of package size and leanness. Significant variations from the sustainable market price have implications for sales.[55] Will a $0.34 price variation make a significant impact?

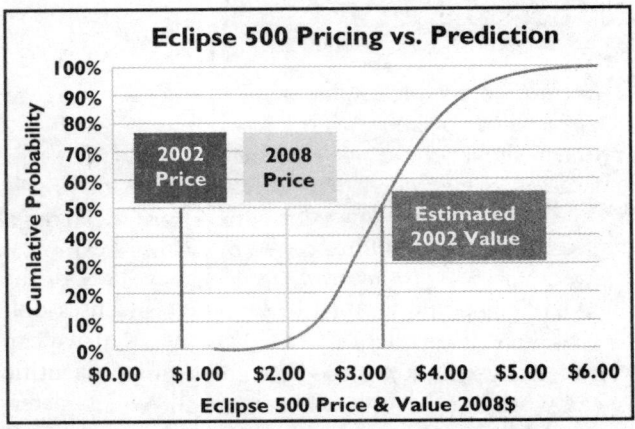

FIGURE 4.16 The underpriced Eclipse 500 bankrupted Eclipse Aviation, losing over $1 billion.[56]

for $30,000 and then immediately broadcast to anyone who would listen that you want to sell it for $10,000; the number of would-be buyers would swamp you. Such was the case with the Eclipse 500. The initial meager price brought orders by the hundreds and the low thousands. Eclipse Aviation initially took orders for its Eclipse 500 at $775,000 per model in May 2000,[57] then their price rose over time as they eventually reached 2,600 orders.[58] Eclipse Aviation, apparently thinking that the price had to match their rising costs, finally raised its price for its Model 500 to $2.15 million in 2008.[59]

At the same time, the company found itself beset with similarly massive production problems akin to those they created with their faulty, cost-based pricing. They built a prototype vehicle, only to discover that it did not meet their target specifications, and they had to redesign the aircraft nearly from scratch. This caused delays in deliveries, leading to their cash flow slow-downs. With the costs to produce the vehicle above estimates as well, Eclipse filed for bankruptcy in late 2008, having lost over $1 billion.[60]

Eclipse Aviation failed to recognize that manufacturers' costs have little to do with customers' values.[61,62] When you walk into an electronics store looking for a new television, you will consider the screen size, resolution, and the sound quality of the sets offered. Not once will you wonder if the firm selling you the $400 set spent $4,000 to build the set, $400, or $40. That is immaterial to you. You want what you want. Taken together, we can find what everyone in a given market wants. As we have seen, we can discover those desires and how they manifest themselves.

Suppliers offering products without performing value analysis enter markets at their peril. Often, they will find that what the market will bear won't be enough to make a profit.

SUMMARY

People demonstrate physical characteristics, such as their heights, that we can depict with a mean and a standard deviation, which forms a bell-shaped curve. We wonder if we could describe economic behavior in the same way. Classic economics, once measured, and in some cases still, take stock of the usefulness of goods and services in terms of utils. Hypernomics uses dollars to express the value of those same items, testing the idea that we can find a way to predict the average price products may fetch. The scientific method validates the value determination hypothesis that consumers determine prices based on product features and rejects the null hypothesis that the product attributes have nothing to do with sustainable prices. Many features can come into play in value determination. Studies incorporating more features important to consumers relative to the products they buy can improve the accuracy and precision of value estimates. Improper pricing can lead to lost profits, lost sales, or in the worst cases, bankruptcy.

VIGNETTE: THE VALUE OF EXPANDING ONE'S LIMITS

"Don't stop when you're tired. Stop when you're done."
David Goggins

"Speed is not an aspect of life, it is life."
Alain Prost

Rocky Bleier (Figure 4.17) graduated from Notre Dame in 1968 after taking his football team to the national championship as a junior and playing as its captain as a senior. A relatively slow-moving running back with a personal best 40-yard dash time of 4.8 seconds, the Pittsburgh Steelers picked him in the 16th round of the National Football League (NFL), which made him the 417th selection.

After being drafted by the U.S. Army in 1968, he volunteered for duty in South Vietnam in 1969. While on patrol that August, he was shot in the left thigh, and moments later, had a grenade go off near his right foot, which was severely damaged. Doctors told him he'd never play football again. Not long after that, Art Rooney, the Steelers owner, wrote him a postcard that read, "Rock—the team's not doing well. We need you. Art Rooney"

FIGURE 4.17   Rocky Bleier, in 2017, addressing the Metropolitan Washington-Baltimore United Service Organizations (USO).[63, 64]

Bleier returned to training camp in 1970, over 30 pounds below his playing weight and barely able to walk. Placed on injured reserve that year, he got into a few games on special teams in 1971. But Bleier still hadn't regained his form. He continued to play in 1972 and 1973, but only had four rushing attempts in two years.

Then Rocky gave himself a tough question: What would happen if "some time in the future you didn't have to ask yourself 'what if?'"[65] Faced with his self-challenge, he returned to the Steelers' 1974 training camp to his old playing weight of 212 pounds.

When he ran the 40-yard dash, he did it in 4.6 seconds.[66] With part of his right foot blown off. His previous best had been 4.8 seconds. He became a 1,000-yard rusher in the 1976 season and a four-time Super Bowl winner.

Added speed added several years to Rocky Bleier's career. What does going faster do for modern NFL wide receivers? As you might guess, we can figure that out with Hypernomics.

What's the value of added speed for veteran wide receivers? We can find out if we remove the rookie contracts and draft halo effects by looking at pros in the league for six or more years. As Figure 4.18 shows us, the total compensation for NFL wideouts increases with receptions per game.[67, 68]

At the same time, their value falls dramatically with age. Speed plays a role too. A 28-year-old receiver with four catches a game running a 4.65 40-yard dash is worth about $6 million annually.

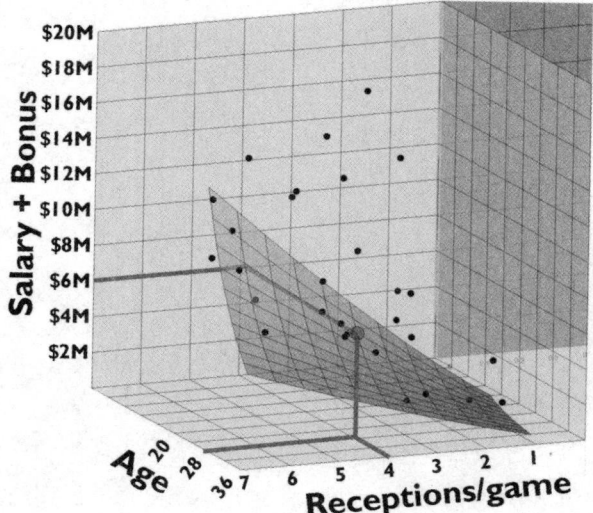

FIGURE 4.18 An NFL wide receiver's Value goes down with age, but up with receptions per game.[69]

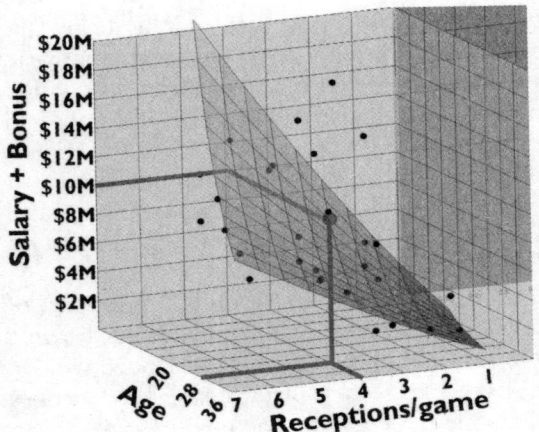

FIGURE 4.19   An NFL wide receiver's Value goes up dramatically with added speed.[70]

But, as we discover in Figure 4.19, being able to run that distance a quarter second faster, or 4.4 seconds (a 0.25-second drop, just a little more than Rocky Bleier's 0.20 improvement), a receiver the same age and number of catches, finds the extra speed adds another two-thirds to his compensation, bringing it to about $10 million per year in salary and bonuses.[66]

It's hard to improve speed. But if you can do it in the NFL, it pays off. Just ask Rocky Bleier.

CHAPTER 5

Demand

"And he writhed inside at what seemed the cruelty and unfairness of the demand."

C.S. Lewis

DEMAND FRONTIERS

You have many demands levied on you. Your parents, significant other, friends, teachers, job, it's always something; the list seems never-ending. There are innumerable demands upon your time and energy. People are demanding. They always want something. A large portion of those things we find in markets. Markets are built on demand, and demand means money. Hypernomics takes a deep interest in the demands on your money and everyone else's. There are numerous ways to look at demand, and we will examine several of them. Perhaps the most primal of these is the demand frontier.

In the early history of the United States, the American frontier was a way to describe the outer wave of westward expansion that began with the first English colonial settlements in the early 1600s. Geographical boundaries do not generate as much discussion now as in the past, but they are still very much with us. Figure 5.1 reveals that you cannot drive east of Florida's outer banks. That's a frontier.

Humanity, of course, has its ways of dealing with geography. We use oceans, seas, rivers, lakes, and mountain ranges to define international borders; when that is not enough, we draw a line in the sand. Sometimes, one side of a territorial dispute might suggest where the line should go and then find harsh opposition. World War I found people fighting for new territories, some of which became permanent in ways combatants did not envision before the war ended. Germany sought expansion to the west and got to a malleable line that came to be known as the Western Front, only to find its army stagnated. Ultimately defeated, Germany would lose the parts of

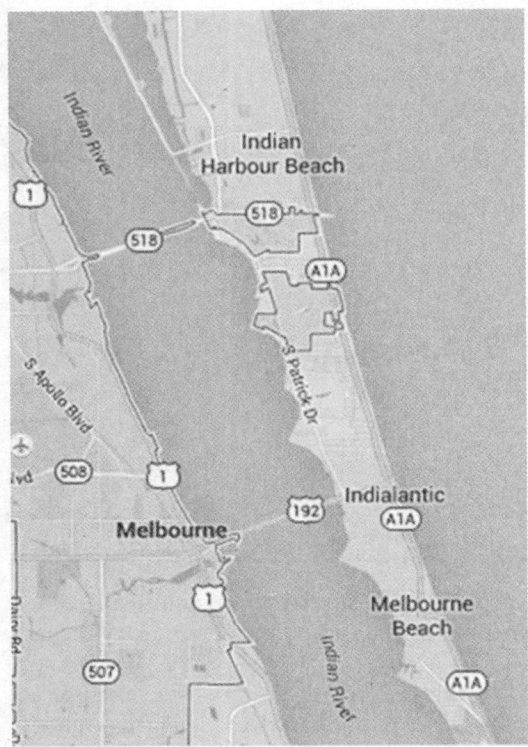

FIGURE 5.1   Nature poses frontiers for us. Driving
a car east of the barrier island of Melbourne, Florida,
is impossible.[1]

Belgium and France it had conquered and parts of what had been within its
borders before hostilities.

It is easy to see physical boundaries when they are right before us. Nothing says to stop driving quite like the ocean right in front of you. The difference between dry land and water is clear-cut. No one had to tell you that
the bad guys were on the other side of no-man's land in World War I, as
Figure 5.2 discloses. Going beyond your frontiers was at once unambiguous
and laden with danger.

Market economics must be vastly different. Or is it?

No one will likely die if you do not perform demand frontier analysis.
However, many projects perished for lack of it.

So, how do we go about it? First, we need to understand the components
of demand. This analysis requires two classes of information: quantities

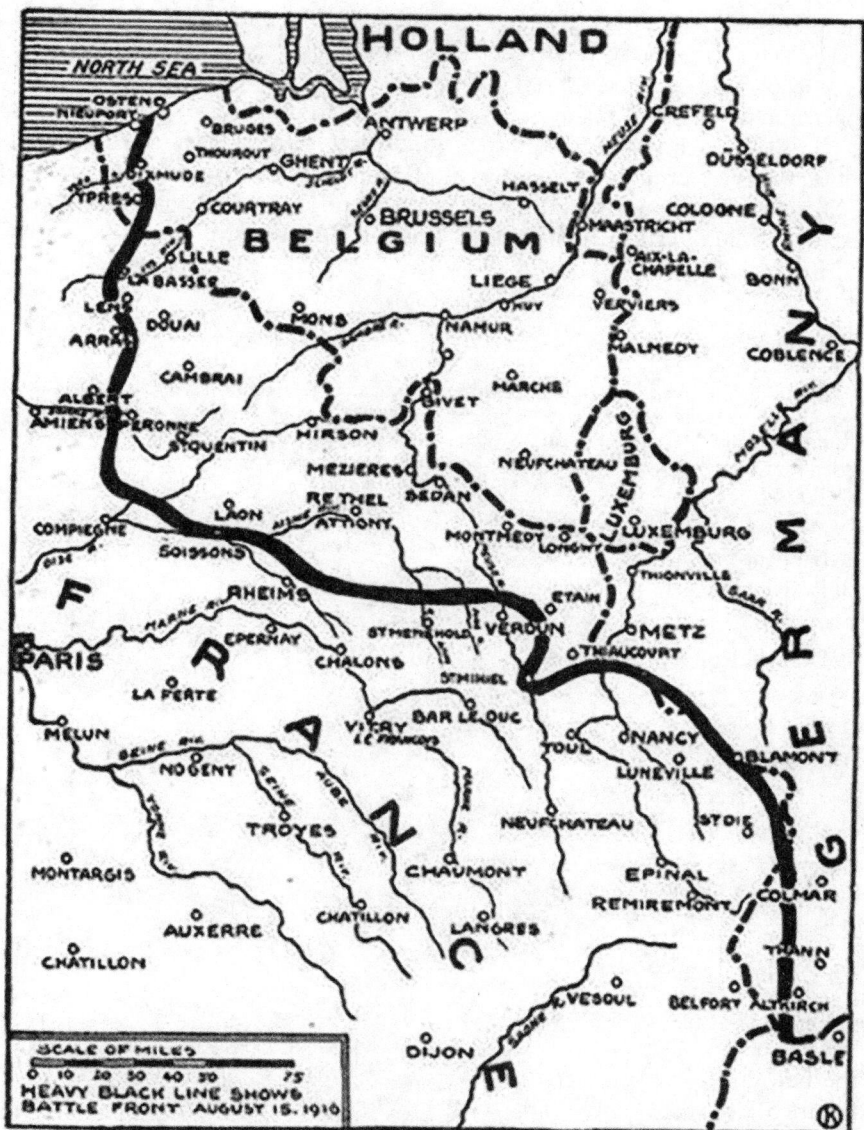

FIGURE 5.2 People create their frontiers. In World War I, the Western Front divided Germany in the East from the Allies in the West.[2]

and prices. Some people think that governments need not abide by demand curves. This is entirely incorrect. Thus, for our first foray into demand, since it is among the easiest data sets to assemble, we will examine the U.S. government's demand for fighter, bomber, and attack aircraft.

Table 5.1 shows us 24 different aircraft models that various U.S. military service branches bought over 60+ years (we use such a long period because it takes time to get a large enough sample size in this market and because some old models, first built in the 1950s, are still in use as of this writing in 2023).

TABLE 5.1   Long-lived U.S. fighter/bomber/attack aircraft purchases, 1957–2021.[3–31]

Manufacturer	Aircraft Model	1957 to 2021 Qty	2021 Flyaway $M
Boeing	B-52H	744	$100.00
Rockwell	B-1B	100	$475.66
McDonnell Douglas	AV-8B	323	$44.30
McDonnell Douglas	FA-18AD	1480	$50.90
Boeing	FA-18EF	563	$64.90
McDonnell Douglas	F-15AE	1415	$50.10
Lockheed	F-117A	59	$86.90
General Dynamics	F-16CD	4600	$30.30
Lockheed Martin	F-22	187	$217.23
Northrop Grumman	B-2	21	$1,209.24
Grumman	A-6	693	$69.38
Fairchild Republic	A-10	716	$16.35
Grumman	F-14	712	$107.54
General Dynamics	F-111	563	$47.62
McDonnell Douglas	F-4	5195	$19.50
LTV	A-7	1545	$21.09
Vought	F-8	1219	$36.25
Douglas	A-4	2960	$8.05
Northrop	F-5	2246	$8.82
Lockheed Martin	F-35A	388	$94.45
Lockheed Martin	F-35B	167	$136.87
Lockheed Martin	F-35C	65	$127.55
General Atomics	MQ-9	337	$17.88
General Atomics	MQ-1	360	$4.91

We should note that the quantity column has a date range, meaning that versions of the models in this column built before or after the date range are not included. Also, note that the price column states that we are examining the "flyaway" cost, which is the recurring price to the U.S. government *after* its significant investment in the development costs of these projects. Observe that the United States bought a few costly models (only 21 sales of the B-2, which went for about $1.2 billion a copy), but many more of the less costly ones (4600 F-16s sold at a little more than $30 million each). This is crucial—we instantly know that this table indicates that the United States bought fewer of this type of product as the price goes up. What other sense can we make of this information?

Suppose we plot these data using quantities sold as our horizontal component and prices for our vertical element. If we do this, we get the view in Figure 5.3. Here, we have our 24 models as individual round dots on the chart. With this picture, it is easy to see that some models are more toward the right and the top of this map than others.

In Figure 5.4, we identify the outermost points (the B-2, B-1B, B-52, F-4, F-14, F-15, F-16, F-18, and F-22) and characterize their positions in both 2021 and 25 years earlier, in 1996. Note that they collectively form a boundary without much movement. When we find the lines of best fit in Figure 5.5 (here, the upper one for 2021, the lower one for 1996), we

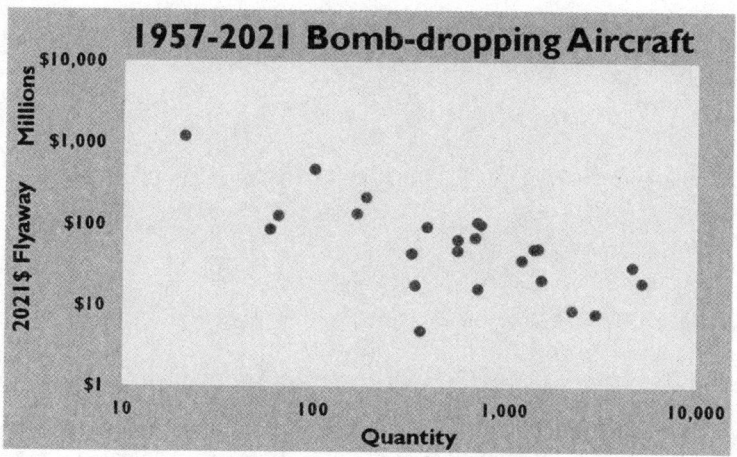

FIGURE 5.3 From 1957 to 2021, the United States purchased more of the less expensive bomb-dropping aircraft than the more expensive models.[32]

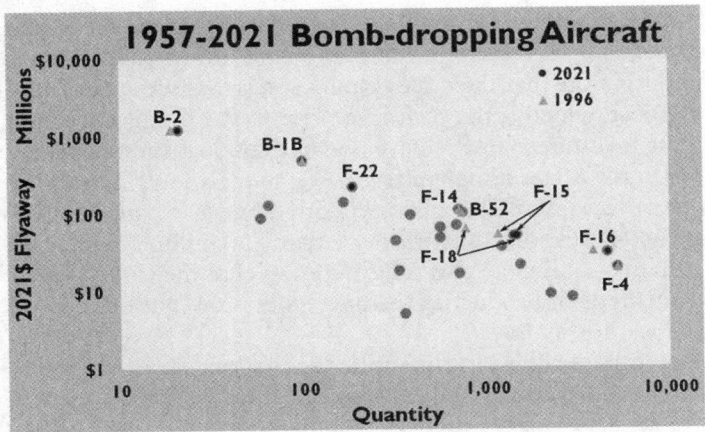

FIGURE 5.4   The darker dots within the lighter dots are the 2021 quantities at the market limit, while the triangles inside or next to those dots represent the limit in 1996.[33]

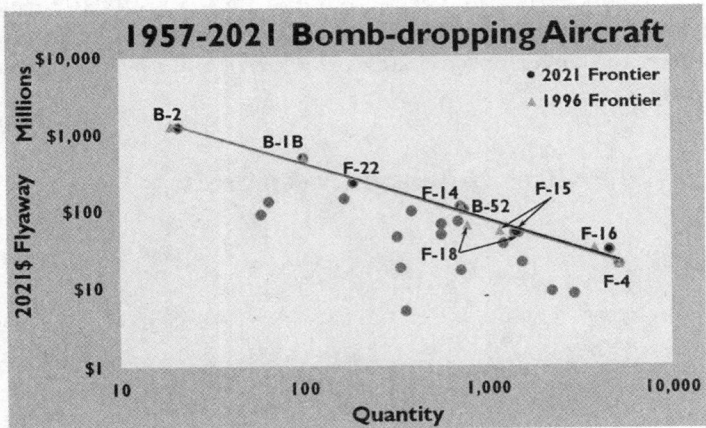

FIGURE 5.5   Between 1996 and 2021, the Demand Frontier for bomb-dropping aircraft moved up about 2%.[34, 35]

discover that they are highly significant, and thus, form good predictors of The Demand Frontier a crucial concept for us, and we must define it.

Demand Frontiers: These are the outer and upper market boundaries for quantities and prices, respectively.

Demand Frontiers are not immutable. Growing markets, like those for cell phones in the early 21st century, are expanding upward and outward. Contracting markets, like those for cathode ray television sets during the same timeframe, see their markets contracting downward and inward. Furthermore, these lines are "fuzzy." They are not deterministic and have distributions, just as we saw with heights and economic values. The Demand Frontiers ranges give us the likelihood of projects exceeding them. However, while other markets are highly dynamic, the Demand Frontier for fighters, bombers, and attack aircraft is highly correlated and stable, as it has not moved much in decades. It is folly to suppose that a program could best it by a substantial margin.

However, Figure 5.6 shows us that one can try. In the 1980s, Northrop Grumman proposed building 132 B-2 Stealth Bombers, estimated in 1981, which were thought to have a flyaway price of $649 million each (in 2013 dollars); the price grew to $981 million for the same quantity in 1989. Eventually, the company settled for 21 units at $1,091 million each. The U.S. Air Force wanted more. So did Northrop Grumman. But, the U.S. Congress, the purse keeper, ultimately forced them to abide by the Demand Frontier they had organized for themselves.

A few years later, also in Figure 5.6, Lockheed Martin attempted to exceed the Demand Frontier with its F-22 fighter. It ran the same course, with its initial estimates within the limits of the market. Its price grew, and the company eventually found itself with about a quarter of the quantities it first sought.

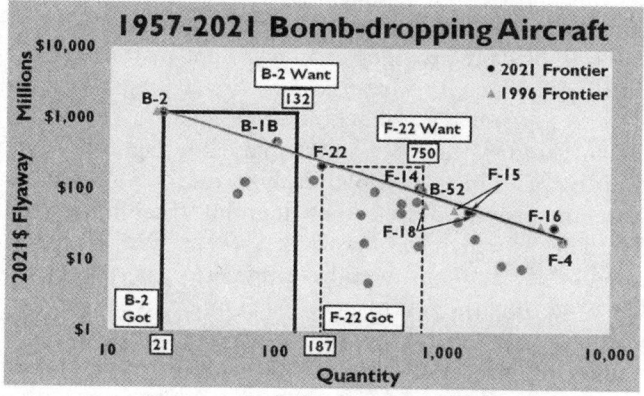

FIGURE 5.6 Northrop Grumman wanted to sell 132 B-2 bombers, but was stopped for lack of funding at 21 units.[36] The original target for F-22s was 750 units; Lockheed Martin sold 187. Both firms ran afoul of their collective Demand Frontier.[37, 38]

Lockheed Martin aims to sell a vast number of its new fighter, the F-35, but will find its sales similarly limited by the Demand Frontier if the price does not fall sufficiently.[39, 40]

AGGREGATE DEMAND

While the Demand Frontier gave us market limits, we will undoubtedly be interested in other measures of the price responsiveness of markets and the nature of the revenues they produce. What happens when prices go up? How much more will the market absorb if products sell for less? In the fighter, bomber, and attack aircraft market, the U.S. government often ties large portions of profits directly to costs. Contractors typically make, say, a 10% profit on top of the cost of each aircraft sold. One can imagine that there might be a bias to let costs rise since the profits per plane will increase. Why take 10% on a plane with a base cost of $100 million and make $10 million in profit when we could add some features, sell it for $120 million, and earn $12 million? That is good for the contractor's bottom line, right? Or is it? What would happen if the thought that adding features to add profits was shortsighted? Suppose instead that doing that would *decrease revenues and profits* with them. After all, in the short exercise we have been pondering, we have completely neglected any discussion of quantities sold. We already know that quantity is necessary—after all, we have an entire axis dedicated to it. Our work with the Demand Frontier showed us that quantities and prices tie at the limit. We must understand how quantities and prices relate, specifically to the case in front of us. We will find that we can discover those market relationships using aggregate demand.

To aggregate means to bring together as a collection, a whole. We will find that gathering groups of data provides crucial insight in the form of Aggregate Demand Curves, which in Hypernomics are aggregations for individual markets and do not consider the whole economy.

Using the data we gathered in Table 5.1 and displayed in Figure 5.3, we can separate the models by price bins, as shown in Figure 5.7.

Here, we have three horizontal dotted lines denoting three bins, each equally spaced by price. The price increment is about $406 million. With that complete, we find each bin's total quantity and average price, as revealed in Figure 5.7. We do that by adding the revenues for each model in its bin and dividing that number by the sum of all the models sold in that range. We then represent those points as a series of circular open dots for each bin.

Finally, in Figure 5.7, we find the line of best fit through the data—this one is particularly good.[41] Not only do we need to examine how well this curve fits, but we also must know its slope. This curve is relatively flat or

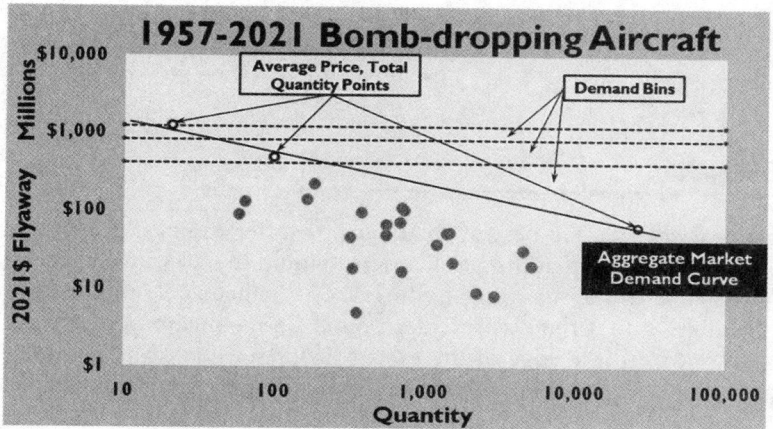

FIGURE 5.7   Aggregate Demand estimates price responsiveness and may be used to discover the revenue in different ranges in a market.[42, 43]

elastic, meaning there is more money in the lower reaches of this market than in its upper regions.[44] Demand curves with slopes less than −1.0 are also called inelastic.[45]

When we work out the revenues in the bins from Figure 5.7, we get Figure 5.8. Our flat demand curve is such that over half of the revenue went

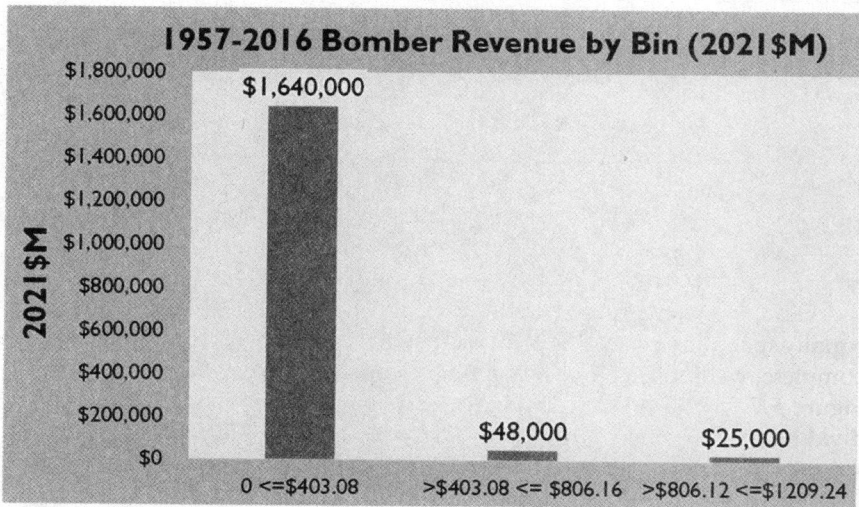

FIGURE 5.8   The lower-priced end of this market contains far more revenue than its upper end.[46]

into our lowest price bin; those aircraft models sold for $50 million or less. Had the aggregate demand curve been steeper, we would find more money in the higher-priced bins.

AVERAGE DEMAND

Companies strive to be the best of their type, to offer the best goods and services, and to be leaders in their fields. They would like to push frontiers, including the edge of the markets in which they compete. The thing about demand frontiers is that they represent an outer limit—meaning that some products do not push the edge of the sales envelope. If we want to understand the realm of the possible, we should look at the nature of the probable.

The most likely outcomes, as we know from our work on height, are closer to the center of distributions, the average. Any five women you see walking down the street are more likely to be closer to five feet four inches rather than six feet four inches. The same thing happens with goods and services—their sales are more likely to be nearer the average than the market frontier. We should find that average in advance of launching a new product.

Once we have all the data in our market, we again find the line of best fit through them, which we depict as the Average Demand Curve in Figure 5.9. This represents the average sales line for this particular market over the period. Some programs did better, others not as well, but on balance, the average quantities sold were along this line.

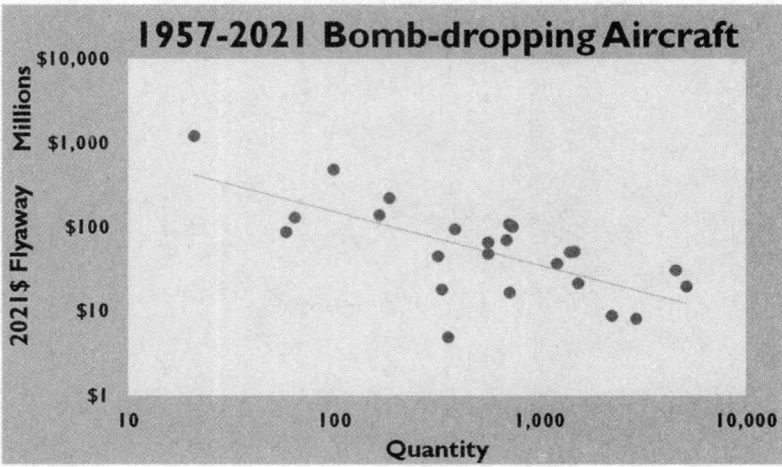

FIGURE 5.9   Average Demand calculations take a line of best fit through all the data.[47]

Again, as with all markets, these curves shift. What is the Demand Frontier this year may be the Average Demand in a few years. That happens in growing markets. However, while planners may hope for more sales than the average, they should know at least what they are more likely to expect.

MINIMUM DEMAND

Occasionally markets exhibit a trait relative to the products, with sales ranges closer to the bottom of the market relative to quantities sold. We call this phenomenon Minimum Demand.

The case we have been studying, fighter/bomber/attack aircraft purchased by the U.S. government for six decades, offers us such a case of Minimum Demand. In Figure 5.10, we find the leftmost and bottommost programs and plot them as white Xs over their original black starting points. Then, we see the best-fit line as statistically significant in our now familiar fashion. Minimum Demand is the opposite of the Demand Frontier; while the latter measures the maximum number of sales we could expect, the former addresses, as the name suggests, the minimum.

Importantly, we should *not* take Minimum Demand as a guarantee. There are no assurances that our product will have a market simply because

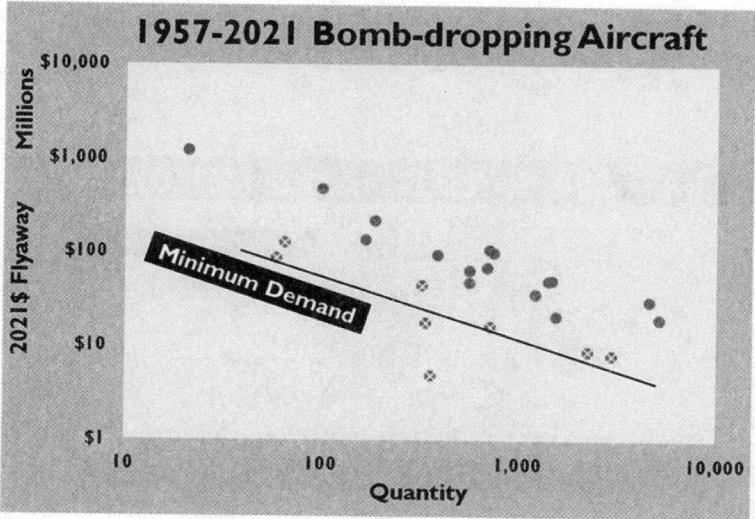

FIGURE 5.10 Minimum Demand examines the least expected number of sales given a product's price and general acceptance by the market.[48]

we decided to build it. Indeed, this market for U.S. warplanes abounds with models that never made it into production, with the McDonnell Douglas/General Dynamics A-12,[49] the Northrop F-20,[50] and the North American B-70[51] being just a few examples. We should instead view Minimum Demand as a lower threshold for sales *given* that we have made products that the customers in our markets want. We should also remember that if we can find such lower limits, they will necessarily be fuzzy as they are lines describing averages with distributions.

PROXY DEMAND

Sometimes people wish they knew how an entire market works but only have access to some of its data. You may want to know how the market for, say, flat-screen televisions works, but very likely, only some people have or can get all the data on its market.

In such cases, we may rely on Proxy Demand. In the case of Figure 5.11, we may want to know the Demand Frontier for the S&P 500.

In Figure 5.11, we can calculate and know the Demand Frontier for all outstanding shares for the entire market. But, if we didn't know that and could find the Daily Volume, we could use its Demand Frontier to offer an approximation of the like slope of the market. In this case, the slopes were within 5% of one another. One could imagine using this technique to discover, say, the Demand Frontier for the number of reviews for flat-screen televisions and their prices as a proxy for the slope of the Demand Frontier for the total sales in the market.

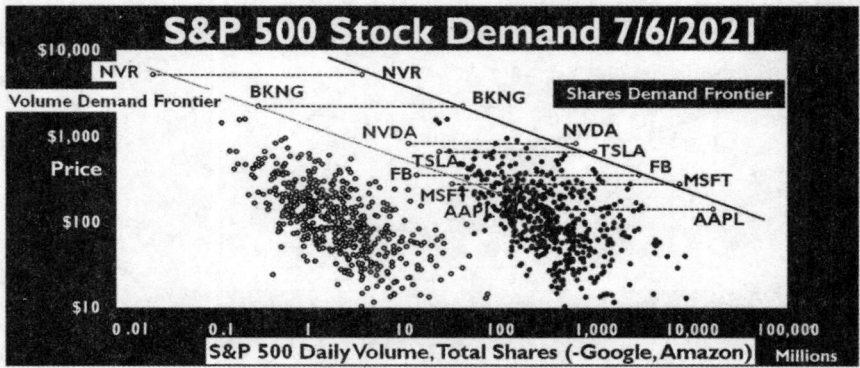

FIGURE 5.11   If we use the S&P 500 daily volume Demand Frontier as a proxy, we get a decent approximation of the Demand Frontier for all outstanding shares.[52]

SUBMARKET, SUB-SUBMARKET, AND MISSION MARKET DEMAND CURVES

While knowing what is happening in our markets is essential, we should also know that they are tiered. We just examined a particular class of military aircraft. Still, there are several other types of military planes—reconnaissance, tankers, patrol, and cargo or transport planes, to cite just a few. As we attempt to crack new realms for products that we intend to build, we often need to know the structure of the markets in as much detail as we can muster.

Figure 5.12 shows that we could consider the different civil and military aircraft markets as submarkets making up the larger aircraft market. Below these submarkets, on the civil side, we have a sub-submarket consisting of helicopters, general aviation (civil aviation operations that are not for hire), regional aircraft, business aircraft, and airliners. These individual categories of civil aircraft work together and form the larger market. As Figure 5.13 shows, the entire aircraft market has well-defined curves for the its Demand Frontier, Aggregate Market Demand and Average Demand.

And as Figure 5.14 reveals, each submarket has its aggregate demand curve. Note that none of the slopes of the sub-submarkets match that of the submarket.

Below this level, within the helicopter sub-submarket, we have the mission (or functional) markets that take up an additional eight categories, which we see in Figure 5.15.

Here, it is crucial to understand that while the sub-submarket has demand curves by which it abides, these aggregate mission demand curves are just as real as the other demand curves we have seen. We should also understand that we can find aggregate, frontier, minimum, and average demand curves in each of the mission markets.

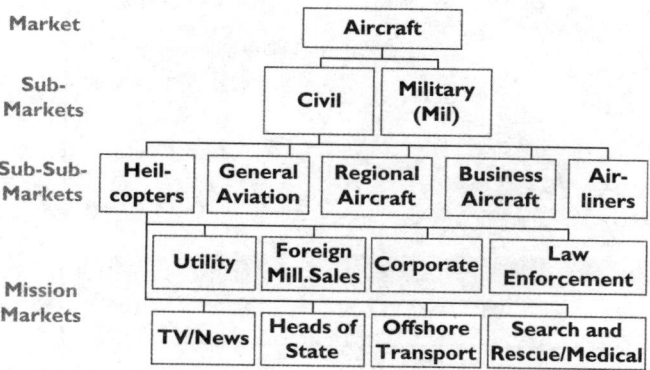

FIGURE 5.12 Markets may consist of several layers within them.[53]

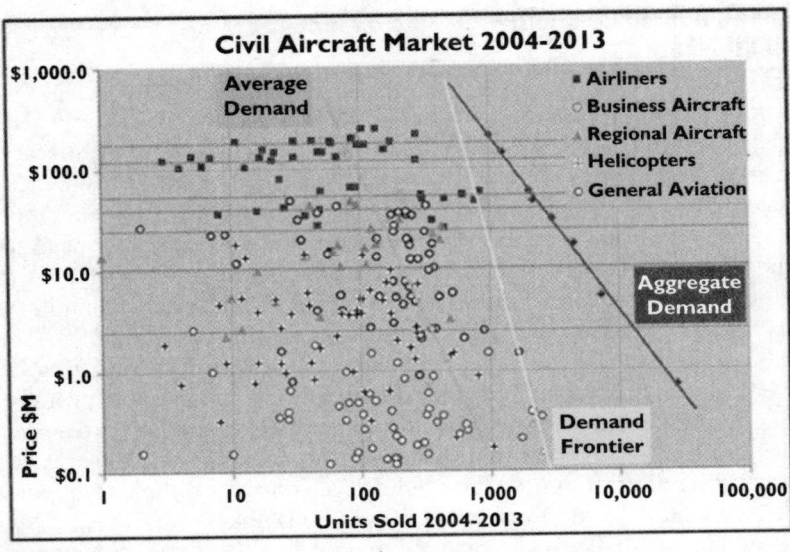

FIGURE 5.13 The Civil Aircraft submarket has its own Aggregate Demand, Demand Frontier, and Average Demand Curves. This submarket is built up from five sub-submarkets: airliners, regional aircraft, business aircraft, helicopters, and general aviation aircraft.[54]

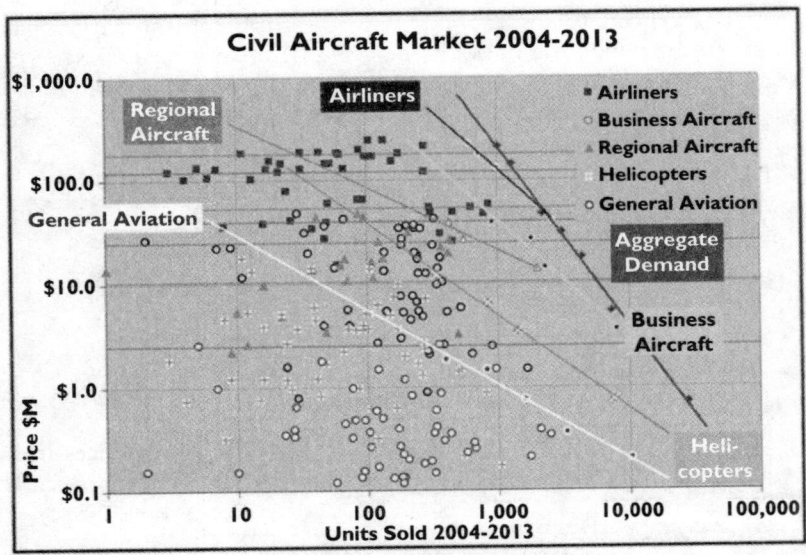

FIGURE 5.14 The Civil Aircraft Aggregate Demand Curve sums up like curves from airliners, regional aircraft, business aircraft, helicopters, and general aviation aircraft.[55]

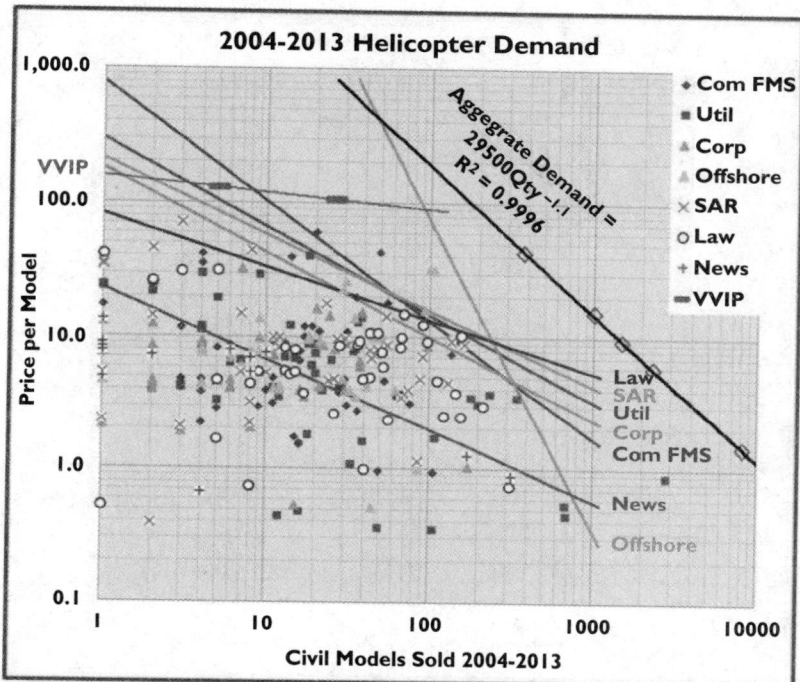

FIGURE 5.15   The individual mission markets contribute to the Aggregate Market Demand of this sub-submarket.[56]

Additionally, if we wanted to build a helicopter made especially for news reporting, if we did our analysis to produce Figure 5.15, we would find out that this mission segment has the least demand of all eight market types. That market segment might need to be more significant to break even or make money with a model designed only to report the news. Perhaps we might consider making the new model capable of taking on multiple missions or figuring out how to live with a small share of a tiny market.

PRODUCT DEMAND CURVES

In some cases, typically, when there are only a few goods or services in a given market, we find that product demand curves appear. These curves are part of the definition of the product's value, as they effectively state that the more the product enters the market, the less it is worth to the customers. In the case shown in Figure 5.16, the Northrop Grumman B-2 Stealth Bomber's value fell quickly as more units entered the market. As we will see

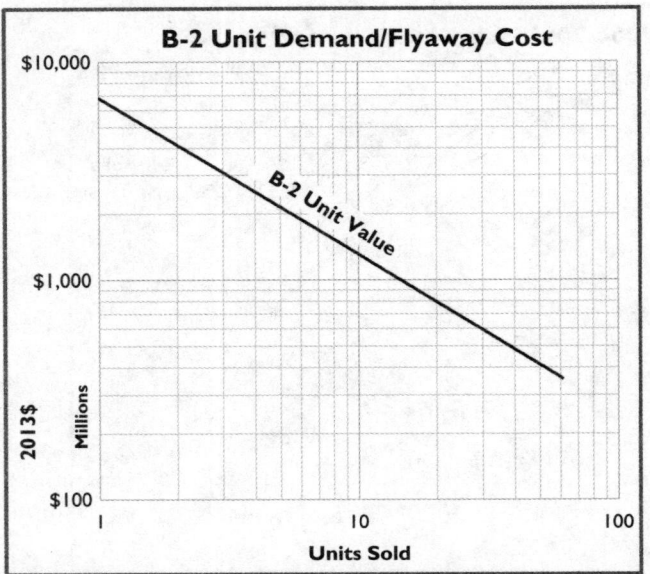

FIGURE 5.16 Sometimes, a product's Value falls substantially as more of it enters the market. In such cases, Product Demand Curves may form, such as this one pictured for the Northrop Grumman B-2.[57, 58]

when we get into our next chapter, it is crucial to know how value compares to cost in the Value Space and along the Demand Plane.

SUMMARY

Nature gives us barriers, and markets do as well. Market limits, as Demand Frontiers, form in all sufficiently well-established markets. Sometimes, a product attains only minimal viability. In that case, it may form part of a Minimum Demand line, showing the smallest sales products expected for a given period. We need to find Aggregate and Average Demand curves to understand how markets react to price changes. Aggregate Demand Curves also relate to where the bulk of the market monies lies. We may break markets into sub-elements, including submarkets, sub-submarkets, mission markets, and several others. Product Demand Curves reflect a particular part of a value equation in which sustainable prices for a given product fall significantly as quantities increase.

A HYPERNOMICS VIGNETTE: THE VALUE OF AND DEMAND FOR MONEY

"Money changes everything."

Cyndi Lauper

While all U.S. denominations are the same size (2.61 inches wide, 6.14 inches long, and 0.0043 inches thick) and color,[59] countries that form the European Union find multiple shapes for their Euros as they range in size from 4.7 by 2.4 inches to 6.3 by 3.2 inches and have a variety of color schemes.[60] But even though we are familiar with its look, feel, and dimensions, and handle it all the time, either as hard currency, coins, cards, or tokens that work in their place, money often seems fuzzy. How much is there? What's it worth? How does the market determine its Value? Now that we know something about Hypernomics, we want to see what this new discipline reveals about these long-standing mediums of exchange.

One of the great things about our modern age is the ease with which we can assemble large masses of information. That ability extends into the currency holdings of most of the larger nations on the planet.

In Figures 5.17 to 5.19, we combine information from four internet sites to form a consolidated database on money. (Please note that the information in these figures changes constantly.)

We define the following columns in Figures 5.17, 5.18, and 5.19.

Total Units are the numbers of "M-1" currencies issued by the country. M-1 is defined as "Notes and coins in circulation (outside Federal Reserve Banks and the vaults of depository institutions) (currency), traveler's checks of nonbank issuers, demand deposits, and other checkable deposits (OCDs)."[61]

The **Exchange Rate** is "how much one currency is worth compared to a different one."[62]

The **Inflation Rate** refers to "the general level of prices is going up,"[63] here, as typically used, on an annual basis.

Foreign Exchange Reserves "are a nation's holdings of other countries' currencies that can be converted into its own currency through the foreign exchange market as well as holdings of foreign assets in government securities, such as bonds and gold that can be easily turned into cash."[64] If we plot the Currency Units horizontally and use their Exchange Rate against the U.S. Dollar vertically, we end up with Figure 5.20.

CODE	Country	Total Units	Exchange Rate	Inflation %	Foreign Currency Reserves
ALL	Albania	694,521,000,000	0.0086252	7.4	4345
ARS	Argentina	5,240,520,000,000	0.0078902	60.7	39139
AUD	Australia	1,705,000,000,000	0.6858711	5.1	55396
EUR	Austria	332,568,000,000	1.0183299	8.7	28513
BSD	Bahamas	3,728,000,000	1.0000000	4.1	1758
BHD	Bahrain	4,494,000,000	2.6525199	3.5	3415
BDT	Bangladesh	4,032,695,000,000	0.0106947	7.42	42202
EUR	Belgium	311,900,000,000	1.0183299	9.65	31762
BZD	Belize	2,177,000,000	0.4962779	6.6	277
BTN	Bhutan	106,126,000,000	0.0126768	5.79	1238
BOB	Bolivia	75,458,571,000	0.1452011	1.41	4624
BRL	Brazil	602,637,000,000	0.1902950	11.89	357740
BND	Brunei	5,861,000,000	0.7168459	3.8	3664
BGN	Bulgaria	104,172,000,000	0.5202914	15.6	32881
CAD	Canada	1,623,740,000,000	0.7727975	7.7	105618
CLP	Chile	65,949,000,000,000	0.0010266	12.5	42593
CNY	China	67,440,000,000,000	0.1493652	2.5	3305419
COP	Colombia	182,341,000,000,000	0.0002286	9.67	58161
KMF	Comoros	134,375,000,000	0.0021104	3.59	202
HRK	Croatia	192,530,000,000	0.1355197	10.8	28416
CZK	Czech Republic	5,011,404,000,000	0.0413360	16	174994
DKK	Denmark	1,504,466,000,000	0.1369113	7.4	78004
DOP	Dominican Republic	674,549,000,000	0.0183278	9.47	12611
EGP	Egypt	1,496,662,000,000	0.0530223	13.2	37909
SVC	El Salvador	4,982,000,000	0.1143511	7.76	2510
XAF	Equatorial Guinea	749,725,000,000	0.0015530	2.9	48
EUR	Estonia	22,199,000,000	1.0183299	21.9	2216
EUR	Euro Area	11,525,664,000,000	1.0183299	8.6	85602
EUR	Finland	185,267,000,000	1.0183299	7	16552
EUR	France	1,902,839,000,000	1.0183299	5.8	226316
GMD	Gambia	37,539,000,000	0.0184976	11.58	191
EUR	Germany	2,914,000,000,000	1.0183299	7.6	277782
EUR	Greece	195,219,000,000	1.0183299	12.1	10895
GTQ	Guatemala	147,935,000,000	0.1290989	7.55	18807
GNF	Guinea	40,142,000,000,000	0.0001152	10.99	1418

FIGURE 5.17 Database of the world's major currencies, Part 1 of 3, as of July 12, 2019.[65–69]

CODE	Country	Total Units	Exchange Rate	Inflation %	Foreign Currency Reserves
HNL	Honduras	117,110,000,000	0.0408297	9.09	8462
HKD	Hong Kong	3,436,022,000,000	0.1274048	1.2	465704
HUF	Hungary	33,940,000,000,000	0.0025143	11.7	36593
ISK	Iceland	803,000,000,000	0.0073009	8.8	6860
INR	India	52,862,000,000,000	0.0126060	7.04	588314
IDR	Indonesia	2,114,754,000,000,000	0.0000668	4.35	135550
IQD	Iraq	27,887,000,000,000	0.0006883	5.4	64000
EUR	Ireland	288,959,000,000	1.0183299	7.8	7717
ILS	Israel	704,592,000,000	0.2891009	4.1	199808
EUR	Italy	1,578,628,000,000	1.0183299	8	211419
JMD	Jamaica	369,356,000,000	0.0066578	10.9	3905
JPY	Japan	1,027,514,000,000,000	0.0073481	2.5	1322193
JOD	Jordan	13,230,000,000	1.4104372	4.4	19044
KZT	Kazakhstan	8,378,061,000,000	0.0021205	14.5	35438
KES	Kenya	1,867,000,000,000	0.0084681	7.9	8870
KWD	Kuwait	13,286,000,000	3.2573290	4.52	48202
EUR	Latvia	17,665,000,000	1.0183299	19.3	5404
LBP	Lebanon	57,729,000,000,000	0.0006644	211	12500
LSL	Lesotho	7,120,000,000	0.0593472	7.8	774
EUR	Lithuania	30,432,000,000	1.0183299	18.9	4848
EUR	Luxembourg	373,000,000,000	1.0183299	7.4	1191
MOP	Macau	72,014,000,000	0.1236705	1.1	25849
MWK	Malawi	796,100,000,000	0.0009788	19.1	471
MYR	Malaysia	603,888,000,000	0.2259376	2.8	115762
MVR	Maldives	22,442,000,000	0.0644745	2.46	762
EUR	Malta	21,799,000,000	1.0183299	5.8	928
MXN	Mexico	6,434,540,056,000	0.0488568	7.99	209567
MDL	Moldova	56,693,000,000	0.0521186	29.1	3453
MNT	Mongolia	5,768,183,000,000	0.0003191	15.1	3697
MAD	Morocco	1,101,211,000,000	0.0986680	5.9	35439
NAD	Namibia	69,280,000,000	0.0614137	5.4	1924
EUR	Netherlands	612,148,000,000	1.0183299	8.6	54016
NZD	New Zealand	138,682,000,000	0.6195787	6.9	14544
NIO	Nicaragua	80,700,000,000	0.0279940	10.61	4000
NGN	Nigeria	20,392,537,000,000	0.0023933	17.71	40660

FIGURE 5.18 Database of the world's major currencies, Part 2 of 3, as of July 12, 2019.[61–64, 70]

CODE	Country	Total Units	Exchange Rate	Inflation %	Foreign Currency Reserves
NOK	Norway	2,833,493,000,000	0.0993345	5.7	88058
OMR	Oman	5,783,000,000	2.5974026	2.4	18000
PKR	Pakistan	21,447,783,000,000	0.0048447	21.3	9816
PYG	Paraguay	38,358,442,000	0.0001462	11.5	9880
PEN	Peru	138,128,000,000	0.2582645	8.81	78501
PHP	Philippines	6,321,233,000,000	0.0179115	6.1	106757
PLN	Poland	1,666,787,000,000	0.2133106	15.6	142252
EUR	Portugal	203,155,000,000	1.0183299	8.7	29050
QAR	Qatar	160,715,000,000	0.2745744	5.41	40978
RON	Romania	404,691,000,000	0.2058460	14.49	50971
RUB	Russia	34,720,000,000,000	0.0153846	15.9	586800
RWF	Rwanda	1,511,000,000,000	0.0009746	14.8	1465
SAR	Saudi Arabia	1,569,744,000,000	0.2663825	2.2	451587
SCR	Seychelles	8,018,000,000	0.0757404	2.1	566
SLL	Sierra Leone	7,714,024,000,000	0.0000738	22.44	532
SGD	Singapore	288,656,000,000	0.7153076	5.6	365177
EUR	Slovakia	71,600,000,000	1.0183299	12.6	9305
EUR	Slovenia	31,284,000,000	1.0183299	10.43	1217
ZAR	South Africa	2,378,735,000,000	0.0594495	6.5	54473
KRW	South Korea	1,387,581,000,000,000	0.0007724	6	449300
EUR	Spain	1,381,061,000,000	1.0183299	10.2	91106
SEK	Sweden	4,540,978,000,000	0.0953289	7.3	54020
CHF	Switzerland	778,280,000,000	1.0235415	3.4	1033369
TWD	Taiwan	10,279,100,000,000	0.0335988	3.59	548850
TZS	Tanzania	16,454,000,000,000	0.0004286	4	6714
THB	Thailand	2,931,000,000,000	0.0278924	7.66	242430
TND	Tunisia	45,157,000	0.3236246	8.1	8840
TRY	Turkey	2,662,061,648,000	0.0578938	78.62	107660
UGX	Uganda	14,728,000,000,000	0.0002673	6.8	4300
UAH	Ukraine	1,391,157,000,000	0.0338662	21.5	31614
AED	United Arab Emirates	712,116,000,000	0.2722570	2.5	129428
GBP	United Kingdom	2,427,138,000,000	1.2033694	9.1	231293
USD	United States	20,633,000,000,000	1.0000000	8.6	241975
UYU	Uruguay	199,341,000,000	0.0248262	9.29	16952

FIGURE 5.19 Database of the world's major currencies, Part 3 of 3, as of July 12, 2019.[61–64, 71]

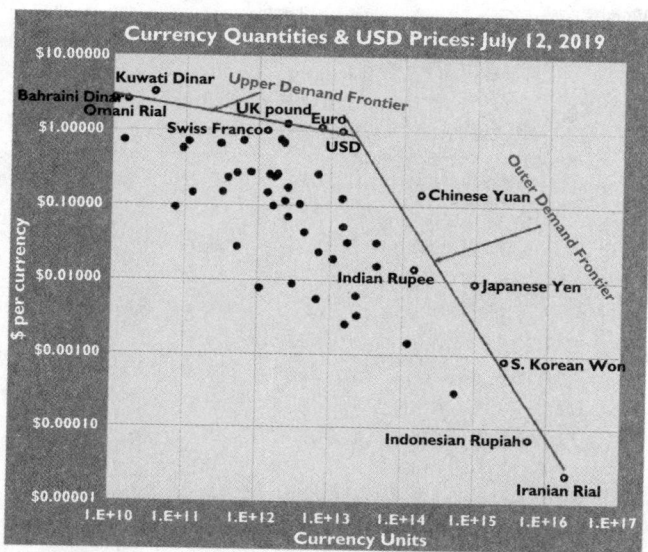

FIGURE 5.20 Fiat currencies units versus price in U.S. Dollars, July 2019.[69, 72]

Figure 5.20 unveils Upper and Outer Demand Frontiers in the fiat currency market. The Upper Frontier was built from the Bahraini Dinar, the Omani Rial, the Kuwaiti Dinar, the Swiss Franc, the British Pound, the Euro, and the U.S. Dollar. At the same time, the U.S. Dollar is also part of the Outer Demand Frontier, along with the Chinese Yuan, the Indian Rupee, the Japanese Yen, the South Korean Won, the Indonesian Rupiah, and the Iranian Rial. The Outer Demand Frontier is particularly interesting here, as its slope is both highly negative (at −1.42) and significant (with a *p*-value of 7.88E-05). We might guess this means the Value of currencies will depend, in part, on how many units have been issued.

When we consider the rest of the data in Figures 15.17 through 15.19, and add subsets of that data which contains the prime rate at the time (as Figures 5.21 and 5.22), we can test what sustains currency Value, which we do in Figure 5.23.

Figure 5.23 shows that currency value decreases as more units are produced, but increases as countries hold more foreign exchange reserves. In this case, we have the country's prime rate set to 2%, which was Sweden's rate at that time. What happens if we change the prime rate? We find out in Figure 5.24.

Country	Total Units	Exchange Rate (to US Dollars)	Prime Rate%	Foreign Currency Reserves ($M)
Albania	6,934,870,578,800	0.02407	7.20	3400
Australia	2,259,050,820,000	0.70207	5.30	58676
Bahrain	10,422,720,000	2.65957	5.70	4657
Botswana	73,093,303,070	0.09430	6.50	7546
Brazil	6,541,589,250,000	0.26752	63.30	388090
United Kingdom	2,438,705,598,000	1.25722	4.30	168206
Bulgaria	91,161,083,700	0.57689	5.80	24318
Canada	2,027,688,726,000	0.76639	2.90	2714
Chile	118,756,940,399,300	0.00147	4.60	39553
China	171,878,312,260,000	0.14534	4.30	3119000
Colombia	535,659,945,840,200	0.00031	13.80	46798
Croatia	321,474,300,000	0.15242	3.91	14307
Czechia	4,313,828,400,000	0.04404	3.90	145978
Denmark	1,336,816,835,200	0.15096	2.90	64016
European Union	7,212,619,882,000	1.12830	0.25	857965
Hong Kong	14,146,495,312,000	0.12781	5.00	437788
Hungary	23,354,889,586,940	0.00346	1.60	31367
Iceland	1,070,996,405,694	0.00794	7.60	6186
India	141,443,639,119,000	0.01459	9.45	430376
Indonesia	5,614,794,089,982,000	0.00007	11.70	123823
Israel	793,091,273,900	0.28130	3.30	118208
Japan	963,564,653,262,000	0.00925	1.50	1322279
Kazakhstan	16,162,413,561,730	0.00261	14.10	30993

FIGURE 5.21 Well find we can estimate a country's exchange rate to the United States Dollar using these attributes. Part 1 of 2, as of July 12, 2019.[61–64, 69–71]

Figure 5.24 shows the effect of raising that loan rate to 63%, which is what Brazil's was at that time. Observe that the whole plane has fallen relative to the picture in Figure 5.23.

In recent times, we have had the emergence of cryptocurrencies. They were especially ascendant in 2019. When we compare the Demand for them against that for traditional fiat currencies, we get Figure 5.25.

We're interested in how the markets for cryptocurrencies and fiat currencies may relate to one another. Cryptocurrencies began to become

Country	Total Units	Exchange Rate (to US Dollars)	Prime Rate%	Foreign Currency Reserves ($M)
Kuwait	36,964,431,000	3.28694	5.20	33130
Malaysia	1,670,971,320,200	0.24315	4.50	102287
Mexico	14,671,730,197,500	0.05265	7.45	175029
New Zealand	298,600,824,900	0.66946	4.90	22183
Norway	2,328,685,446,100	0.11719	1.50	64960
Pakistan	22,493,754,950,000	0.00631	7.00	7611
Philippines	10,890,799,482,000	0.01956	4.19	85400
Poland	1,417,648,093,400	0.26396	4.80	117801
Romania	379,315,647,720	0.23822	5.70	41110
Russia	43,374,928,864,800	0.01587	10.30	520300
Singapore	618,308,454,000	0.73669	5.28	273943
South Africa	2,566,566,106,600	0.07161	10.40	51641
South Korea	2,550,949,211,690,000	0.00085	3.40	403100
Sri Lanka	6,485,057,226,710	0.00568	11.80	8590
Sweden	3,708,987,971,200	0.10671	2.00	59558
Switzerland	1,313,872,290,000	1.01608	2.60	804323
Taiwan	42,669,800,832,000	0.03220	2.70	773
Thailand	16,872,632,713,900	0.03237	6.20	212183
Trinidad and Tobago	125,522,900,820	0.14770	9.00	8111
Turkey	2,544,678,210,000	0.17488	15.20	96300
United States	14,000,000,000,000	1.00000	4.30	126026
Venezuela	1,593,006,250,000	0.10013	23.80	9591

FIGURE 5.22 Well find we can estimate a country's exchange rate to the United States Dollar using these attributes. Part 2 of 2, as of July 12, 2019.[61–64, 69–71]

popular with the advent of Bitcoin. As it happens, regarding Demand, both payment forms have something important in common.

Figure 5.25 shows that their Demand Frontiers slopes are nearly identical using a fiat currency study from July and one on crypto 20 days later. On the left, the crypto Demand Frontier slope is −1.47 (p-value 1.28E-04), while that for fiat currencies is −1.42 (p-value 7.88E-05, as previously mentioned). At that time, at the Demand Frontier, cryptocurrencies had reached about 1/1000th of the fiat currency extent. Observe the steep cryptocurrency

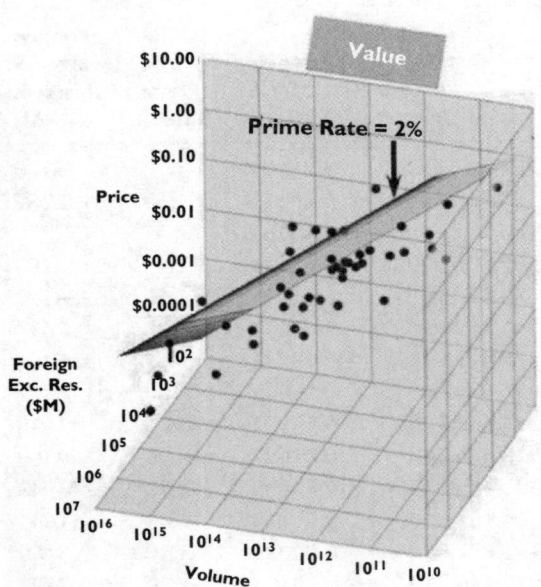

FIGURE 5.23 The fiat currency value on July 12, 2019, was a function of currency volume, foreign exchange reserves, and the prime rate.[75]

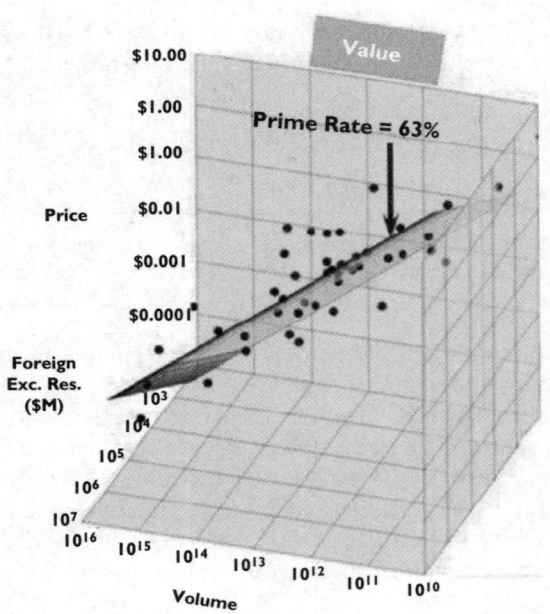

FIGURE 5.24 In July 2019, as the prime rate rose, currency value fell.[76]

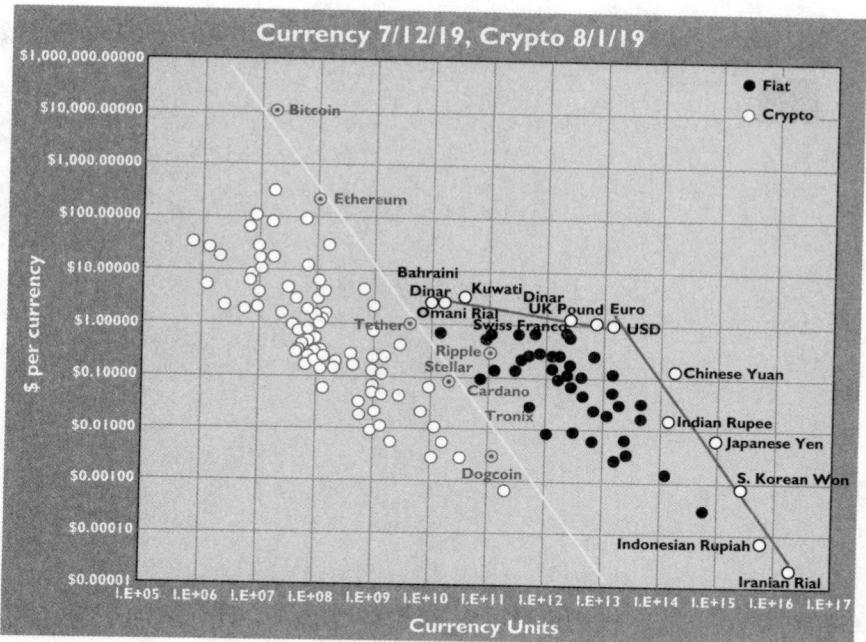

FIGURE 5.25   In the summer of 2019, cryptocurrencies and fiat currencies had similar slopes.[77]

Demand Frontier; more money is at the upper end of this curve at its limit. At that time, Bitcoin's market capitalization was nearly twice that of the rest of its market combined.

While Hypernomics got its start in the analysis of individual markets, the work here shows that it has the potential to provide deep insight into global economic issues as well.

CHAPTER 6

Price and Quantity Determination

"It isn't that they can't see the solution. It is that they can't see the problem."

G.K. Chesterton

THE GENERAL PROBLEM CALLS FOR SPECIFICS

Price. Quantity.

If you are a producer, you are deeply concerned with these figures for your offerings.

If we hope to profit from any good or service, we must predict both reasonably accurately. To figure that out, we first must characterize the problems facing us. If we are to produce something, it will always have some *specific* features. The new electric car you make will have a particular horsepower and range. A novel cross-town transport service you offer to a major city must have specific delivery times by distance and weight. An innovative dairy you put up might offer new product types with your distinct specifications, such as 3% milk in a three-quart container. Producers like you and others are concerned with the profit potential of specific unique offerings. Average prices for similar goods and services might prove interesting to you and your fellow entrepreneurs. However, you and they will find that you will need more guidance for their product formulations or sales potential. Eventually, we have to get down to *specifics*.

Interestingly, we observe that most market characterizations to date tend to address the *average* products in any given industry, leaving the details buried in the conglomerate that makes the whole. Such analyses offer correct answers in the sense that they are defensible in their assumptions and math. However, they leave us with scant more understanding and nary a glance into actionable intelligence. They get the right answers to the wrong questions.

THE NEOCLASSICAL VIEW: THE LAW OF SUPPLY AND DEMAND

As of this writing, the dominant school of economic thought, the neoclassical economists, very much like the idea of equilibrium. They often begin their analysis by fleshing out a demand curve. In the case of ground beef, for example, they might research and discover, as we can see in Figure 6.1, that from 1980 through 1986, *average* prices for beef in the United States fell as the quantities sold rose. This history enables us to draw a predictive

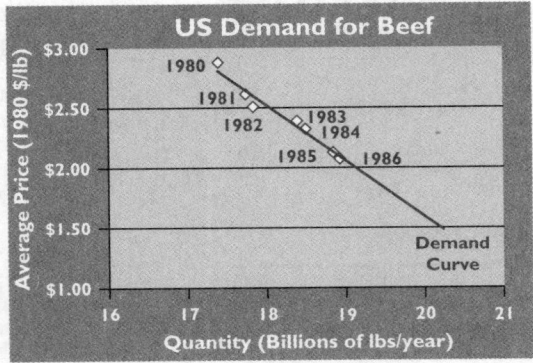

FIGURE 6.1 The United States experienced a downward trend in average beef prices from 1980 to 1986.[1, 2] Neoclassical economists go a couple of steps further in Figure 6.2.

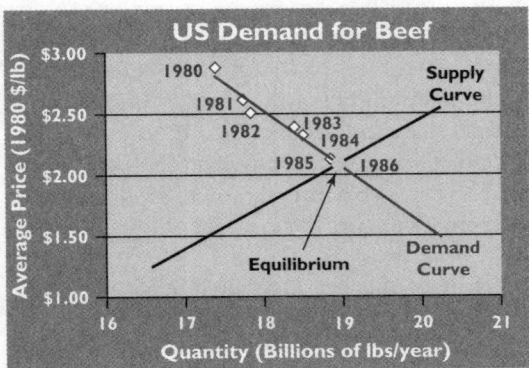

FIGURE 6.2 Neoclassical economists imagine an upward-sloping supply curve intersecting a downward-sloping demand curve, forming a single equilibrium point.[3–6]

line through it, which we call a demand curve. Given the trend, it is apparent that more beef would be demanded if the average price fell.

There, they posit an upward-sloping (from left to right) supply curve, which "shows the relationship between the market price and the amount of that commodity that producers are willing to produce and sell, other things held constant."[7] This, in turn, leads to "a market equilibrium," which "represents a balance among all the different buyers and sellers."[8] In combination with downward-sloping demand curves, the notions of upward-sloping supply curves and the resulting equilibriums form the core concept of the Law of Supply and Demand.[9] In Figure 6.2, therefore, neoclassical economists find an equilibrium in the U.S. market for beef in 1986 at 18.9 billion pounds (the horizontal component) and $2.08 (the price as represented by the vertical axis), shown by the dot at the intersection of the supply and demand curves.

At least four massive errors are buried in the Law of Supply and Demand.

The first error relates to its use of average prices. In Table 4.2, we found data relative to the value surface of beef prices that we plotted in Figure 4.15. When we plot the average price of that Table 4.2 data as a horizontal surface in Figure 6.3, we see that that surface, an outcome of the Law of Supply and Demand that neoclassical economists favor, tends to be much further away from the observed data points (the spheres) than the corresponding

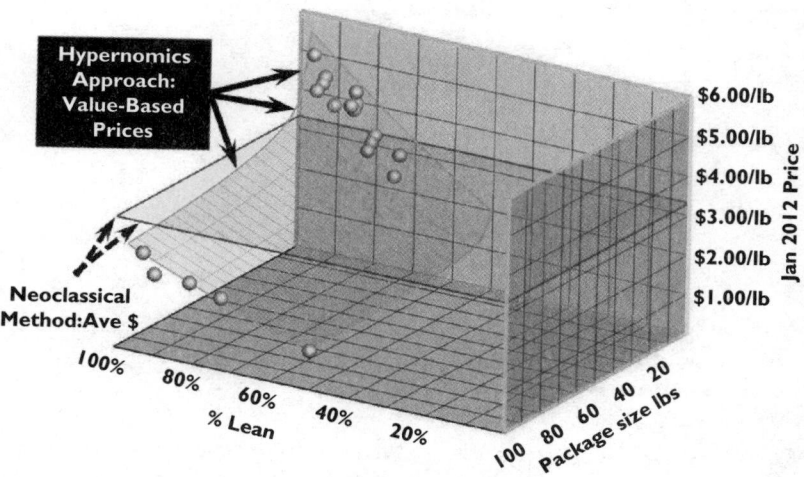

FIGURE 6.3 Neoclassical economists use average prices (the horizontal, flat surface) to find equilibrium. That approach ignores that most prices are not close to the average. Hypernomics, use of Value Analysis (the curved surface) provides much better accuracy than the neoclassical average prices.[10, 11]

Value Surface that Hypernomics offers. That isn't good if you need accurate estimates of what your product is worth.

Neoclassical economists use average prices (the horizontal, flat surface) to find equilibrium. That approach ignores that most prices are not close to the average. Hypernomics, use of Value Analysis (the curved surface) provides much better accuracy than the neoclassical average prices.

We can see the differences in predictive ability more clearly in Figure 6.4. In this view, we depict errors from Neoclassical Economics as solid horizontal bars, while we show those from Hypernomics as cross-hatched horizontal bars. The object here is to be as close to the vertical $0.00 (no error) line as possible. A glance at the data indicates that the Hypernomics analysis does far better. Its average error is about a fifth that of the Neoclassical approach.

The second error relates to the notion of "single point equilibrium" in the first place. In Figure 6.3, *each* sphere is a fully functioning member of

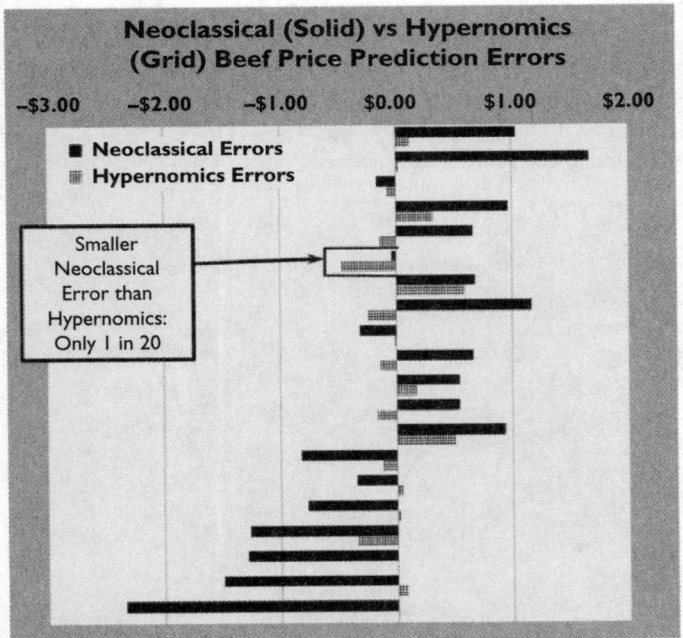

FIGURE 6.4 Using average prices, Neoclassical economists develop errors characterized by solid bars. At the same time, using Value Analysis, Hypernomics finds its errors depicted with crosshatches. The closer each bar is to $0.00 (no error), the better predictor it is. The average Hypernomics error is $0.18, while the neoclassical average is $0.88. Hypernomics estimates are closer to the actual values 19 out of 20 times.[12, 13]

the market product set. Every product has multiple sales that the market supports based on its value, as customers define it. There are numerous sales of various products. Moreover, no one comes to the market and says aloud, "What was the cost of this product, and how did they come up with the price?" You do not care if the market makes a $0.25/pound profit on your purchase or loses $0.50/pound. You and everyone else know that the product in question satisfied your value to price threshold. You do not care about a balance between price and cost. You only care about the products' features relative to their prices. Nothing else matters concerning value. This is true for every product sold outside of a monopoly.[14]

A third problem with the Law of Supply and Demand is the caveat concerning "other things held constant." This clause would have us limit our analysis to the Demand Plane only. As a matter of logic, if every element a market needed to consider were found in an arrangement such as Figure 6.2, we could undoubtedly get insight into "equilibrium states" and the effect of shifting supply and demand curves on changing "equilibrium." But we don't see that in the real world. And we know better than that now. Price and quantity determination requires simultaneous insight into the Value Space and the Demand Plane. To rely solely on the Demand Plane and ignore Value Space is worse than your shooting guard shooting pool at center court in the middle of your basketball game. He may be taking a shot it's true. But his sinking the eight ball in the side pocket won't help when you and your teammates want him to knock down a three-pointer. He is busy playing the wrong game; while he aims his cue stick, he aims at the wrong goal.

Meanwhile, you are playing in dimensions he can't see, and to properly score, you'll have to shoot a basketball through a hoop at which he's not seeing. The pool table won't get you there. You can't play a four-dimensional game in a two-dimensional setting. Engaging a four-dimensional game that every market plays requires an environment the two-dimensional Law of Supply and Demand does not recognize.

FERROUS BLUNDER: UNIVERSAL CLAIM OF UPWARD-SLOPING SUPPLY CURVES

This fourth problem with the Law of Supply and Demand differs from the three others in that there are, in markets for commodities, solid foundations for upward-sloping supply curves. What that slope means in practical terms is that as producers of a specific commodity want to make more of it (i.e., more units of the item along the horizontal axis), especially in the short run, it becomes relatively more expensive per unit (with respect to the cost of the commodity measured along the vertical cost axis) due to increased labor costs and the increased difficulty of extracting or producing

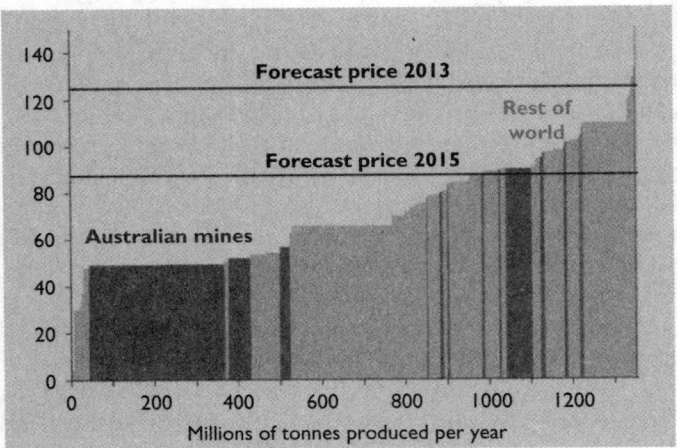

FIGURE 6.5 An upward-sloping supply curve for iron ore reflects the added costs that producers incur as it becomes harder to retrieve the metal from the ground as well as the differences in the wages these producers pay.[15]

the commodity. We see this in markets like the one for iron ore, as shown in Figure 6.5. In this case, going from left to right, the costs go up as it becomes harder to dig up the ore, as labor costs rise, or both, according to the nature of each site.

The problem here is that while this approach may work well for iron, we cannot necessarily apply it to all commodities, let alone all the other goods and services available to consumers. Beef is a commodity. We have just witnessed how someone could characterize a single point for beef along a hypothetical supply line, finding an average price at which there might be an average equilibrium. However, when we did, we found that it had little meaning. The reason is that there are so many variations from the average that it makes it meaningless. In our little experiment in Figures 6.3 and 6.4, we found that the would-be "equilibrium price" predicted the individual product prices more accurately than value analysis only once in 20.

The notion of upward-sloping supply curves is more than insulting and an idea that strains credulity when we think just a little about it. Labor is a significant cost component and is usually the dominant term in most products. If a supply curve is going up, it means that people are becoming less capable the more times they produce something. When you perform a task repeatedly, do you become less adept at doing it? You learned how to tie your shoes at a very young age. Does it take you more time now? Of course not. However, this is what an upward-sloping supply curve would have you believe—it suggests that people get *dumber* as they do a task repeatedly.

We know from experience that the more knowledge we have with a particular task, the more adept we become. We see this reflected in Figure 6.6, which addresses the market for solar panels over nearly 40 years. The trend, marked by the dotted line, shows that from 1976 to 2019, the cost of solar cells dropped 20% every time the cumulative amount of shipped modules doubled. This phenomenon, known broadly as the Learning Curve and more narrowly characterized in this field as Swanson's Law, worked its way across an entire industry over nearly four decades. That means that workers learn this process all over the world. As some solar panel assemblers left

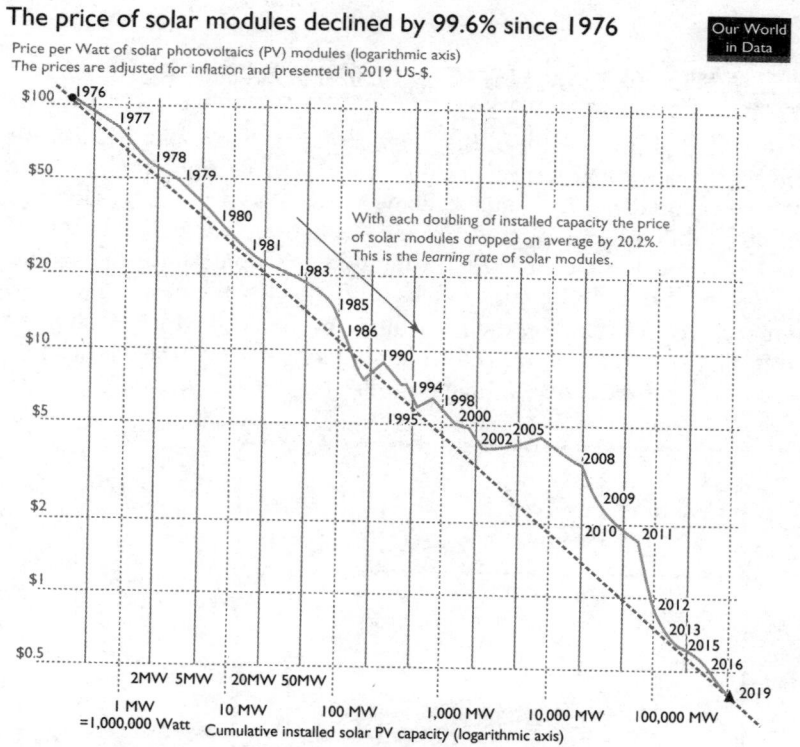

The price of solar modules declined by 99.6% since 1976

Price per Watt of solar photovoltaics (PV) modules (logarithmic axis)
The prices are adjusted for inflation and presented in 2019 US-$.

With each doubling of installed capacity the price of solar modules dropped on average by 20.2%. This is the *learning rate* of solar modules.

Our World in Data

Data: Lafond et al. (2017) and IRENA Database; the reported learning rate is an average over several studies reported by de La Tour et al (2013) in Energy. The rate has remained very similar since then. Licensed under CC-BY
OurworldinData.org – Research and data to make progress against the world's largest problems.   by the author Max Roser

FIGURE 6.6 A downward-sloping learning curve reflects that people get more competent at doing something the more times that they do it. These improvements can spread across an entire industry and last for decades. Swanson's Law is an observation that the price of photovoltaic modules tends to drop 20% for every doubling of the cumulative shipped volume.[16, 17]

the industry, they passed their knowledge along to their replacements, who continued the trend, learned more, and became even more productive.

Thus, perhaps the only markets for which the Law of Supply and Demand makes an undeniable case for itself are uniform elements such as silver, gold, and platinum. Its claim that it can adequately address all commodities goes belly-up when we do the simplest of studies on cattle. Neoclassical economists are trying to answer four-dimensional problems in a two-dimensional world. They want to impart wisdom to us but believe that we get dumber as we go along. But we are more intelligent and get smarter the further we go down the curve. The irony of the would-be ubiquity of the Law of Supply and Demand is that it is best suited for elements like iron but little else.

THE HYPERNOMICS VIEW: THE LAW OF VALUE AND DEMAND

Even though we cannot get all of our answers from the Demand Plane, we will find many uses for it, especially for quantity projections for products given their estimated values. Demand Plane analysis is a crucial predictor of product profitability in many cases once we have done our Value Analysis.

The key to proper Demand Plane analysis is people's knowledge, and they will learn how to do repetitive tasks more quickly the more they do it. Furthermore, workers pass on their learning. As the Ford Motor Company showed in Figure 6.7, it could produce millions of units of the Model T at progressively lower costs over a long period.

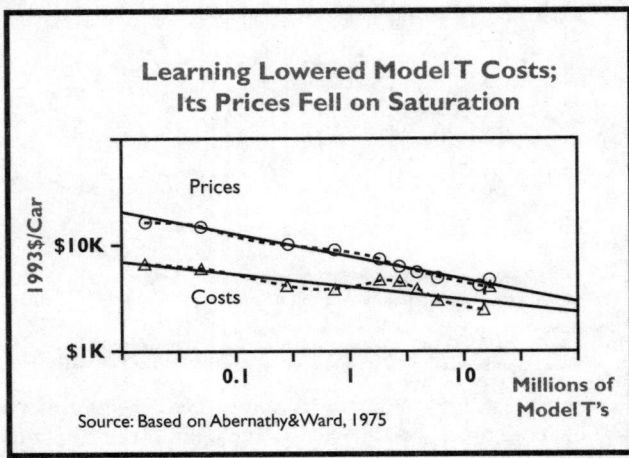

FIGURE 6.7 Decades before the solar industry began, Ford Motor Company demonstrated learning for millions of Model Ts.[18]

It is crucial to compare cost projections to demand projections as part of our Demand Analysis. Figure 6.8 shows that Ford continued to make its Model T as long as its costs were below the price the company could command. This continued for 16.5 million units and almost 20 years.[19] Then, as the company began the move to sell its new Model A, its Model T costs went up and finally matched the demand curve for it. If the company had made more of this vehicle, they would have lost money from that point forward, as the costs for the Model T would have exceeded its prices. We call this condition where prices exceed costs a *sustainable disequilibrium*, so designated for two reasons: 1) this condition is sustainable, perhaps for a long time, as long as demand exceeds the cost; and 2) the two equilibriums of Demand and Cost have vastly different meanings in Hypernomics than they do in neoclassical economics.

The Learning Curve is a pervasive phenomenon that frequently comes into play in determining quantities sold in Hypernomics. The curve, expressed as a percentage, indicates how much of the work remains as the amounts double. Table 6.1 shows three such curves, all beginning with 1,000 hours of labor for the first unit. In the second column, an 80% curve means that every time the number of units doubles, 80% of the cost remains. Thus, going from the first unit to the second, we have 80% of the first unit costs for the second unit or 800 hours. If we double the units again to four, the hours required are 80% of the hours for the second unit (80% of 800 hours), and if we double the units one more time, the eighth unit takes 80% of the hours for the fourth unit (80% of 640 hours).

TABLE 6.1 An 80% Learning Curve means as the product quantity doubles (as from 1 to 2), the cost go down by the Learning Curve Percentage. Thus, moving from the first to second unit in this example drops the cost from 1000 hours to 800 hours (That is, the second unit costs 80% of the first unit, the fourth is 80% of the second, and so on).[20, 21]

Curve	80%	77%	70%
Unit	Hours	Hours	Hours
1	1000.0	1000.0	1000.0
2	800.0	770.0	700.0
3	702.1	660.8	568.2
4	640.0	592.9	490.0
5	595.6	545.1	436.8
6	561.7	508.8	397.7
7	534.5	480.1	367.4
8	512.0	456.5	343.0
9	492.9	436.7	322.8
10	476.5	419.7	305.8

Learning Curves indicate the new amount of labor to do a task every time the quantity produced doubles. An 80% curve states that we have 80% of the labor at Unit 2 compared to Unit 1 and 80% at Unit 4 compared to Unit 2.

As the Learning Curve percentage falls, the amount of work remaining after doubling falls, as shown in the columns marked "77%" and "70%" in Table 6.1. After only eight units, the difference in the hours required to do a job is dramatically lower for a 70% learning curve compared to an 80% learning curve, given that they have the same starting value.[21] Notice in Figures 6.6 and 6.8 that real-world learning may follow a trend but need not be entirely consistent. People and groups learn more quickly and slowly as novice and experienced workers enter and leave the workforce. As Figure 6.6 reveals, learning may slow down (as, say, immediately after management offers new tools for workers to use). But then it may go faster (at a lower learning curve) just as the Learning Curve temporarily moved upward in the solar module market from 2001 through 2006, only to become steeper than the average from 2006 through 2012.

When Unit Demand or Product Demand Curves appear, as one did for the B-2 bomber in Figure 6.8, it should pique our interest to compare it to the Unit Cost Curve that describes the learning curve for the same product. The B-2 Unit Demand Curve in Figure 6.8 fell rapidly, much faster than the corresponding B-2 Unit Cost Curve. The market hit equilibrium when Value equaled Cost at the 21st unit. Past that point, Cost exceeds Value, meaning it is no longer worthwhile for the customer (here, the U.S. government) to buy it.

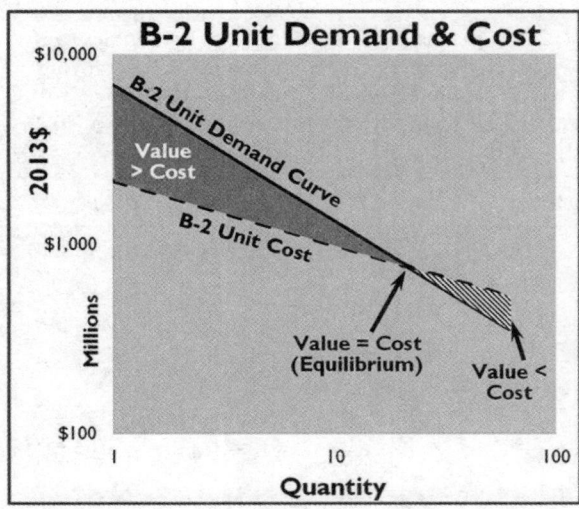

FIGURE 6.8 The B-2 bomber's value fell faster than its cost. At the 21st unit, the cost matched the value, and the program stopped.[22, 23, 24]

This market condition for a Northrop Grumman B-2 bomber purchased by the U.S. government in the public sector is much like the end of production for the Ford Model T market in the private sector. In Figure 6.8, we found that Ford Model T prices (collectively making up elements of the Model T Unit Demand Curve) fell consistently from the 10,000th version (0.01 million of Model Ts along the vertical axis) of it going forward to about 16.5 million versions of it sold. At that point, costs (depicted by the line with triangles) rose to meet prices (the line with circles), and profits fell to zero as the Model T hit the "end of product run equilibrium." No producer wants to make products past this point.

A completely different type of equilibrium relates to conditions nearer the beginning of a new product rather than its end. Imagine that you have designed a new electric car ready for production for your first sale. Because you have done your Value Analysis, you know that you can charge a certain amount for the first one and that the price you can command will fall predictably but slightly over time. At the same time, your analysis shows that the ongoing costs to produce your car start above the sustainable price and that those costs fall faster than the vehicle value. Because of these differences, you will eventually reach a point where cost equals value, the breakeven point, another kind of equilibrium, as Figure 6.9 displays. Before this point, you sold each car at a loss. Beyond this point, you will sell each one at a profit.

Not all product classes are new, of course. While the electric car is a relatively recent invention, clothing is not. As Figure 6.10 shows us, the

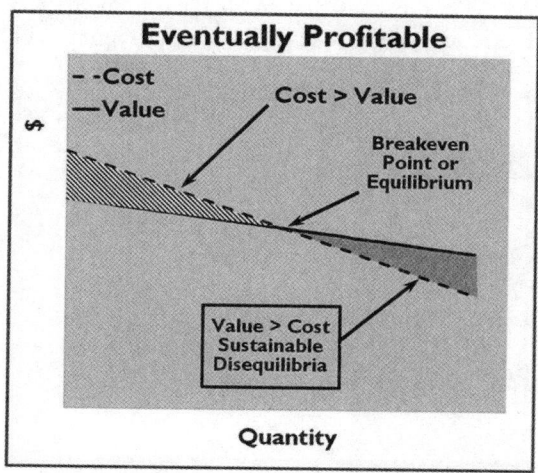

FIGURE 6.9 For some products, their recurring costs are initially higher than their values. If costs fall faster than values, those products will reach breakeven and profitability.[25, 26]

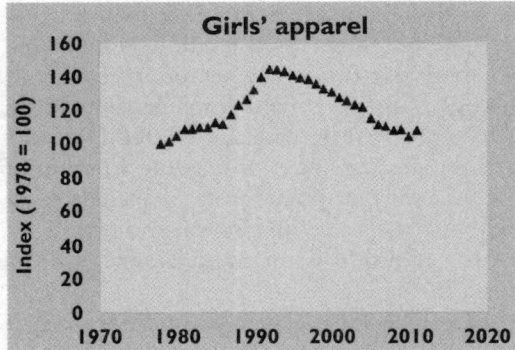

FIGURE 6.10 Product value can fall for some time, as girls' apparel did in the United States from 1992 to 2011.[27, 28]

U.S. Bureau of Labor Statistics tracks how prices change in apparel. Using an index with a baseline value of 100 in 1978, prices in constant 1978 dollars crept upward from 1978 to a peak in 1992. This means that if girls' socks matched the overall trend, a pair of socks that cost $1.00 would run $1.45 in 1992, in 1978 dollars. From that point forward, the indexed price fell to $1.04 in 2010, increasing slightly to $1.08 in 2011.

For well over the 20-plus years the Bureau of Labor Statistics tracked it, the price of girls' socks fell. For the companies that made such items to stay in business, their costs must have fallen as well, as we discover in Figure 6.11.

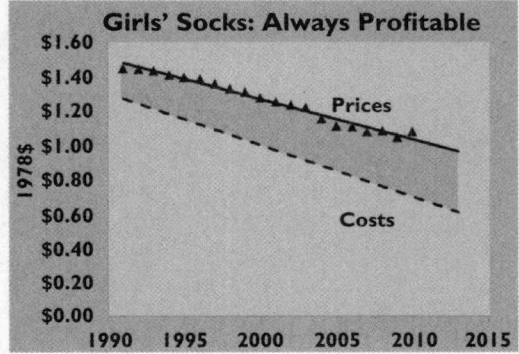

FIGURE 6.11 Some products are profitable over indefinite periods as long as costs are below prices.[29]

Over the same period, producers made those socks for less than the prices they retrieved; otherwise, they would not be in business. Girls' socks are just one product category in which prices exceed viable producers' costs over long periods. There are numerous markets where producers offer goods and services for which their customers gladly pay and offer ongoing profits to their providers.

SUMMARY

Neoclassical economists believe in the Law of Supply and Demand, in which a downward-sloping demand curve intersects an upward-sloping supply curve at a single point that they call equilibrium. Hypernomics finds at least four massive problems with this theory. One is their use of average prices for analysis—very few prices in most markets mimic the average, as Value Analysis shows. The second relates to the "single point equilibrium," Hypernomics indicates that there can be any number of fully functioning product forms within any market, including commodities. A third problem relates to the Law of Supply and Demand's caveat relative to "other things being held equal." This would have us limit our work to the two-dimensional Demand Plane, but we have repeatedly discovered that the adjacent Value Space offers a deeper analysis of markets' workings. The fourth and final problem relates to an upward-sloping supply curve. This curve implies that people get dumber as they do a task repeatedly. On the contrary, learning curve histories depict precisely the opposite—people get more innovative about jobs the more often they repeat them.

Learning Curves are ubiquitous and an essential part of Hypernomics. Despite the widespread misuse of the term, steep Learning Curves indicate that people learn quickly. If Learning Curves fall slower than Product Demand (or Unit Value) Curves, the cost will eventually meet the price. The intersecting lines will attain the end of product equilibrium, as did the Northrop Grumman B-2 bomber and the Ford Model T. Another type of equilibrium in Hypernomics exists when product costs, initially higher than product value, finally fall to meet value. This is a breakeven point beyond which products are profitable. Some products, such as girls' socks, are always worthwhile for suppliers that can make them for less than their prices. There is no consideration of equilibrium for such products. Other goods and services, such as public transportation, are never profitable and require subsidies to keep them going.

A HYPERNOMICS VIGNETTE: THE LAW OF VALUE AND DEMAND

Several years ago, I began tracking the progress of a new business jet called the Aerion AS-2.[30] Designed to be the first supersonic private jet, going about 1,000 miles per hour at its maximum, Aerion conceived it to revolutionize air travel. It would help fill the gap left in the air travel market by the Concorde, a supersonic commercial transport (Figure 6.12).[31]

Robert Bass, a Texas billionaire, founded Aerion in 2003 and began developing the Aerion AS2 in 2004. In December 2020, I wrote on LinkedIn that the plane was worth every penny of its $120 million price tag, but there needed to be more pennies worldwide to hit its demand target. Aerion wrote a firm retort on LinkedIn a few days later, claiming new orders, which came in after I wrote my piece about them. I repeated my position, citing my evidence.

The company halted development in May 2021. In September of that year, it went into liquidation.

They're not writing to me anymore.

How could I know in advance that it would fail? Plotting Demand Frontiers over time offers some deep insight into the workings of markets.

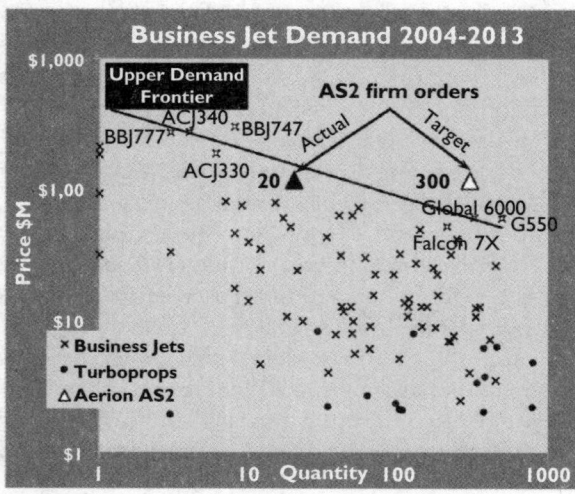

FIGURE 6.12   The 20 orders Aerion had for its AS in 2014 were in line with the Demand Frontier for the past 10 years.[32]

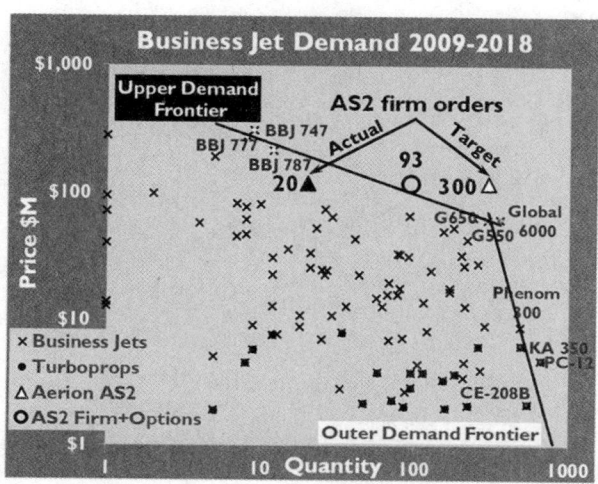

FIGURE 6.13 The 93 orders and options Aerion claimed for the AS2 in 2020 were still in line with the Demand Frontier for the past 10 years, but far below their target of 300 sales in a decade.[33]

As shown in Figure 6.12, the Demand Frontier from 2004 to 2013 suggested a limit of 47 aircraft over a decade at their price. Five years later, from the beginning of 2009 to the end of 2018, the Frontier had moved in their direction and could support 63 planes in 10 years as Figure 6.13 clearly reveals. But, if you were to do the math, you'd find that it worked out that the company had a 1 in 40 chance of making its sales goal of 300 supersonic business jets at $120 million in 10 years (Figure 6.13).

As they entered liquidation, Aerion said, "In the current financial environment, it has proven hugely challenging to close on. . .large new capital requirements to finalize the transition of the AS2 into production." That hints that they were pointing to the pandemic as their primary source of the financial dilemma.

But the Demand analysis showed that given the slow acceleration of the Demand Frontier, the market was decades away from being able to buy the plane in quantities sufficient to make a profit.

Yes, it was worth every penny spent on it, as its buyers confirmed when they placed firm orders for the plane. But there wasn't enough money in the world to make the AS2 fly financially.

Demand analysis lets you know that before you spend $1 billion and find out the hard way.

CHAPTER 7

Market Mapping and Financial Cat Scans

"We're all pilgrims on the same journey—but some pilgrims have better road maps."

Nelson DeMille

GOT EGGS?

There is an apocryphal story about Christopher Columbus, which, despite its questionable authenticity, has deep meaning for those who have done or created something new and vital and how the public views the feat (depicted in Figure 7.1). It was recounted in 1565 by the Italian historian Girolamo Benzoni,[1] who wrote:

> Columbus was dining with many Spanish nobles when one of them said: "Sir Christopher, even if your lordship had not discovered the Indies, there would have been, here in Spain, which is a country abundant with great men knowledgeable in cosmography and literature, one who would have started a similar adventure with the same result." Columbus did not respond to these words but asked for a whole egg to be brought to him. He placed it on the table and said: "My lords, I will lay a wager with any of you that you are unable to make this egg stand on its end like I will do without any kind of help or aid." They all tried without success and when the egg returned to Columbus, he tapped it gently on the table breaking it slightly, and, with this, the egg stood on its end. All those present were confounded and understood what he meant: that once the feat has been done, anyone knows how to do it.

FIGURE 7.1   *Columbus Breaking the Egg* by William Hogarth.[1, 2]

Columbus's trips were all the more remarkable since he made no "use of intelligence, mathematics or maps."[3] He went off into a great unknown, risking life, reputation, and everything in between. Not satisfied with doing it once, he did it four times, choosing a different route for each voyage, as Figure 7.2 shows. In the process, he developed his intelligence and mapped

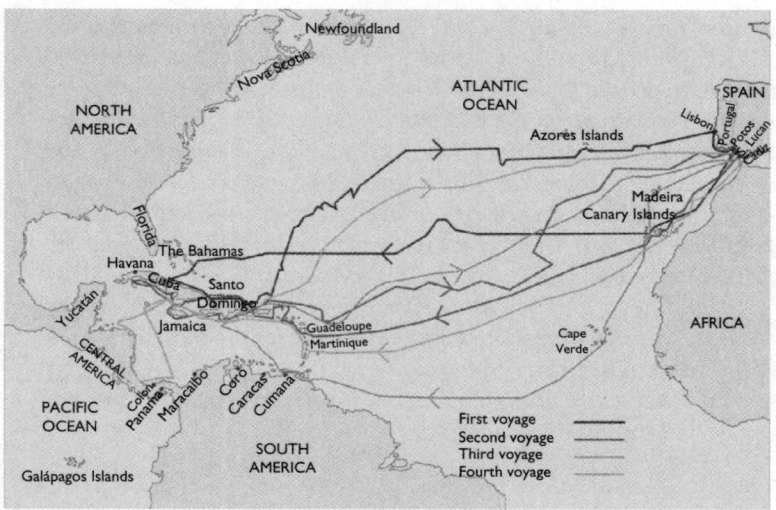

FIGURE 7.2   Columbus made four round trips from Europe to the Americas, each expanding the boundaries of what was known in Europe then.[4]

it for posterity. Very importantly, he got down to specifics, replacing conjecture with knowledge. Many people had ideas about how to get to the new world, but it took Columbus to implement a plan with defined actions that formed specific directions.

In many respects, the discipline of Hypernomics is like a series of broad expeditions to previously unknown and only recently revealed locations. This is because as it shuns physical dimensions for mathematical ones, it nonetheless appeals to analogies to geography. Any one of the roughly 108 billion people who have lived to date[5, 6] could have made these discoveries, and once unveiled, anyone can replicate the results by cracking the egg just so. Unlike geographical discoveries, however, revelations in Hypernomics are seldom end-alls. Still, they more often are gateways to insight into markets that others will not possess if they do not do similar work. In these respects, Hypernomics is more like a new optical instrument, available to anyone who wants to use it. It is best used with extensive knowledge of constructing, manipulating, and utilizing the new dials. This apparatus can help practitioners optimize market entry and profitability, and like the best of tools, proper use of it will enable users of it to be more productive. For new market entrants, its use of maps offers visual guidance on producing products that customers want while avoiding competition to the fullest extent possible. We find ourselves again appealing to geography to get a historic feel for this.

In 1893, the U.S. government held its fourth Oklahoma Land Rush, in which a crowd of roughly 100,000 people raced into a region called the Cherokee Outlet in search of one of the 42,000 parcels to which they could lay claim (Figure 7.3).

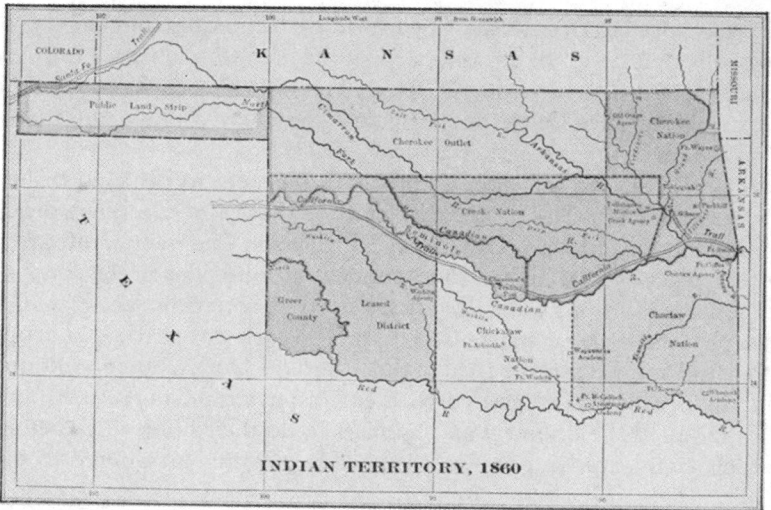

FIGURE 7.3 The Cherokee Outlet, the center shaded parcel below the northern extent of Oklahoma, was the site of the fourth Oklahoma Land Rush in 1893.[7]

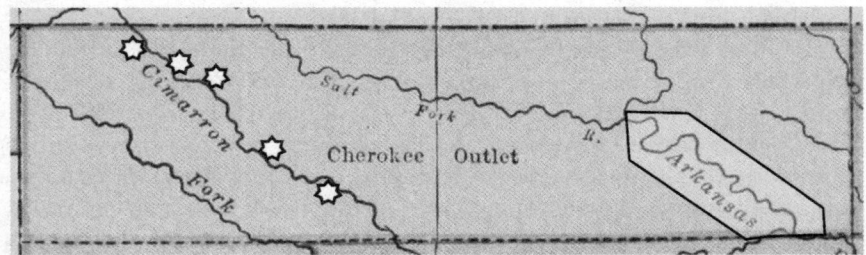

FIGURE 7.4 As the fourth Oklahoma Land Rush began, some good sites, notionally shown as starbursts toward the western end of the Cherokee Outlet along the Cimarron River, were already taken. There were good remaining sites, hypothetically in the shaded area about the Arkansas River to the east, with good access to water and transportation.[8, 9]

The folks who dutifully waited until the cannons sounded, known as "Boomers," raced into the Cherokee Outlet. They found many people, the "Sooners," had jumped the gun hours and days earlier and taken some prime locations (Figure 7.4) with access to transportation and seemingly copious amounts of water.

The apparent ongoing abundance of water was something of an anomaly. Hawkers of the land told settlers that based on an unusually wet period in the Great Plains in the years before the land rushes, the "rain would follow the plow." That claim was an instance of correlation (rain supporting farming) without causation (farming did not cause the rain, which was the hypothesis), with no evidence to support that claim, which was later discredited.[10] Decades later, because of bad farming techniques and the inevitable dry spells that beset the region, parts of the area turned largely barren and formed the Dust Bowl of the 1930s. As Figure 7.5 reveals, the western portion of the Cherokee Outlet was affected particularly badly, and many fled the region entirely in search of a better life.

Figures 7.3, 7.4, and 7.5 offer analogies to markets, as the land rushes were precisely that, a market of free real estate to those who got their corner of Oklahoma the quickest. Figure 7.3 reveals that the Cherokee Outlet was a property market limited in size and bounded on four sides. In Figure 7.4, we see that some locations were already taken—trying to claim those would result in a physical or legal struggle or both. The easiest way to get a property was to find an unclaimed parcel in the Cherokee Outlet. Some locations are better than others, and getting to them faster would take speed and guile. This required the Boomers and Sooners to do their homework before making their claim, studying the maps the U.S. government offered to the

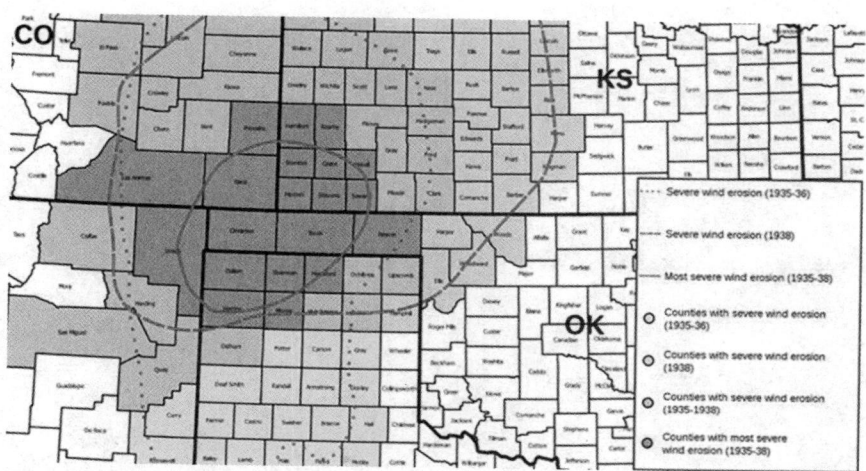

FIGURE 7.5   A few years after the fourth Oklahoma Land Rush, it was evident that the western part of the Cherokee Outlet was not a settler's best option.[11]

public prior to each land grab. Those who could make the best sense of those maps landed the best properties.

Figure 7.5 shows that, due to the ongoing Dust Bowl, a portion of the Cherokee Outlet became barren decades after its proud owners claimed land there. This was at odds with the conventional thinking that the lands would be forever fertile. It makes clear that we need to see corresponding market maps from the past to get a more comprehensive grasp of their dynamics.

MARKET MAP BOUNDARIES

The Cherokee Outlet, a geographical market for land set up by the U.S. government, had distinct boundaries in four directions: north, south, east, and west. All markets have similar limits, albeit in mathematical space.

The General Aviation market has a few dozen models, including several vehicles specialized as "bush planes." These planes fly cargo and passengers to remote locations, such as the aircraft shown in Figure 7.6, and are vital to their regions' economies.

As always, we can plot the quantities sold and their associated prices on the Demand Plane, which we do in Figure 7.7.

We are already familiar with the outer boundary to the right and in yellow, shown as the Quantity Limit Line, which we know as the Outer

FIGURE 7.6 General Aviation aircraft, like this Aviat Husky, includes bush planes that fly cargo and passengers to remote locations.[12]

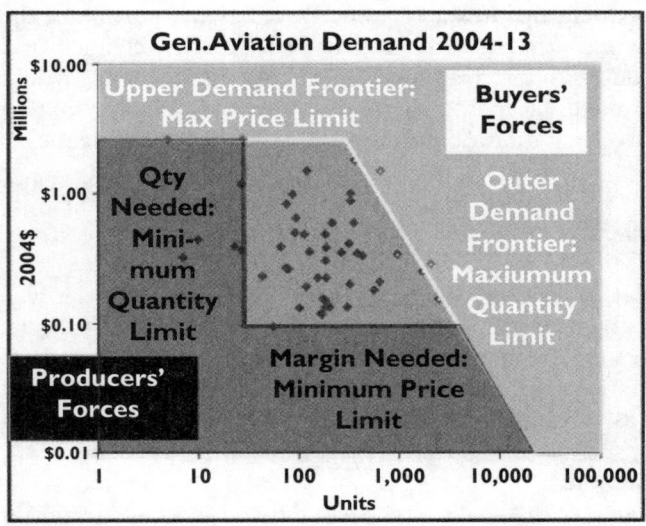

FIGURE 7.7 The General Aviation market has Upper, Outer, Lower, and Minimum limits that bind it.[13]

Demand Frontier, which buyers self-impose on the market—this relates to the maximum amount of product the market will consume at the agreed-upon prices. While the slope of the buyers' Quantity Limit Line suggests that there might be a single unit sold at an extraordinary price, in practice, the market runs up against an upper boundary known as the Upper Demand Frontier, the maximum anyone will pay in this market, which is the upper-most nearly horizontal line in Figure 7.7, also set in place by the buyers. Products priced beyond this limit will find few or no takers and fail for lack of sales.

Producers face limits, too. Each market has its lowest price good or service, one below which no product exists. At this point, the producers find that the difference between the price they get and the cost they incur yields a minimal profit, a Margin Limit, and the most negligible difference between revenues and expenditures acceptable to producers. Any product priced lower than this would not produce a sufficient profit to stay in business. While this Margin Limit changes over time, going up or down, depending on producers' economics, it exists in every market. These margins may be thousands of dollars in the General Aviation aircraft shown in Figure 7.7 or as slim as a few pennies for a pair of girls' socks.

Producers face a different barrier than buyers, as revealed by the leftmost Quantity Limit. Producers need to keep lines going, meaning they need a minimum amount of product to 1) keep their workers gainfully employed, and 2) keep the Learning Curve going in their factories and offices. As shown here, some products fall short of this inner Quantity Limit, not producing sufficient quantities to keep their lines going over time. These planes may be out of production, and their suppliers deliberately slow down or stop their lines over these 10 years. Alternatively, manufacturers may have just begun production during this period, and sales have yet to ramp up to satisfactory, sustainable levels. While the minimum number of planes required for profitability may be few as three per year, for a factory producing girls' socks, the minimum number of socks for a given line may be in the tens or hundreds of thousands of pairs. Producers' forces work in opposition to buyers' forces.

FEATURE AND PRICE GAP MAPS

In the fourth Oklahoma Land Rush, we discovered that staking a claim was more complex than placing a pin on a map. Some people took spots even before the game began, even though that was against the rules. If we could have a map showing us the best remaining parcels, even as we raced toward them, we would have some intelligent direction to guide our decision on where to put down stakes.

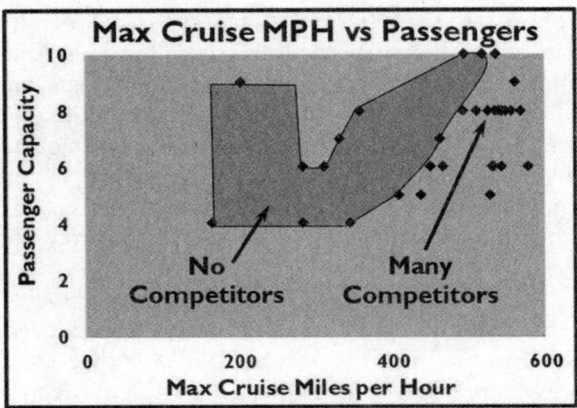

FIGURE 7.8   The business aircraft market has open feature space for speed and passenger capacity.[14]

Such maps might exist for markets—if only we take the time to draw them. As Figure 7.8 shows us in a feature map comparing maximum cruise speed to passenger capacity in the business aircraft market, some regions had great competition. Several planes offer eight-passenger accommodations with top speeds of 480 to 580 miles per hour. However, there is a large unoccupied area where we find no competition concerning these critical features.

We find the same phenomenon in Figure 7.9, in which a broad swath of the market has no competition regarding the maximum range and the cabin heights. Other parts of the market are chock-full of competition for these two attributes, but we find only a few products in that region.

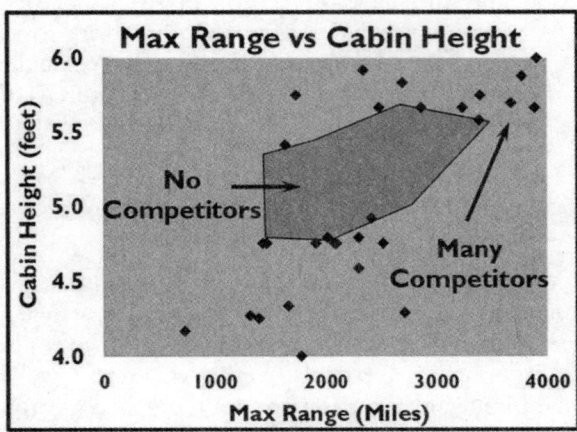

FIGURE 7.9   A similar gap exists for range and cabin height.[15]

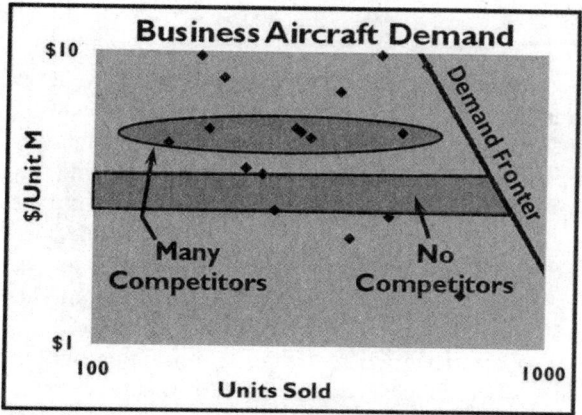

FIGURE 7.10 This Demand Plane has a large gap concerning sales price.[16]

While Figures 7.8 and 7.9 deal with elements of the Value Space, Figure 7.10 addresses a gap concerning the Demand Plane in the business aircraft market, one between $2.9 million and $3.9 million. One could imagine that a new model, with more features than the aircraft at or near $2.9 million, but with fewer valued attributes than the competitors, near $3.9 million, would find some ready buyers, given the appropriate features. Minus a few decimal places, this is akin to the market for flat-screen televisions offering products ranging in price up to $2,900, offering no products for the next $1,000, and then skipping up in price to the following flat-screen televisions at $3,900. Surely, someone would want something in between.

Thus, we can see that dot-maps and gap analyses of Value Spaces and Demand Planes have analogies to geographical maps but with some critical differences. In the Cherokee Outlet, there is only a geographic map of available parcels at any one time, determined by latitude and longitude. In mapping Value Space, there are roughly half as many feature maps as features that contribute to Value. Note that each feature map has two elements; thus, the total number of feature maps we want to draw will likely be the total number of valuable features divided by two. Hypernomics would also like to entertain at least one price gap map of the Demand Plane and perhaps many more for each significant price gap. The idea here is that there is no need to take competitors head-on—we can find regions where we have minimum competition and instead direct our new products to those regions and avoid the competition to the fullest extent possible.

FINANCIAL CAT SCANS

There are many analogies between Hypernomics and geography, as we have discovered. The discipline makes use of computed tomography (CT) as well.

Tomography includes "any of several techniques for making detailed x-rays of a predetermined plane section of a solid object while blurring out the images of other planes."[17] You likely heard the word tied to the phrase CT (computed tomography) or CAT (computed axial tomography) scans. It's a process in which a series of x-ray images are taken from many angles to produce virtual cross-sectional (tomographic) object images without surgery, as shown in Figure 7.11.

While medical CAT scans are designed to examine anomalies within the skull, Financial CAT Scans are concerned instead with distances from one surface (as a Value Surface or Demand Limit) to another (as a Cost Surface). This is akin to noting that the vertical distance between the front and the back of the skull is greater near the middle of the head (as in the first panel of the third row in Figure 7.11) than it is nearer the top of the skull (in Figure 7.11's rightmost, lowermost panel). Working with Financial CAT Scans is more straightforward than medical CAT scans in one respect.

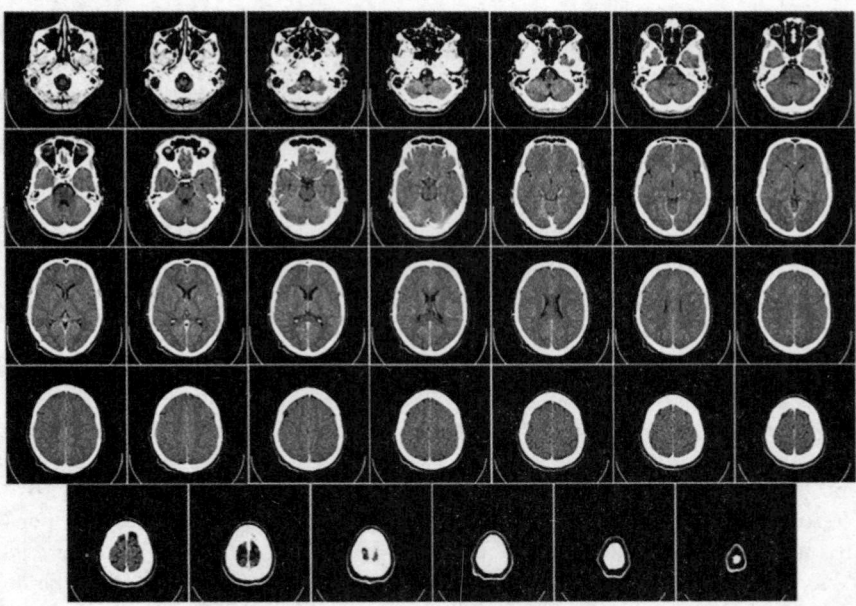

FIGURE 7.11   Computer tomography of a human head, from the base of the skull to the top.[18]

The latter addresses everything within the skull, brain, eyes, nose, sinus cavities, blood vessels, nerves, and everything else. Financial CAT Scans, by contrast, are only concerned with the distances between the analysis boundaries, akin to only being involved with the span of one side of the skull to the other. However, Financial CAT Scans can have numerous parameters for the same market. We change the Valued Features of interest and study numerous price gaps, effectively examining different conditions across multiple boundaries over four dimensions. In this regard, they can be more complicated than traditional medical CAT scans.

Our goal for Financial CAT Scanning is simple: solve for maximum profit potential with the least amount of competition. We will find that given enough passes through the data, not only can we do that, *we ought to be able to optimize profit first and work out our configuration second.* We need to emphasize this—if we understand our costs and our customers' values, we can specifically design products that avoid competition to the fullest extent possible. We can still meet our customer's needs and offer us the maximum profit, not by "seeing what the market will bear" after we built a product, as the neoclassical economists would have it, but by understanding how the market rewards feature compared to our costs for them. We design new products not based on our feelings about them but on our customers' feelings, as demonstrated by their actions.

Financial CAT Scans begin with data. For the example in front of us, we have already retrieved and analyzed the data for the Value Space. We will start the Financial CAT Scan analysis by plotting a market's demand points, as shown in Figure 7.12 (this data set is for General Aviation planes, but it could be any market we choose).

We will want to know the market's responsiveness to price changes, so we draw our demand bins and determine our Aggregate Demand curve in

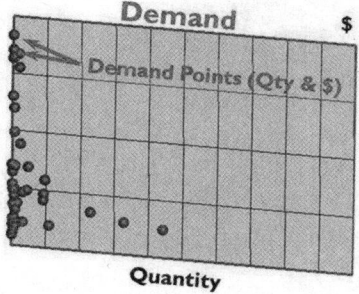

FIGURE 7.12 Financial CAT Scans begin with plotting Demand Points.[19]

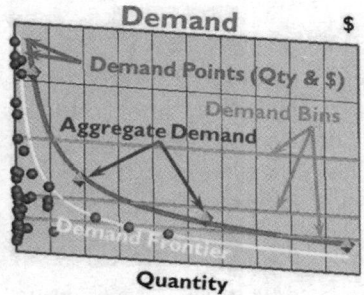

FIGURE 7.13 Once we have the Demand Points, we can perform a Demand Analysis.[20]

Figure 7.13, and we find our farthest points there as well and figure out our Demand Frontier.

We seek gaps in the market where we need more competition. After a nearly continuous string of prices from the lowest regions of the market, we see an opening just below the second horizontal line. We draw a horizontal line through the middle of this gap from quantity origin to where that line meets the Demand Frontier, and then create a vertical line from that point down to the Quantity Axis. On the Demand Plane, then, we have a target quantity and price. As we have realized, that price extends into Value Space, as Figure 7.14 further indicates. The question then becomes which features we will use to describe our Value Space.

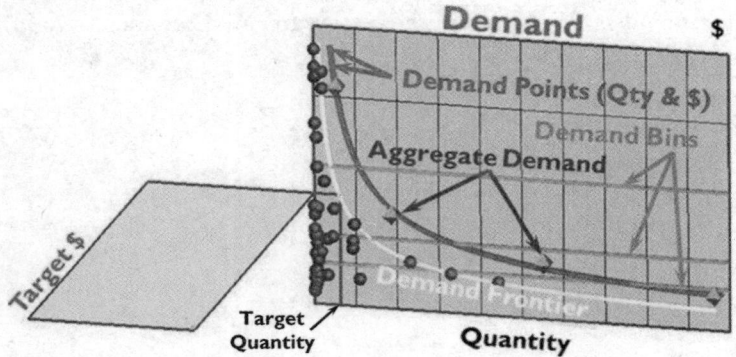

FIGURE 7.14 With the Demand Analysis complete, we find the middle of a price gap and use it as a Price Target. By doing this, we also gain a quantity target.[21]

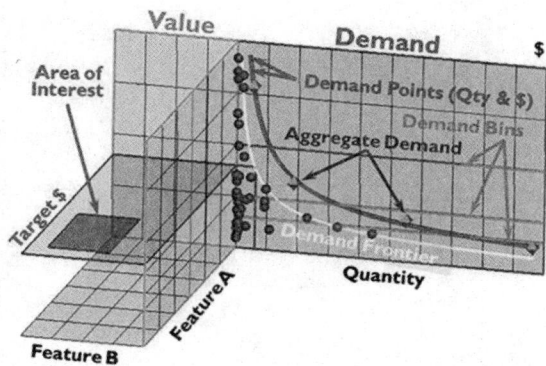

FIGURE 7.15 We bound the Target Price with a pair of Features, here A and B, to create a Value Space and a four-dimensional environment. We pare the problem down to an Area of Interest.[22]

Figure 7.15 describes any market problem in terms of essential Features A and B. In this case, Features A and B for General Aviation relate to the model's speed and passenger capacity. Still, they could be two dominant valued features in any market. Because our origin begins at (0,0,0,0), we will, in practice, never consider all options. This is because the market will never want zero of any feature they like, but instead will want more than zero to have enough of the features they like to buy, but not so many that the product exceeds their budgets. This mandates that we narrow the problem to an Area of Interest, the darkened region on the Target Price Plane in Value Space, which has a minimum and maximum level of each Feature A and Feature B.

In Figure 7.16, we add the Value Surface for this product for a single-engine plane, which we had already done in advance. Very importantly, if we describe Value with three or more variables, we will need to fix the other variables not considered by Feature A or B as constants—more on this later in this chapter. At the same time, we need to derive the costs of varying product quantities and place those cost surfaces into the analysis. In this case, we have estimated the cost of providing one unit and 500 units. One of the first checks we can do with this analysis is to see if the value exceeds the cost for some part of Value Space—which it does. This observation means that profit is possible with this product.

Since we have a Target Price, we will be very interested in the curved line that describes where the Value Surface intersects this self-imposed Demand Limit, which we see in the Area of Interest.

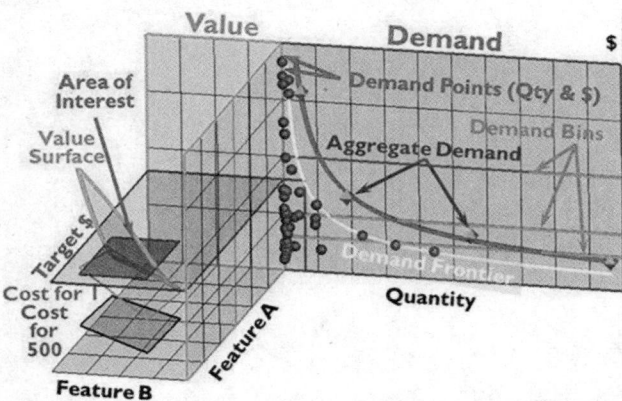

FIGURE 7.16 Using the Value Analysis we completed in advance, we lay in the surface describing how the market responds to Features A and B, and add the cost surfaces for 1 and 500 units.[23]

When we get deeper into a problem, we often encounter other issues restricting where to place new products. For example, concerning Feature B in Figure 7.17, we may discover that, as a practical matter, we will abide by the minimum amount suggested by the Area of Interest. Still, our facilities will not permit us to go to the outermost limit in the Feature B direction. Therefore, we constrain ourselves along the Feature B axis with a minimum and maximum feature amount, with the constraints as vertical, limiting walls.

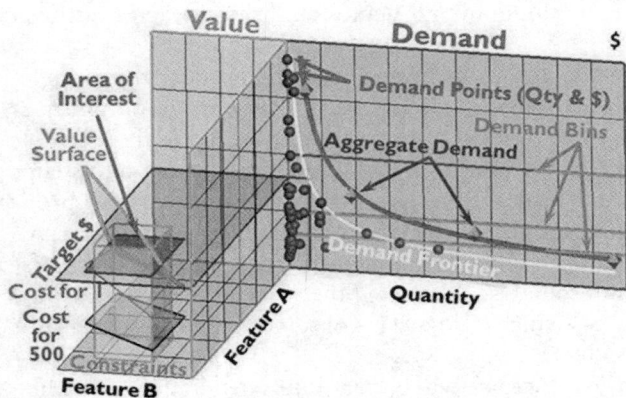

FIGURE 7.17 Here, we find additional constraints, such as technical, legal, or practical limits, that further restrict the viable product region.[24]

Along the Feature A axis, we find a different condition. For Feature A, we can tolerate the maximum amount suggested by the Area of Interest but find that it would be more beneficial to our company if we offered more than the minimum amount recommended by the Area of Interest. In this case, we limit ourselves to something more than the Area of Interest Feature A but abide by its maximum.

This sets us up for Financial CAT Scanning, which we begin in Figure 7.18. In Figure 7.11, a CT scan of a human head started at the skull's base and went toward the top of the skull, which would be in the vertical direction if the patient were seated. In our case, we perform these section cuts first, going with one Feature axis and then the other. In Figure 7.18, we begin by taking section cuts along the Feature B axis, using the black Financial CAT Scan plane to mark where we have been. We start at one edge of our constraints and continue the process in steps to the far edge of our limits. We may set the increments between scans to be wide at the beginning and then narrow the scans as we zoom in on our best option, first along one axis, then the other.

While scanning in one direction is good, we will want to scan in the other direction for good measure. We do that in Figure 7.19, where we turn the scanning 90° and run section cuts down the Feature A axis. Again, we can take as many slices as we find appropriate, looking for one that maximizes the profit line. That is the difference between its value, which we set as its price, and its costs, times the expected quantities to be sold, which we derived from our analysis.

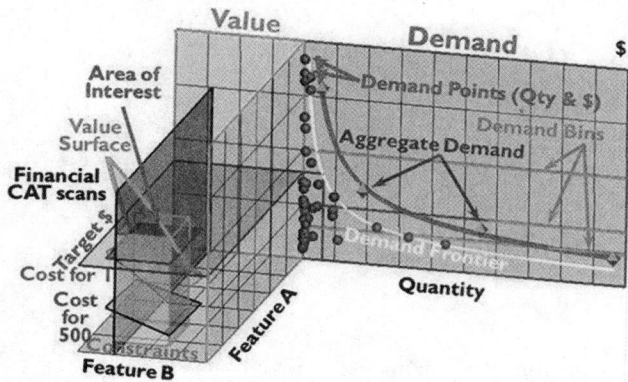

FIGURE 7.18 Now we have a region bounded on the top by the lower of our demand limit or our Value Surface, bounded on the bottom by cost and four sides by our constraints. That permits us to perform section cuts, or Financial CAT Scans, through the data.[25]

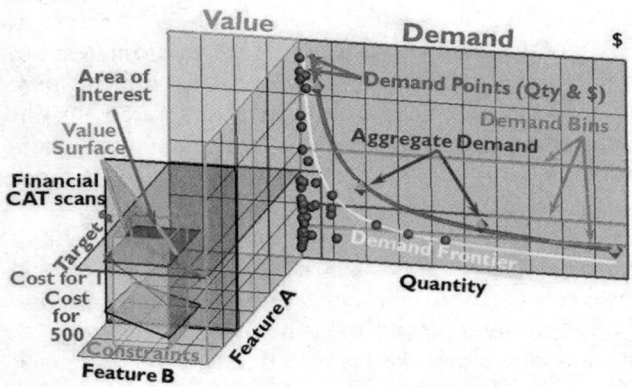

FIGURE 7.19 We continue with Financial CAT Scans along the Feature A axis.[26]

When we find a Financial CAT scan of particular interest, we will want to examine it in detail, as shown in Figure 7.20. Here, we have pulled a section cut to the left of the four-dimensional environment and are looking "end-on" down the Feature A axis in Value Space. We can see the horizontal bars representing the distal limit of the Feature B axis and the vertical

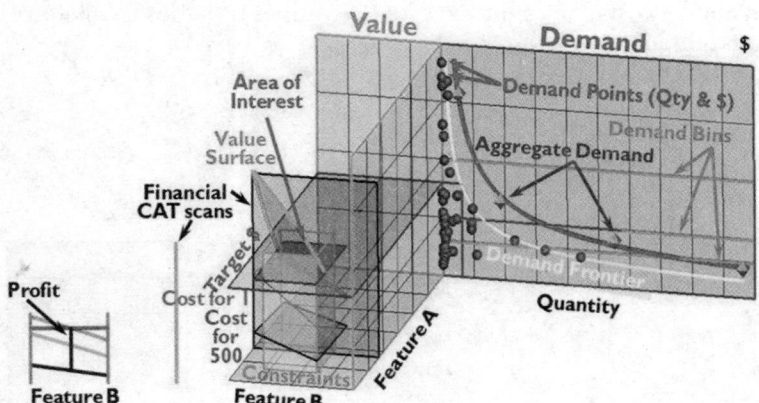

FIGURE 7.20 We find a promising section cut here. The vertical Profit Line on the left shows the per unit profit potential as the distance from where the Value Surface intersects the Target Price to the Costs for 1 Unit (light-colored line) and 500 Units (dark line).[27]

element of the Feature B axis on the left and right, respectively. We are interested in where our Demand Limit, the horizontal line, intersects the Value Surface, as this forms a point on a production possibilities curve. Note that this point solves for the price (which we set), Demand Frontier quantity (which we derived once we set the price), Feature A, Feature B, and the cost and profit for one or 500 units.

Thus, we started with four dimensions—Feature A, Feature B, Price, and Quantity. By setting the price, we derived quantity, thereby taking quantity temporarily out of the picture, leaving us with three dimensions. Since we set the price, giving us two remaining dimensions, we were only interested in finding Feature A and Feature B. By picking a profit line, we determined both Feature A and B. Working backward, the single-dimension profit line lets us determine all four dimensions. We keep resetting the variables and fixing the constants until we have exhausted all options until we are confident we have a configuration with the minimum amount of competition and the most significant profit potential.

The Value Surface in Figure 7.20 intersects the Target price along a curved line, as shown in Figure 7.21. All combinations of maximum speed and seats yield the same (Iso-) predicted value. Since that expected value (here, $742,000) is our price target, we can support that price with any

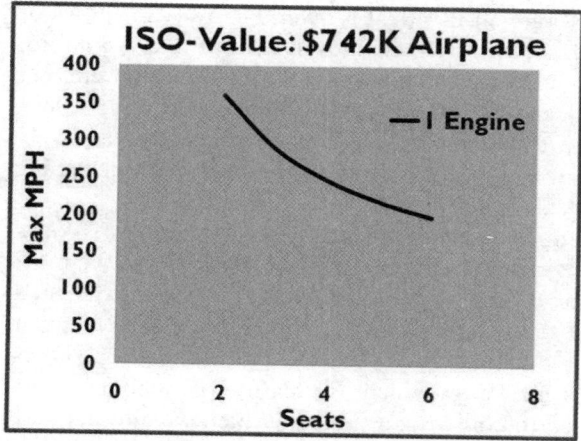

FIGURE 7.21 ISO-Value Curves depict where Value Response Curves intersect self-imposed Demand Limits. This curve represents where the Value Surface in Figure 7.20 intersects our Demand Limit.[28]

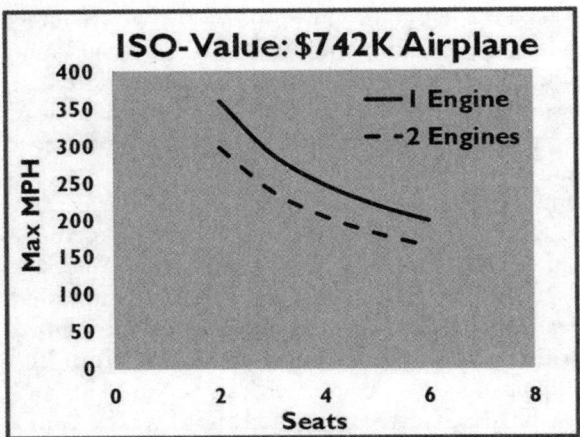

FIGURE 7.22 More engines add safety. The ISO-Value Curve for a two-engine plane shows that it does not need to go as fast as the single-engine plane to have the same value.[29]

combination of features, though as we have seen, we will want to distance ourselves from our competition (not shown here).

There are other ways to get an identical answer. Figure 7.22 shows us that if we used a Value Surface with two engines instead of one, we do not have to have our plane go as fast as a single plane with the same number of seats to get the same value. This is because the added engines add safety. If one engine goes out in a two-engine plane, you still have power, likely enough to get where you are going. If one engine goes out in a one-engine plane, you now have a glider.

More than just analyzing a single pair of features for a market is required if many more features contribute to a value within it. To that end, we must fix some features and let the others vary, and only when we have exhausted all combinations and done the Financial CAT Scanning for all the relevant outcomes may we consider this part of our work done. Figure 7.23 shows us how we could analyze a market in which five features contribute to the value of a product. We need to construct a table in which we alternatively fix some variables and let others vary to find the best possible collection of product features. It turns out that these multiple contributors to value are common to many markets. Some markets have as many as nine contributors to value, all working simultaneously.

Case	Engines	Pass	MPH	Height	Range
1	Fixed-1	Fixed	Fixed	Vary	Vary
2	Fixed-1	Vary	Fixed	Vary	Fixed
3	Fixed-1	Fixed	Vary	Vary	Fixed
4	Fixed-1	Vary	Fixed	Fixed	Vary
5	Fixed-1	Fixed	Vary	Fixed	Vary
6	Fixed-1	Vary	Vary	Fixed	Fixed
7	Fixed-2	Fixed	Fixed	Vary	Vary
8	Fixed-2	Vary	Fixed	Vary	Fixed
9	Fixed-2	Fixed	Vary	Vary	Fixed
10	Fixed-2	Vary	Fixed	Fixed	Vary
11	Fixed-2	Fixed	Vary	Fixed	Vary
12	Fixed-2	Vary	Vary	Fixed	Fixed

FIGURE 7.23 A thorough analysis will allow us to fix some features and allow others to vary. Systematically doing this allows us to exhaust market opportunities.[30]

SUMMARY

Maps are vital to understanding geography. Cartographers show us where the sea ends and the land begins. They depict latitude, longitude, and geographic features such as lakes, canyons, and mountains; they can also reveal aspects such as roads and highways, navigable rivers, annual rainfall, mineral content, and population density. All of these characteristics and much more influences how people value land.

Hypernomics relies heavily on maps. Demand maps show us market bounds determined by customers, which relate to the maximum prices and quantities they can afford. In contrast, producer bounds reveal the minimum amounts needed to maintain learning and the like margins required for continued profitability. Demand maps also show gaps in the market, regions where no product competes relatively to price. Such areas may respond well to new products that seek to differentiate themselves in terms of their prices, offering producers a way to gain the minimum amount of competition.

Feature maps for products reveal gaps in which no competitor has an offering. Complete market analysis often requires multiple feature maps to account for all the attributes that customers find appealing. Combining Feature maps and Demand maps, gap analysis offers visual proof that new products have minimum competition, subject to these new products being within market limits.

Financial CAT Scanning takes advantage of both Demand and Feature maps. One way to begin such analysis is to pick a pair of essential features for the horizontal axes in Value Space and fix any other valued features as constants. Then we could find a price gap on the Demand Plane and choose the center of that void as a target price. This takes our four-dimensional analysis down to three-dimensional, as we have solved for maximum quantity. With an Area of Interest identified in the Value space, we add a completed Value surface, which we compare to an associated cost surface, and then bound the region with any constraints we face. We then run a series of 2D section cuts through the analysis along the Feature A and Feature B axes. Now we have reduced the problem to a series of 2D images. Within these images, we find the one with the most significant profit potential while remaining free of the competition—this is a 1D solution. We can find the best possible market entry point by varying the other vital features and exhausting the data for relevant combinations. In the process, we have solved for maximum profit first and the configuration required to support it second.

CHAPTER 8

Aiming and Missing

"A goal is not always meant to be reached; it often serves simply as something to aim at."

Bruce Lee

Markets, as we have come to realize, have boundaries and limits, densely populated regions and some much less so, and relationships that buyers form in reaction to the products offered to them. Just as an armed unit invading a foreign land strives to conquer a part of it, a producer entering a market aims at a segment of a highly bounded region, whether that producer realizes it or not. Thus, producers must understand what it means to aim and how to plan for the inevitable misses that come from taking shots.

NEOCLASSICAL AIMING

The current or neoclassical school of thought makes many predictions about the economy and the markets that make it up. Regarding their market projections, they often forecast a series of single elements—such as the prices of agricultural items such as wheat, corn, or soybeans (in the commodities market). In contrast, others estimate what buyers will spend to acquire heavy or light crude oil in the future. The errors associated with such estimates usually form a straight-line error of a single dimension—the prediction is higher or lower than the actual Value, as shown in Figure 8.1. Neoclassical analysts spend much time and effort on these forecasts, but they are often incomplete, as they fail to account for all the variables in action. Primarily this is because they lack a framework with sufficient dimensions to perform their analysis thoroughly, as called for by prudence. We now know we

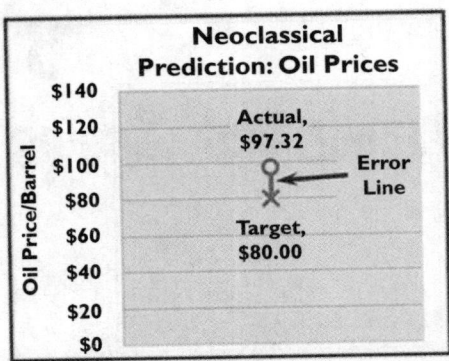

FIGURE 8.1 A neoclassical prediction for oil futures results in a one-dimensional error term.[1]

have a four-dimensional market system with which to contend. What would make us think that a single-dimensional error will account for the entire scope of our misses? Furthermore, what should we make of the differences in the time required to react to various market needs? Is responding to a given market's needs today the same as anticipating its requirements five years from now? Clearly not. We must have ways to distinguish timelines in our aiming.

IMMEDIATE AIMING

In most industries, markets have pressing needs. A convenience store owner must have the price posted for every item in the store. Patrons of the store will eventually want to know next week's Value of an apple but if they are in the store at this very moment, however, they rightfully expect to see the current prices. These are instantaneous prices that vendors and producers offer their clients at that particular moment. In the apple example, they effectively aim at an optimal point in space, just as the archer aims at the target in Figure 8.2. This is *immediate aiming*.

A bullseye is the best option, and the rings around it indicate progressively worse shots. Targets like this offer discrete ways to demonstrate the goodness of the aim. Closer to the center is always better. Time for the archer has immediacy. She may well get better over time. But, on any day that she practices, she will get instant feedback about how close she is to the mark at that moment in time.

FIGURE 8.2 This archer draws on a target directly before her, using immediate aiming.[2]

From the standpoint of the archer, the time elapsed from when she loosed the arrow until it reached its target was virtually instantaneous. If she were indoors, the wind would not concern her. But, being outdoors, she'll have to correct for windage. Having a short shot with an arrow, she had none of the long-distance concerns that permeate long-range riflery, such as gyroscopic drift or the Magnus, Poisson, Coriolis, or Eötvös effects.[3] But she will likely have an error of some sort. Seldom, if ever, will she hit the exact center of the bullseye.

Furthermore, when she misses, she will not do so in the same fashion as the neoclassical economists when they attempt to predict oil prices. Her misses will have horizontal and vertical components, or, as they are called in riflery, elevation, and windage (or Azimuth) errors. When we pair the inaccuracy relative to up and down to the one dealing with left or right, the combined terms form an *error triangle*, shown in Figure 8.3 as the lines from the middle of the bullseye going down to the elevation error and over to the windage error. She must account for both directions of the error to correct subsequent shots. However, producers and store vendors have not been afforded such clear-cut targets and errors.

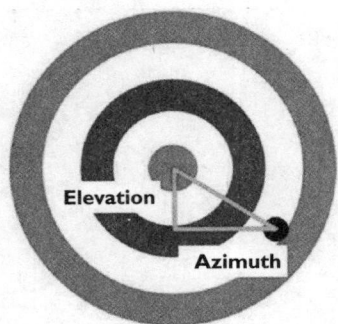

FIGURE 8.3   A miss yields an error triangle with inaccuracies for both the vertical (elevation) and horizontal (azimuth) directions.[4, 5]

Armed forces everywhere put much effort into aiming, which was never more evident than in World War I, where the battles stretched from Europe to Asia Minor. Figure 8.4 reveals shells from a single day's bombardment.

FIGURE 8.4   The Allies launched millions of artillery rounds against enemy positions during WWI. These are the shells from a single day's bombardment. Many missed their marks. They sent reconnaissance planes to assess the damage, with many sorties conducted during artillery barrages in ongoing battles.[6, 7]

FIGURE 8.5 A pilot sits in a Caudron G.3 training and reconnaissance plane.[8] Note the end of the fuselage aft of the pilot, the
metallic structure to the left of the plane's number.

There was much to investigate, as the battle pictured there hints at the
millions of artillery rounds exchanged during the conflict. With the invention of the airplane, it became easier to assess battles from the air. Given that
some actions went on for hundreds of days and bombardments could last
for hours, it became commonplace for the Allies to send up reconnaissance
planes during the middle of a sequence of barrages. Thus, many brave pilots
went out on sorties with cannon volleys coming in from the opposing Central Powers and shells going out from the friendly Allies as well.

Barely a decade past the first flight of an airplane by the Wright Brothers,
the aircraft of the day typically had open cockpits, as shown in Figure 8.5.
A single pilot sits in the cockpit's rear seat, with the student pilot's front seat.
There was little in the way of creature comforts, as pilots had only a thin
leather helmet, goggles, and a heavy jacket to protect themselves from the
elements and fire from all directions.

Imagine the surprise of the United States pilot in Figure 8.6, who, when
sent on a mission to examine damage to enemy positions created by Allied
artillery during one of their barrages, heard a loud thud as a friendly fire
round took off the rear of his fuselage, missing him by inches.

The Allies were trying to hit a spot on the ground with an artillery shell—
and they missed. The pilot, presumably cruising along at about 60 miles
per hour, or 88 feet per second, avoided getting killed by one-hundredth

FIGURE 8.6   A smiling pilot sits in a Caudron G.3 after a sortie conducted during a bombardment.[9] Note that friendly fire blasted off the aft fuselage, and the pilot lived to tell about it.

to one-tenth of a second.[10–12] While that incident points up how close the margins are in life, it also reveals a different kind of error that we need to be able to characterize.

Suppose the Allied pilot in Figure 8.6 took off to conduct battlefield surveillance, flying over the friendly lines as shown in Figure 8.4. Meanwhile, a gunnery team on his side aims to take out an enemy bridge but instead takes off the tail end of the pilot's plane's fuselage, just missing him. How does that look as an error?

The bridge, the target, is Point 1 in Figure 8.7. Missing it in the manner in which they did has three elements. As measured by latitude, the artillery round missed to the south in the north-south direction, as indicated by Point 2.

Not only did the gunnery team miss the mark from north to south, but they also misfired from east to west, the lateral component indicated by Point 3. Because the bridge had an altitude much closer to the ground than the plane, we found an additional vertical miss at Point 4, where the round finally impacted the plane. These four points trace an *error tetrahedron*, indicating latitude, longitude, and elevation misses.

What it means to miss in the physical world is not a problem limited to a single dimension. On a two-dimensional plane, misfires result in error triangles. In three-dimensional space, miscues leave us with error tetrahedrons. We will need both to study more thoroughly and analyze a pervasive problem in Hypernomics.

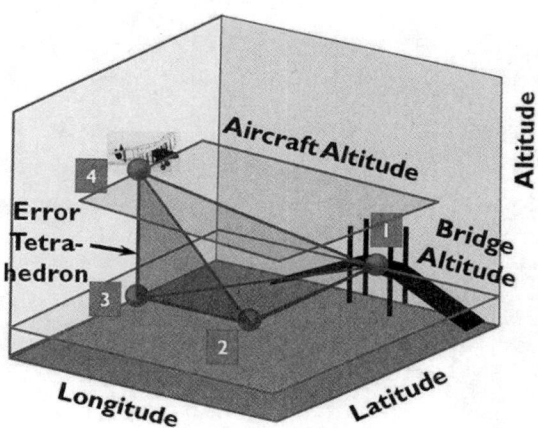

FIGURE 8.7 World War I Allies want to hit an enemy bridge (1) with an artillery round. Not only do they miss the mark concerning latitude (2) and longitude (3), they are off-target for altitude as well, as they hit a friendly aircraft (4). These four points trace out an Error Tetrahedron.[13]

IMMEDIATE AIMING IN HYPERNOMICS

Suppose you lead a team that has done value analysis on a new business aircraft your firm is completing. You have told your people that the new jet will fetch $25 million a copy if they follow the attribute mix you have derived. Then someone suggests several changes to the features—what will happen?

The configuration you had hoped for was to have carried up to eight people, traveled at speeds up to 580 miles an hour, and had a range of up to 5,000 miles, as shown by Point 1 in Figure 8.8.

Now someone removed a seat, and currently, it only holds seven people as we move to Point 2, losing Sustainable Value in the process. Somebody thought it a good idea to reduce the engine rating, which takes the maximum speed down to 540 miles per hour, at Point 3. Yet another person decided to put in a smaller fuel tank than the aircraft could reasonably hold, impacting the plane's maximum range, which moves from 5,000 to 4,000 miles as Point 4. Through each of these changes, the new business aircraft lost Value, becoming worth fewer dollars, and the plane that initially sold for $25 million can now retrieve $18.6 million. As the configuration changed from Point 1 to Point 4 in steps, it traced a Value Error Tetrahedron.

What happens in Value Space must necessarily be reflected on the Demand Plane. Either side of the currency axis always acts in concert. We see the impact of the Value Space in Figure 8.8 on the Demand Plane in Figure 8.9.

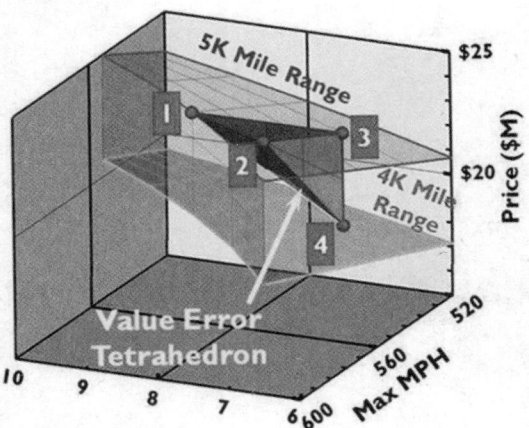

FIGURE 8.8   An airframe manufacturer wants to make a business jet worth $25 million based on its features (1). The plane's Value falls when the company drops the passenger capacity from eight to seven (2). It goes down again when the company reduces the maximum speed from 580 to 540 miles per hour (3), and once more as the company takes the maximum range from 5,000 to 4,000 miles. These four points trace out a Value Error Tetrahedron.[14, 15]

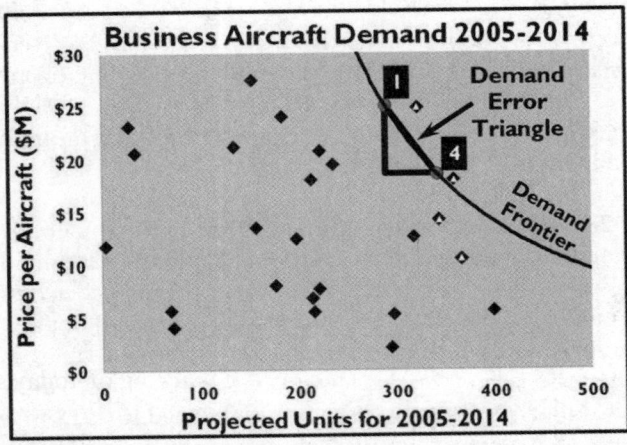

FIGURE 8.9   As prices fall from starting Point 1 to final position 4 due to lower Value, the maximum potential sales quantities increase along the Demand Frontier.[16]

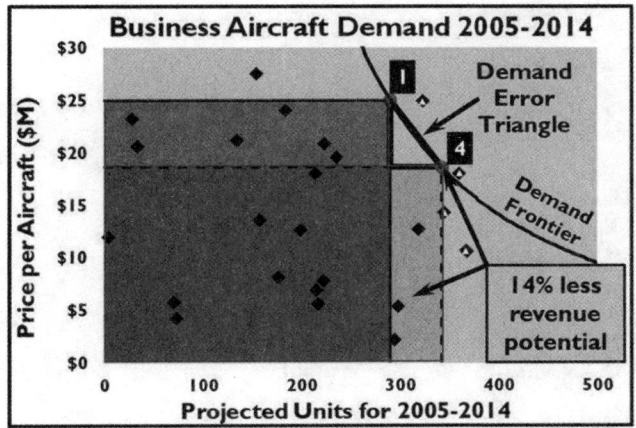

FIGURE 8.10   The price drop from Point 1 to Point 4 lowers maximum potential revenue by 14%.[17]

As the Value fell from $25 million to $18.6 million, the sales potential for additional quantities increased along the Demand Frontier. At first blush, this may sound like a good thing, and sometimes it is. However, this is not one of those times. As Figure 8.10 displays, when we find the maximum potential sales quantities for the initial position and multiply that times the initial price, we get the total potential revenue, shown by the area shaded in light gray. With the price sustainable lower, we perform the same exercise for the lower price and get the area shaded in gray. When we do the math, given the steep slope (at –1.8, much less than –1.0), we discover that we have about 14% less revenue potential at the new price point. Unless the team's costs fall more than the revenue potential, this will not enhance our bottom line and will offer us less revenue and profits. Such conditions, of course, always depend on the slope of the demand curves, which is why it is imperative to understand them.

ULTIMATE AIMING

In many business situations, we will find that we are not working on today's problem but rather the one we will face some time from now. This requires foresight and anticipation. We do not care where the market is but where it will be for these issues. This requires *ultimate aiming*.

Football games often employ ultimate aiming, with quarterbacks anticipating an open space for a receiver. In Figure 8.11, Drew Brees, the

FIGURE 8.11 Drew Brees anticipates Larry Fitzgerald's ultimate spot on the field and will lead him there.[18]

quarterback for the New Orleans Saints, prepares to throw to a spot where Arizona wide receiver Larry Fitzgerald will be, not where he is.

Discovering a space in football is a key to winning games, just like finding a new business opportunity. However, the nature of missing in football and business is much different than it is in archery. We have but two ways to miss in archery—up and down and left and right, as arrows reach a target that is on a flat plane. Working in three-dimensional space requires more as there is more going on. We must account for all of the errors we can feasibly address. This will necessarily include a time component.

When Drew Brees throws a pass, or the unseen soccer player from Figure 8.12 kicks the ball, they intend to send it to the desired target.

Once they have let it go or struck it, the ball travels in a straight line unless acted on by another force. In the physical world where both players find themselves, gravity, friction from the air and ground, and other players can act on their passes or shots. With a well-constructed pass traveling in the absence of another person to shift its direction, intended receivers, especially those with long experience in such matters, make allowances for friction and gravity and can anticipate where the ball will be based on where it has been.

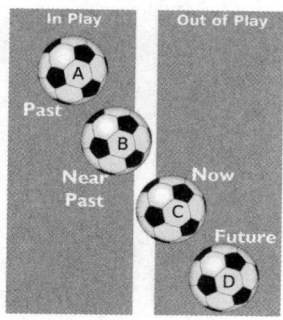

FIGURE 8.12 A soccer ball is a region bounded by leather that makes up the outside of a sphere. Once a force is imposed on it, such as a kick, just before A in the past, it continues to move in its initial direction of travel to the near past (B) and present (C), and will likely move on to a future Point (D), unless acted upon by another force.[19]

Larry Fitzgerald figured this out 1,432 times in National Football League games by the time he retired, second to all-time Jerry Rice. It makes us wonder if there is a similar way to track markets to foresee where they will be before some future date.

ULTIMATE AIMING IN HYPERNOMICS

Things change. Once struck, the ball in Figure 8.12 moves along a path determined by various forces that it faces, changing position all the while.

Markets are much the same. Nascent markets most especially demonstrate more rapid changes in position than long-established ones, as buyers become aware of the products within them, other producers and new products enter them, and technological, physical, and legal barriers transform over time. At this time, the electric car market is in such a state. Figure 8.13 shows us that the market in 2012, indicated by the red quantity-price pairs, had a Demand Frontier drawn with the yellow line.

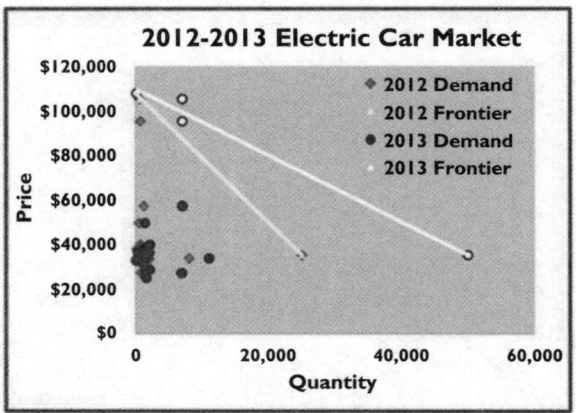

FIGURE 8.13 In 2012, the diamond points made up the Demand for the electric car market, with each diamond depicting the quantity and price for a given model. They made up the left-most Demand Frontier in that year. One year later, Demand shifted to the circular points, which shifted the 2013 Demand Frontier accordingly.[20]

Note that by the following year, 2013, there were many more sales, as indicated by the blue points, so much so that the 2013 Demand Frontier reached 50,000 units at its furthest extent, as the white line shows us. Thus, as a line going through economic space, Demand has a trajectory. More snapshots in time would help us establish its course.

Of course, as we now know, the Demand Plane is not independent of other forces as it constantly moves in concert with its corresponding Value Space, as Figure 8.14 demonstrates. A lot is going on in Value Space over time, we need to account for it, and while we already know most of it, some new pieces have been added.

First, we should examine the upper surface of the irregular red hexahedron (a polyhedron with six sides, a regular version of which is the cube) in the Value Space of Figure 8.14. This plane is the Value Response Surface for the electric car market, which in 2012 showed how the market rewarded range and horsepower for these vehicles.[21] Presumably, beneath the Value Response Surface is another plane called the Cost Response Surface, which shows producers' costs to make these products.[22] If producers cannot get their costs below their prices, they will eventually fail, so this surface must be below the sustainable price at some point. Here, the producer costs are already below the sustainable prices, showing that they are making a profit. There is other important information that the hexahedron reveals to us.

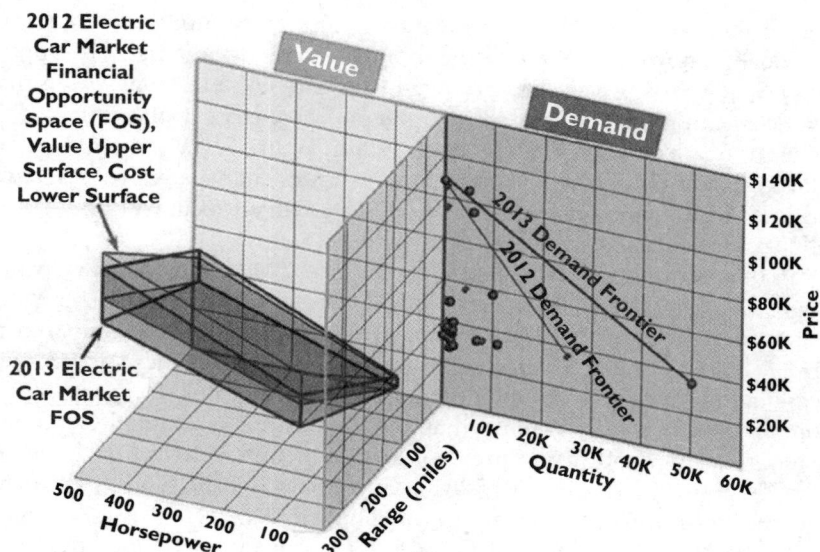

2012 Electric Car Market Financial Opportunity Space (FOS), Value Upper Surface, Cost Lower Surface

2013 Electric Car Market FOS

FIGURE 8.14 Changes on the Demand Plane reflect across to Value Space. In 2012, the electric car market had a particular affinity for the features offered to it, as the uppermost Value Surface in the upper bounded region of Value Space indicates. Producers formed a cost surface below that surface, roughly parallel to it, and part of the same region. Along each Valued Feature axis, there were minimum feature constraints set by the market and upper feature constraints bounded by the technology of the day and the buyers' ability to buy those cars. Combined, these limits define a Financial Opportunity Space (FOS), a bounded moving region where profit is possible. Much like a soccer ball, this bounded region shifted downward to the 2013 electric car market FOS the following year.[23]

Note that along the horsepower axis, there is a minimum amount offered. While producers could theoretically provide less, consumers will not stand for it, so the market finds itself with a self-imposed minimum. At the other end of this axis, producers limit how much horsepower they can install and still sell it for a price that does not exceed the buyers' threshold. Likewise, in the range direction, no consumer wants to be stranded on a trip, let alone a short one. Thus, we find a minimum market value here, just as we did with horsepower. In addition, while consumers may fantasize about some practically unlimited range for their electric cars, it is hard to store that much energy.

Thus, the market bounds itself concerning the currency direction by the vertical difference between price and cost. At the same time, it restricts itself to minimum and maximum feature values going along each horizontal valued feature axis. We call this bounded region the Financial Opportunity Space. It is possible to profit with feature combinations, given that producers can match or beat comparable industry costs. Conceptually, this enclosed region is much like the soccer ball in Figure 8.12, and once struck, will move over time. It will proceed as consumers change preferences, laws, and incentives to buy change, and producers extend technical boundaries and learn how to make the products more efficiently.

In this example, as we moved from 2012 to 2013, the consumers' value proposition changed. The different shape indicates this to the upper-Value Response Surface of the 2013 Financial Opportunity Space compared to 2012.[24] At the same time, producers have "gone down the learning curve," meaning that they have grown more innovative about how to produce each model in the market, meaning that they make the same models for less money than they did in the previous year, which is reflected in the lower Cost Response Surface in 2013 vis-à-vis that of 2012.[25] Note that in this case, the constraints are unchanged for simplicity's sake.

So, as the 2012 Financial Opportunity Space evolved into the 2013 FOS, the market demonstrated movement that we captured, just like slow motion photography captures the path of a struck ball. With enough shots of these spaces moving over time, we can anticipate where to be when we get our products to market as we lead the market after tracking it.

We call the tracking of Financial Opportunity Space over time *Economic Trajectory Analysis* or *ETA*.

SUMMARY

Whether or not analysts or producers realize it, their predictions on new products are equivalent to aiming at one or more markets. Such estimates often only entertain a single component relative to the market, such as a future commodity price. In these cases, those predictions are one-dimensional, producing an error line between the forecast and the actual Value at the time of the projection.

The physical world offers us different examples of errors. When an archer aims at the center of a two-dimensional target and misses, that miss has a horizontal (or azimuth or windage) component and a vertical (or elevation) term. When compared to the target's center, these two elements of the miss form an error triangle. Aiming at a target in a three-dimensional setting is still more complicated. When an artillery round flies off, aimed at a bridge downrange, and hits an aircraft far short of the intended impact point, that miss forms an error tetrahedron. The four sides of this polygon include 1) the error in latitude, 2) the longitude error, 3) the elevation error, and 4) the line from the impact point in space to the intended target.

Errors in aiming in the physical world have analogies in Hypernomics. Missing all three of the only targeted features of a product will cause it to 1) lose its sustainable price along Valued Feature A, 2) do the same along Valued Feature B, and 3) drop to another, lower Value Response Surface, forming a Value Error Tetrahedron. Here, the four sides of this tetrahedron are 1) the error in Feature A, 2) the error in Feature B, 3) the Value Surface elevation error, and 4) the line from actual product point features and price back to its original features and price. Meanwhile, the movement from the intended product price and quantity to another pairing on the Demand Plane creates a Demand Error Triangle. The vertical error relates to price, while the horizontal element addresses quantities sold.

Immediate aiming relates to pointing to positions currently available in markets. The time between finding the targeted area and placing the product within it must be short as the time from arrow release to impact is very short.

Ultimate aiming is the recognition that some targets move over time, such as the receiver in football. Balls used in sporting events are enclosed regions in which players in the game evince great interest—they want to know where the ball is and where it is going. Markets have analogies to these balls, which we call Financial Opportunity Spaces. These Spaces move over time. With enough views of such Spaces over time, we should be able to predict where they will be in the future, which is Ultimate Aiming in Hypernomics.

CHAPTER 9

N-Dimensional Systems

"*There could be more to the universe than the three dimensions we are familiar with. They are hidden from us in some way, perhaps because they're tiny or warped. But even if they're invisible, they could affect what we actually observe in the universe.*"

Lisa Randall

"*Evolution has ensured that our brains just aren't equipped to visualize 11 dimensions directly. However, from a purely mathematical point of view, it's just as easy to think in 11 dimensions as it is to think in three or four.*"

Stephen Hawking

The economic world with any number of, or N, dimensions is as real as any other. While the mere thought of an unlimited number of dimensions displayed simultaneously might appear mentally overwhelming, it turns out that the few mechanisms that form it are akin to a small number of familiar objects and concepts taken from everyday life. Those ordinary things include 1) pie, 2) logarithmic scaling (used to measure earthquake, sound, and light intensities), 3) Rolodexes (a physical filing system typically using card stock), 4) concentric circles, and 5) parallelograms (as in extendable mirrors).

Furthermore, N-dimensional systems exist not only when it comes to the economy but taken together they are the sum of our collective economic output. Thus, to limit the analysis to fit within the framework of this book, N-dimensional systems, as applied here, will only address economics. While aspects of this line of inquiry may well appeal to some other disciplines, we will leave the expansion of those concepts to future works.

As they apply to Hypernomics, N-dimensional systems often deal with multiple markets forming the world gross domestic product (GDP). As we will see, though, we are not limited to that as we could perform similar analyses for world GDP subsets, such as budgets for a nation or a state, or perhaps draw one for a private or publicly traded firm involved in many distinct markets. For brevity, we will limit our N-dimensional discussions to GDP for this discussion. In its simplest embodiment, the GDP concept is nothing more than the collective world pie. N-dimensional systems, therefore, are very interested in the "pie portions" each market has relative to the world total. Each economic sector's "pie piece" measurement is of great interest. For that, we will need to study pie.

COMMON OBJECT 1—PIE

And now, ladies and gentlemen, here's a food item in Figure 9.1 that needs no introduction—pie!

As you may have guessed, we will need to form an N-Dimensional system of many four-dimensional markets to perform some massive but meaningful data compression of our depiction of those markets. This begins with understanding the economy at large, which often begins with understanding the broadest sectors of it. An excellent place to start is with pie.

FIGURE 9.1 Pie has a diameter and a depth to it.[1]

Several features of pie make it mathematically appealing to us. While it is undoubtedly possible to characterize a pie by something other than its traditional circular shape, we will confine ourselves to pies that retain that long-lived feature in this work. When it comes to this circular shape that describes the sum of its pieces, as we will use it to describe GDP, two aspects of the pie become important: 1) its diameter, and 2) its height. These two terms combine to work out the pie volume at hand. In our case, we will further suppose two additional things: 1) that the pie bottom, top, and all cross-sections of it running parallel to its base have the same diameter, forming a perfect cylinder;[2] and 2) we restrict the radius of the pie to 1 foot.[3] What does that do for us?

The first thing that we need to do is find out what GDP is for a given year. For that, we can go to the *World Factbook* of the Central Intelligence Agency (CIA) and find that it was $78.28 trillion in 2014, split into three categories, as indicated in Figure 9.2.

Such a large number is hard to comprehend. One way to look at it is to understand that at $100 million per mile, that amount of money would reach over 249,000 miles, the height of an orbit of the Moon near its apogee (Figure 9.3).

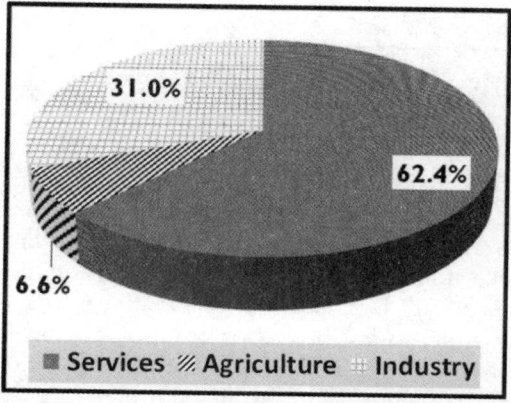

FIGURE 9.2 The U.S. CIA estimated the 2014 world GDP to be $78.28 trillion, broken into these three categories.[4, 5]

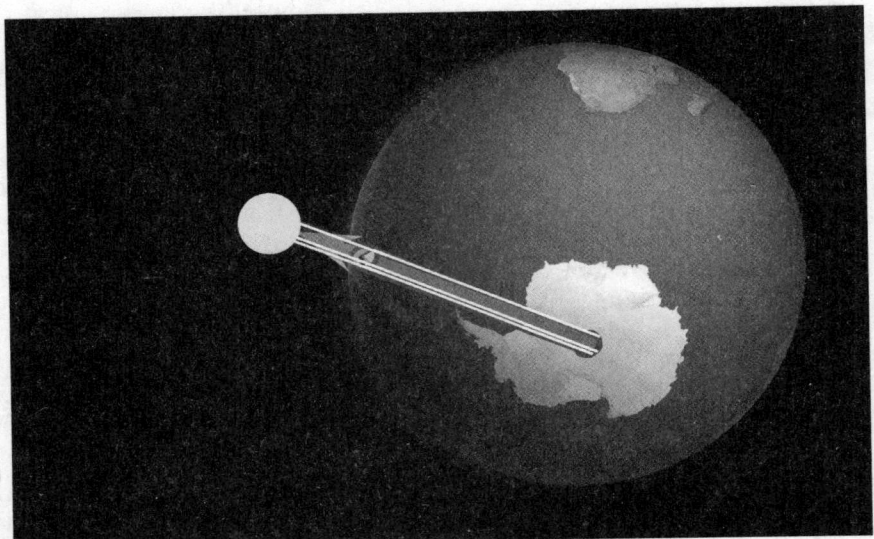

FIGURE 9.3   At $100 million per mile, a cylinder representing total GDP would reach the height of the Moon's orbit.[6-8]

COMMON OBJECT 2—LOGARITHMIC SCALING

As a practical matter, we would never want to consider using conventional linear scaling, as we do not want to work up to the Moon's height. We need to have a way around it. We find that method uses logarithmic scaling, the same scheme used on the Richter scale.

The logarithm is the inverse operation of exponentiation. The logarithm of a number is the exponent to which a base value must be raised to produce that number. Sometimes, the logarithm counts repeated multiplication. For example, the base 10 logarithm of 100 is 2, as 10 to the second power is 100 ($10 \times 10 = 100 = 10^2$). The utility of this process is instantly evident in Figure 9.4, where we find the Base 10 Log of 10 to be 1, and the Base 10 Log of 100 to be 2. This offers us the immense compression we need to see the problem in the scales that we have before us.

In our particular case, at $100 million per mile, we do not want to be working nearly a quarter million miles in space, so we will need to begin with a rescaling first. We will change the GDP column to $100 million per foot, compressing it by 5,280, the number of feet in a mile. That still puts us up to an impractical height, though. As we glean from Figure 9.4, the solution is to take the Base 10 Log of that.

As Figure 9.5 demonstrates, we are only 13.4 feet in the air when we do that.

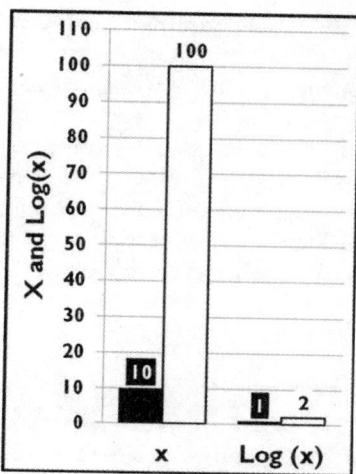

FIGURE 9.4 Log scaling permits us to take large numbers and make them appear smaller. The Base 10 Log of 10 is 1, and the Base 10 Log of 100 is 2. In reverse, we say that 10 raised to the first power (10^1) is 10 or 10 to the second power (10^2 or 10 squared) equals 100.[9, 10]

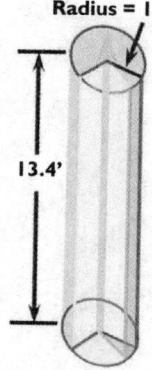

Radius = 1

13.4'

FIGURE 9.5 If we have $100 million of GDP per foot and take that Log, the resulting height is 13.4 feet.[11]

This scaling provides a framework within which we can operate. Note each portion of the economy, the smallest portion for agriculture, the more extensive industry section, and the most prominent element, services, collectively sum up to the total. If we had all the components that comprise each segment, we would have a complete picture of the economy. It would be handy to have a comprehensive view of each market as we rolled it into the total. This means we must think of a way to connect all four-dimensional markets to incorporate the critical features of Figure 9.5, where the parts add up to the sum. For that, we will need to have another everyday object.

COMMON OBJECT 3—ROLODEX

"A Rolodex is a rotating file device used to store business contact information. The name is a portmanteau word of rolling and index."[12] These items were trendy for decades after their invention and before the advent of computers and smartphones (Figure 9.6). They offer a great way to compress

FIGURE 9.6   Rolodex cards store data on a moveable plane—they lose no information as they rotate about their axis.[13]

helpful information into a small, well-organized space. With a few modifications to our purposes, it will show us similar data compression.

With a slight change to the original design, changing the axle direction from horizontal for the floor to vertical, we get the offering shown in Figure 9.7. We have a series of posters mounted up and down relative to the floor, on what is known as a poster rack,[14] upon which we can make some observations and notes.[15]

While there is little remarkable about this physically, this arrangement has some fascinating mathematical appeal, which becomes evident as we characterize its features. Note that as we look at Figure 9.7, each poster has 1) a common vertical axis, 2) a limit on its lower elevation (the height at which each card initially appears over the plane on which it is placed), 3) an upper elevation limit, 4) a lateral or horizontal limit, and 5) information that remains both independent of and stays coherent concerning any position that its angle might take about the central axis. Thus, each card has a dependency common to all others, which is the central axis. Simultaneously, all cards have independence relative to all others as their information stays intact no matter their position as they all cling to the same axis. Still,

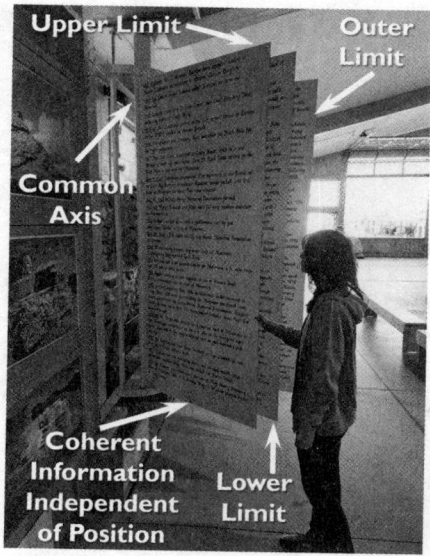

FIGURE 9.7 Information in a Rolodex or this poster rack has a 1) Common Axis, 2) Lower Limit, 3) Upper Limit, 4) Outer Limit, and 5) Coherent Information Independent of Position.

their information does change as they change their radial position. We will find these phenomena to have some advantages for us.

COMMON OBJECT 4—CONCENTRIC CIRCLE

Concentric circles are a collection of circles about the same center point. A rock dropped into a still pond forms waves in concentric circles about its entry point. In the last chapter, Figure 8.3 has a series of concentric circles around the bullseye. One of the reasons that we figuratively migrated some of our analysis to the South Pole was to take advantage of the concentric circles there. Each line of latitude is concentric relative to the axis running through the center of the Earth, the southern end of which is the South Pole. Any circular line with the South Pole at its center is similar to any other drawn. While the increments of 10° of arc in Figure 9.8 represent large distances (the distance between 80° South Latitude and 70° South Latitude

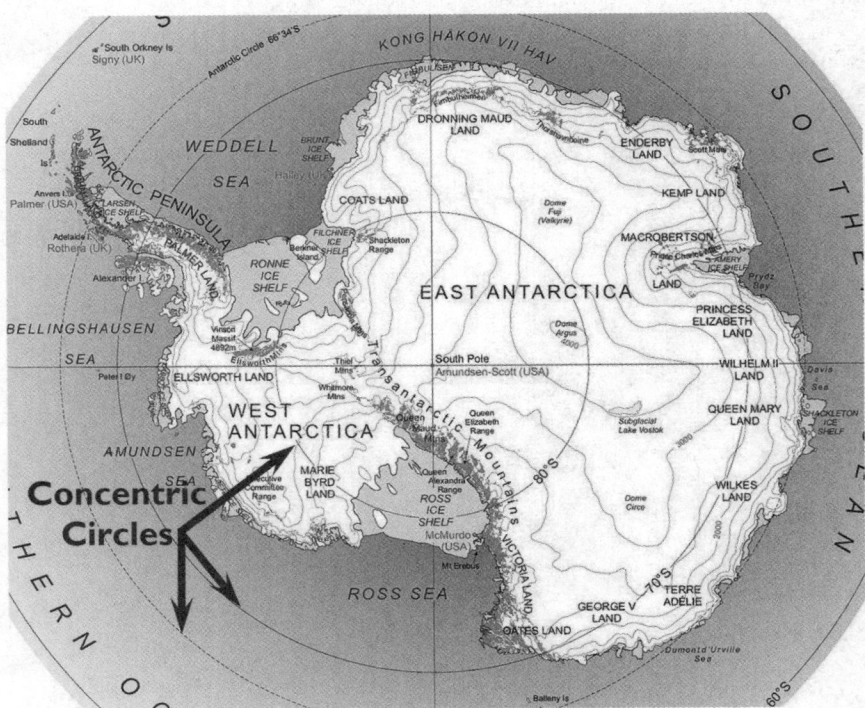

FIGURE 9.8 Upper southern latitudes are a series of concentric circles about the South Pole.[16, 17]

going along a meridian is 693.55 statute miles),[18] we will be entertaining much shorter distances that we will mark in feet.

COMMON OBJECT 5—PARALLELOGRAMS (AS IN EXTENDABLE MIRRORS)

You have likely seen extendable mirrors, even if you did not know their name. Typically, these are wall-mounted units that can extend a mirror away from it using a series of mechanical links, as shown in Figure 9.9.

Many products use this arrangement, including temporary fences, baby gates, and scissor lifts (aerial work platforms). Note that in the case of Figure 9.9, as is the case for all devices of this type, *the link lengths remain unchanged, but the angles between the links change as the mechanism moves*. Note that the links form *parallelograms identical to one another* as they compress or expand and that parallelograms can create squares. The

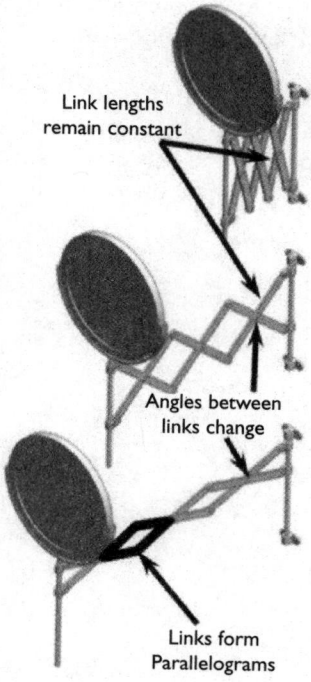

Link lengths
remain constant

Angles between
links change

Links form
Parallelograms

FIGURE 9.9 Extendable mirrors use pantographs to expand their length from a wall.[19, 20]

generic term for such equipment is the *pantograph*, first constructed in 1603 by Christoph Scheiner, who used it to copy and scale drawings.[21] We shall soon discover that despite Jackie DeShannon's pleas to the contrary,[22] the world needs many pantographs now.

STARTING FROM (0,0,0,0. . .0)

To figure out where we are going, we must first remember where we have been. This is seen in Figure 9.10, where we have overlaid our now familiar four-dimensional structure on top of the column depicting world GDP.

Right now, the column has no meaning apart from its radius, height, and cash density, but it soon will. In Figure 9.10, we reiterate that all dimensions are positive and observe that all axes are at right angles to one another, in the tradition of Cartesian systems. Regarding the GDP cylinder in the center of the house, we note that we have only used 180° of arc.

This means we can add another market to the analysis as a duplex arrangement, as Figure 9.11 shows. After the original four dimensions with which we began, we now have the ground beef market, with its "Leanness" Value attribute as the fifth dimension.

Note that this new fifth dimension for Market 2 lies flat against the fourth dimension in Market 1, which is the quantity for the helicopter market. In addition, the market for ground beef also has "package size" as a Valued Feature, which makes up the sixth dimension, and its own quantity

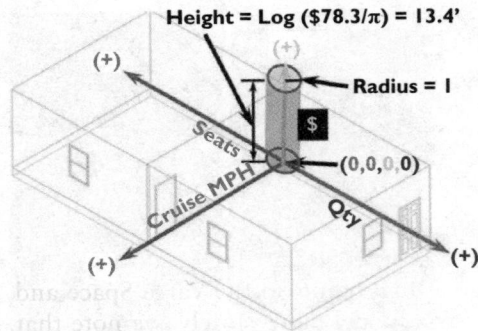

FIGURE 9.10 All markets, including this one for helicopters, have four axes, 1) Valued Feature 1, 2) Valued Feature 2, 3) $, and 4) Quantity.[23]

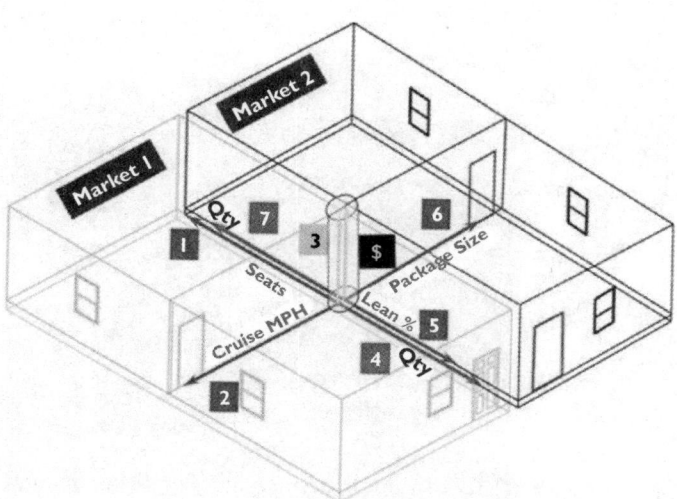

FIGURE 9.11 If we add another market, this one for ground beef, it, too, has four axes, three of which are unique, while it shares a common price axis with the market for helicopters.[24]

term as pounds of ground beef sold as the seventh dimension. Crucially, we do not have an additional axis for the price of ground beef because we already have this axis from our work with helicopters, and the two markets share the central currency axis. If we were to stick to the Cartesian custom of having all axes at right angles to each other, we would be done and unable to press more dimensions into action. What if we were to break with custom?

Recall what we discovered when we studied the vertical Rolodex and its bigger cousin, the poster display rack. We found that the information on each card or poster remained intact regardless of its position on any other card or poster. With that in mind, let's examine Figure 9.12, in which we display three models of the General Aviation market, the Cessna Caravan 1 208B, the Beechcraft Baron 58, and the Cirrus SR22.

Each plane has its standard set of dual points in the Value Space and Demand Plane. When we scrutinize the model more closely, we note that the Demand Plane points have a specific horizontal distance from the common axis, which are their quantities, and a definite height from the base, which are their prices. The Demand Plane's Angle concerning Value Space is immaterial—it adds no useful information, much like changing the

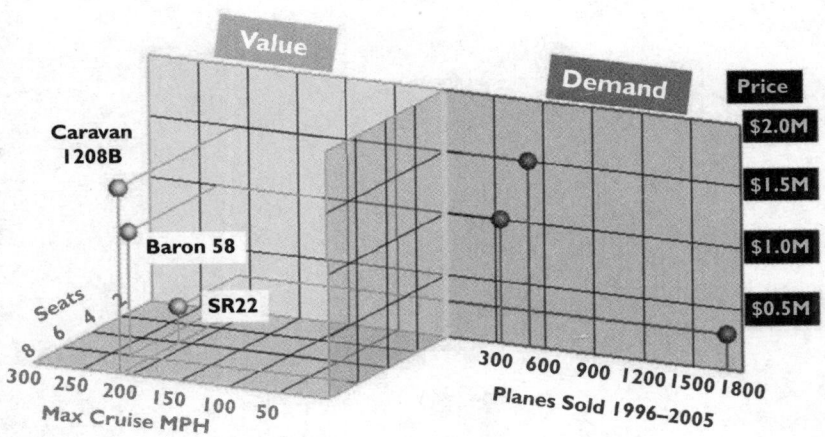

FIGURE 9.12 Demand Plane data relates to Value Space only through their common currency axis. Thus, we can rotate the Demand Plane from its default position.[25]

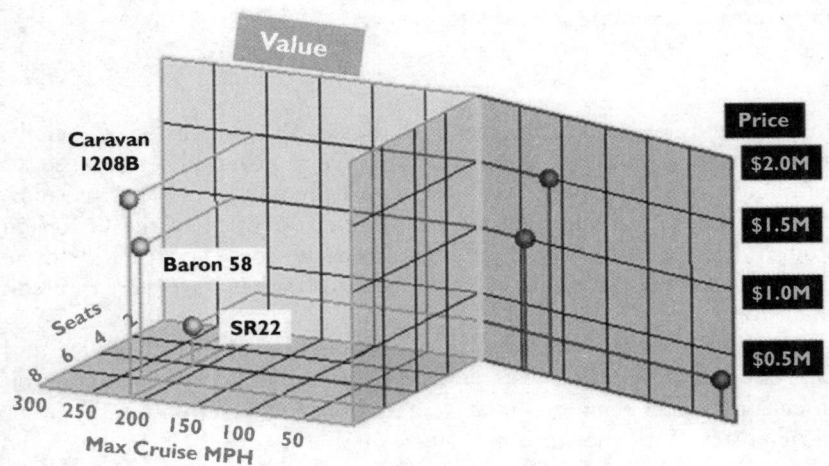

FIGURE 9.13 This Demand Plane rotation about the axis loses no data.[26]

position of any vertical Rolodex cards or posters on a rack does not add information.

Since there is no reason to keep the Demand Plane in its current orientation in Figure 9.12, we can rotate it about the currency axis if we like, as we do in Figures 9.13, 9.14, and finally, in 9.15, where the Demand Plane lies

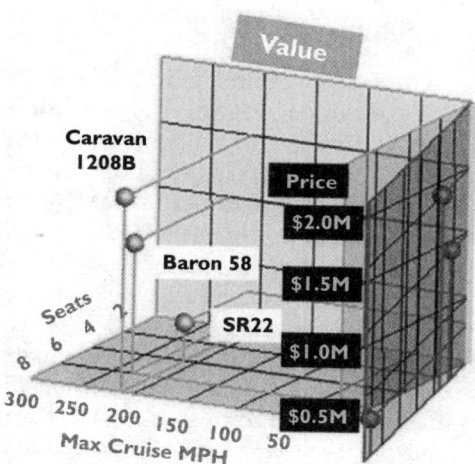

FIGURE 9.14 Extending the rotation still keeps the Demand data intact.[27]

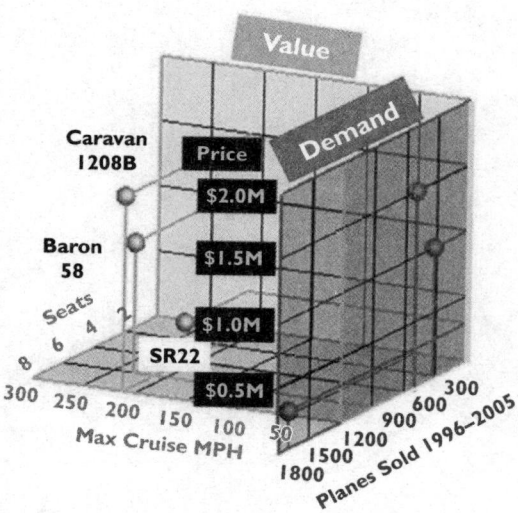

FIGURE 9.15 We still have coherent data with the Demand Plane flat against the Value Space.[28]

flat against its Value Space. Instead of this market taking up 180° of arc, it only requires 90°.

Since this maneuver worked for one market, we presume it will work for two, and we find out that it does in Figure 9.16. Here, we have compressed the two markets from Figure 9.11, taking their space requirements from 360° to 180°.

This, in turn, allows us to add two more markets in Figure 9.17, which also take up only 90° of arc. In Market 3, its Valued Feature 1 is dimension 8, its Valued Feature 2 is dimension 9, and its quantity is dimension 10, while it shares the common currency axis, dimension 3, with all other markets. Market 4 repeats the process while adding dimensions, as its Valued Feature 1 is dimension 11, its Valued Feature 2 is dimension 13, and its quantity is dimension 13, as it, too, shares the common currency axis.

There seems to be a pattern arising here, and we can discover it if we characterize it, as we do in Figure 9.18.

In the first row of data, we see our normal condition with a single market. As we add a second market, we add two more dimensions of value and another for quantity, but keep the same one we had for a single market for the currency dimension. In adding a third market, we repeat the procedure, adding two dimensions for value and one for quantity but not adding any for currency as we continue using that as a common axis. As we go to a fourth market, we repeat the pattern. If we call the number of markets n, we see the generalized terms in the last row.

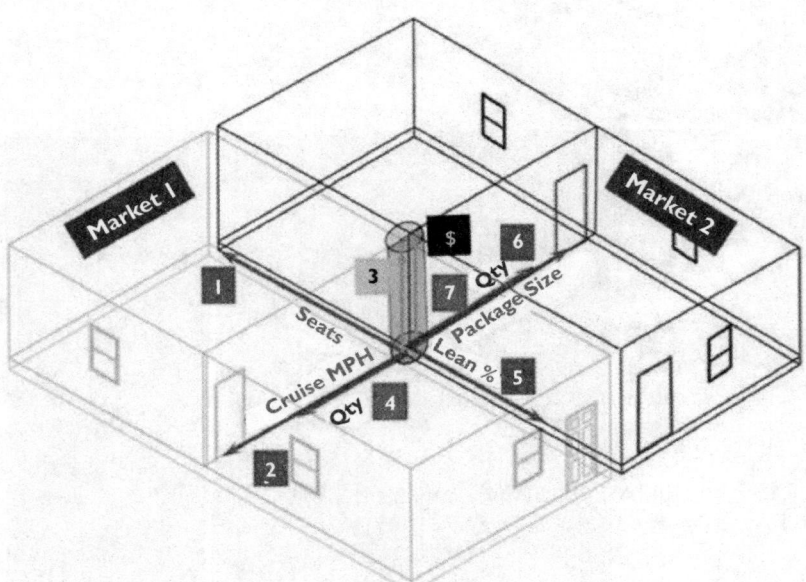

FIGURE 9.16 If we swing the Demand Planes against their Value Spaces, we can compress the two markets in Figure 9.11 into 180° of arc.[29]

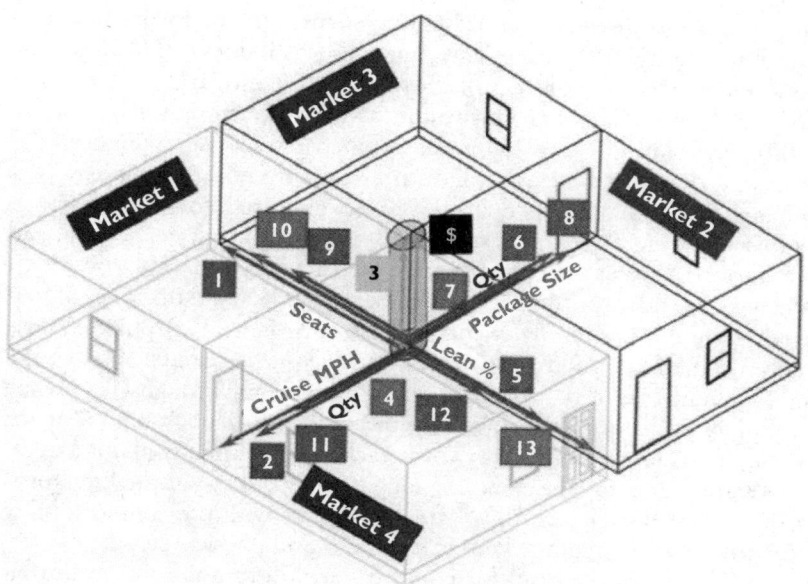

FIGURE 9.17   With 180° of arc remaining, we can add two more markets.[30]

| | Dimensions Required For | | | |
Markets	Value	Quantity	Currency	Total
1	2	1	1	4
2	4	2	1	7
3	6	3	1	10
4	8	4	1	13
n	2n	n	1	3n+1

FIGURE 9.18   There is a pattern for the number of markets considered and the dimensions required to display them.[31]

We might think we must stop here, as we have again used up all 360° of arc. However, then we remember that 1) all coordinate systems do not need to have right-angle geometries, and 2) that the mechanism behind the extendable mirror has some unique features that we could seek to employ to our advantage.

One of our most essential coordinate systems, the one for latitude and longitude, may seem like a grid system, appealing as it does to positions east and west and north and south. Still, the smallest investigations reveal that it is not beholden to Cartesian constraints as we move from north to south along the Earth, latitude and longitude geometries change, as Figure 9.19 shows us that the right angles that Descartes uses are not in effect here.

While it is true that this is not a flat object and, therefore, not designed to be subject to René Descartes's schemes, it points out that we do not need to have Cartesian systems to know where we are relative to other objects.

When we consider coordinates on a globe, we understand that lines of longitude represent a series of *angles* emanating from a pair of set points. Those set points are the North and South Poles, and the lines are indexed from the starting longitude line of 0°, which, by convention, runs through Greenwich, United Kingdom. At one foot from either pole, two lines of longitude 15° apart, a common interval for them, are very near each other, with only about a quarter inch separating them. The same 15° longitude separation at the Equator is over 1,000 miles. In this regard, we are all familiar with the compressibility and expansiveness of longitude lines in a genuine and physical sense.

When faced with the need for compression in our analysis, given that we have already "swung the Demand Plane flat against its Value Space" to gain some working room, what can we do with it to gain even more territory while keeping our information intact?

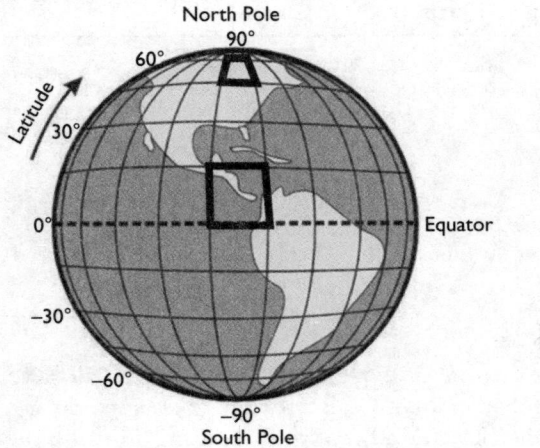

FIGURE 9.19 The geometries of latitude and longitude change based on position.[32, 33]

Taking advantage of the changeable geometries for extendable mirrors and scissor lifts that we examined in Figure 9.9, we gather a series of the whole number ordered pairs to form a pantograph of right angles in Figures 9.20 through 9.24, as shown in the 10 points labeled there. Observe that these pairs are part of a more extensive system that we draw using the standard 90° angle between the axes, a Cartesian system foundation. Additionally, this view contains a series of half-semicircles extending from their whole-number values on the vertical axis to identical settings on the horizontal axis. These quadrant lines reinforce the idea that the distance from the origin (here, [0,0]) to any point away from it may be expressed as a radius, with a fixed distance from the origin and an angle relative to a reference line, as, say, the horizontal axis.

If we were to change the Angle between the axes, as in Figure 9.20, we find that the geometries have changed as well, in the same fashion as they did in Figure 9.9.

While we could focus on any point in Figure 9.21, let's draw attention to the ordered pair (1,1). Its position has changed—it is a little right from where it had been in Figure 9.20 and a little lower. However, its distance from the vertical axis has not changed significantly, as the difference between (0,1) and (1, 1) remains one unit of horizontal distance, as both visual and mathematical checks prove.

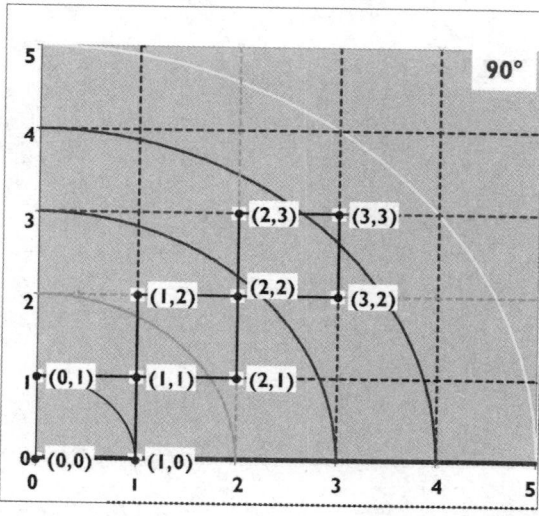

FIGURE 9.20 Here are 10 ordered pairs (as [0,0], [1,1], [1,2], etc.) in a standard Cartesian coordinate system.[34]

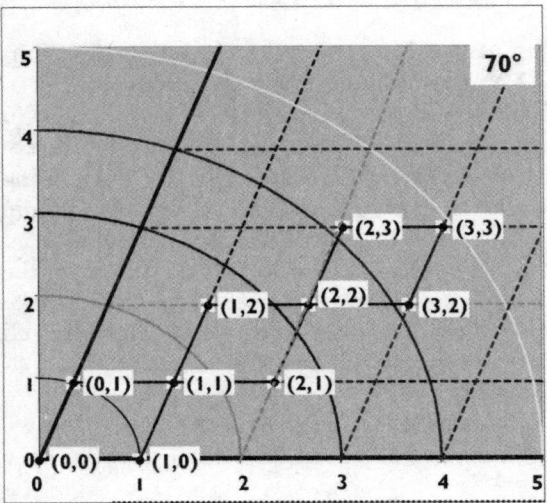

FIGURE 9.21   Changing the Angle of the axes retains the ordered pair information.[35]

In this same fashion, we can take the axes down 20° increments from 90° to 10° as we move from Figure 9.20 to 9.24. Note that while the data compresses, it is not lost. If we want to see it in its original condition, we must reset the Angle between the axes to 90°. We have many pantographs

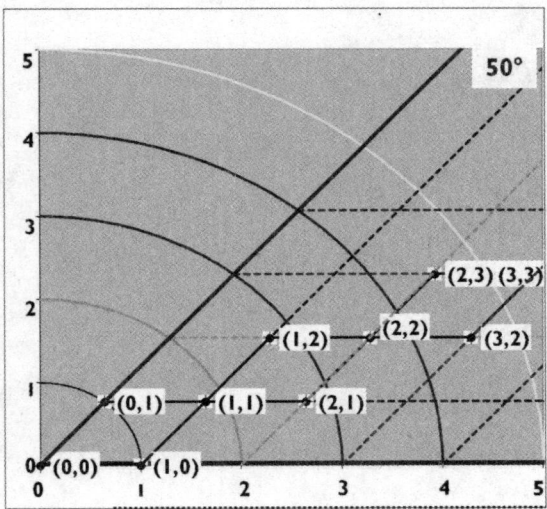

FIGURE 9.22   50° Angle.[36]

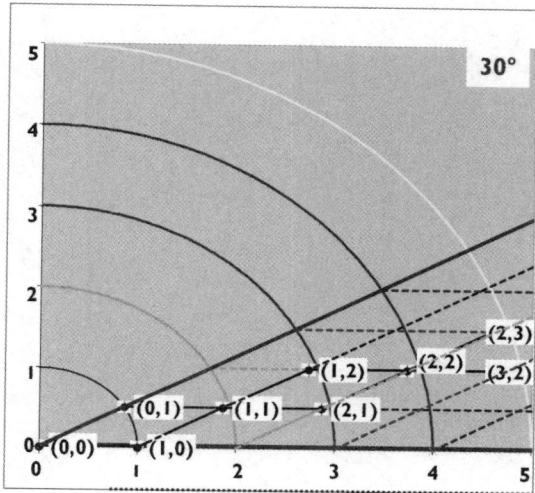

FIGURE 9.23   30° Angle.[37]

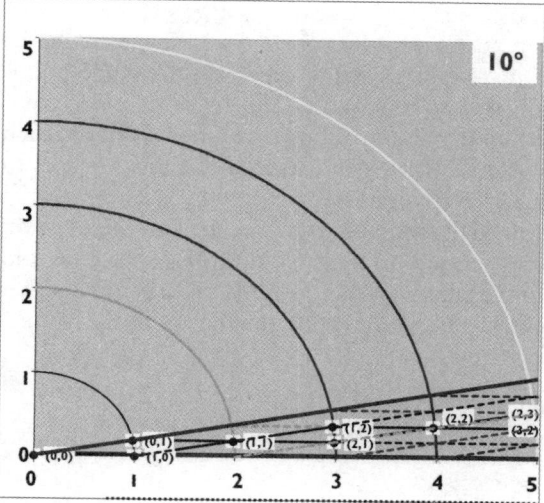

FIGURE 9.24   10° Angle.[38]

hard at work in Figures 9.20 through 9.24. We can verify the angular distance along the horizontal axis with a few right-angle triangles.[39]

Now, let us go back to pie for a few moments. As we saw in Figure 9.1, someone had sensibly cut the pie from its center to its edge and had removed

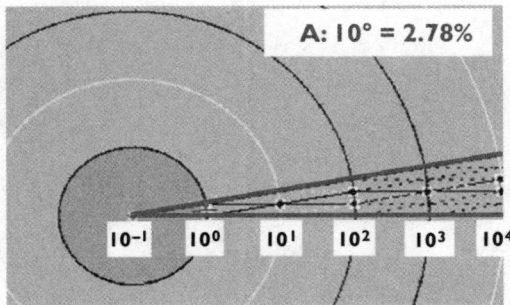

FIGURE 9.25 If we cut our GDP pie column (with a radius of 1) into sections, each representing its portion of world GDP, we could extend the pie cut lines to and through concentric circles surrounding it.[40]

a piece. That's how we all cut pie—we stop when we get to its edge. What if we continued the cut past the border?

Let's begin with a pie of radius 1, as shown as the shaded area in Figure 9.25. As we make two cuts from the center to the edge, with the Angle set to 10°, we will designate that wedge to represent the corresponding market's contribution of 2.78% to the total GDP.

If we cut our GDP pie column (with a radius of 1) into sections, each representing its portion of world GDP, we could extend the pie cut lines to and through concentric circles surrounding it.

If that market's portion of GDP is more extensive, we can make room for it by adjusting the Angle of the pie piece as we do in Figures 9.26 and 9.27. At the same time, we extend the lines that define the size of the market *past* the edge of the inner circle at 1 unit to represent the collapsed Valued

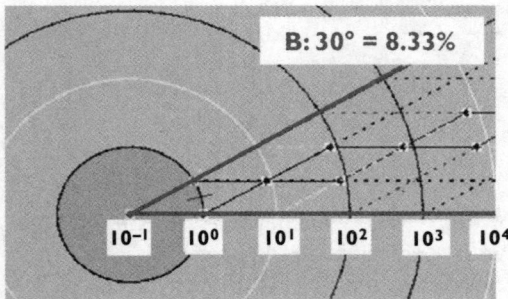

FIGURE 9.26 Changing the Angle changes the market's cut of GDP.[41]

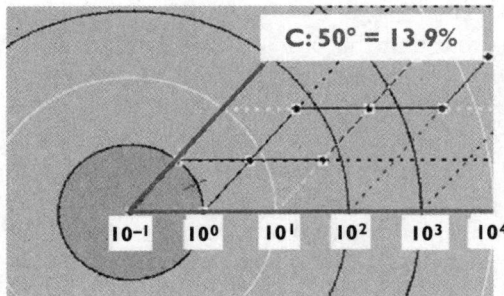

FIGURE 9.27 The Angle is changeable.[42]

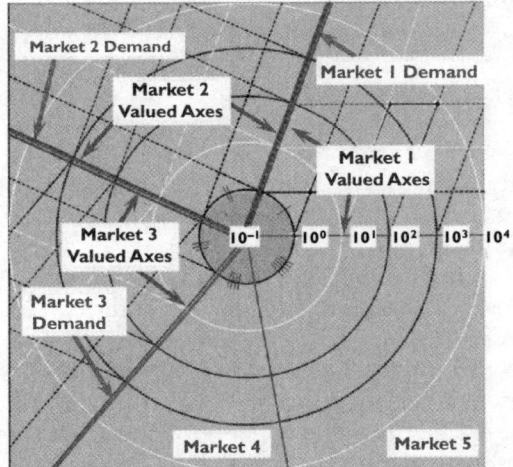

FIGURE 9.28 If we cut our GDP pie column into 5 pieces, one for each of the five markets making up a fictitious GDP total, from the top, it would look like this. Each market would have two Valued Feature Axes defining it and an adjacent Demand Plane.[43, 44]

Feature Axes, as we did in Figure 9.17. We change the Angle to describe this market's share of GDP.

What can we say about other markets' share of GDP? In Figure 9.28, we add four more markets, for a total of five that make up a fictitious GDP. Each market's portion of GDP relates to its portion of the center-shaded GDP pie. Recall that in Figures 9.12 through 9.15, we swung the Demand Plane around until it lay flat against its corresponding Value Space. Now note that for Market 1, the lines extending past 10^0 or 1 represent the Valued Feature lines for that market and that the Market 1 Demand Plane, as viewed from above, once again lies flat against its associated Value Space.

Immediately adjacent to the Market 1 Demand Plane line, we find one of the two Valued Feature Axes for Market 2. After we travel to the required number of degrees of arc within Market 2, we see the other Valued Feature Axis and, immediately adjacent to it, the Market 2 Demand Plane line. The lines separating each section continue in this fashion to accommodate all the markets. Figure 9.28 could represent the GDP of a small country with only five products of note, or it could stand for a company. Eventually, for world GDP, we will need hundreds, if not thousands, of markets. We also need a way to capture all these markets in a single view.

We need a way to account for the position in not only Market 1, but also in all other markets that follow it. Not only that, but we have also seemingly left the Cartesian coordinate system behind, and we should account for our position in our new system, which we must name, as well as our old Cartesian system. We call our new system the *Polar Parallel Coordinate System* because all axes emanate from the common axis, which we call a pole, and several axes will necessarily be immediately adjacent to one another (i.e., there is no space between them) and parallel to one another. With Figure 9.29, we discover what it looks like.

With the floor-to-ceiling "Zero Angle" plane as a starting point, we go counterclockwise to the full-height planes that separate the industry, services, and agriculture sectors in that order. Note that the concentric horizontal values begin at 10^4 and go in powers of 10 to 10^{12}, our arbitrary outer limit. Note the dark inner circle with a radius of 1 (10^0), which is our GDP pie column. The plane that reaches from the center horizontally out to 1 and up from 10^{-2} (our bottom) to $10^{13.4}$ forms a wedge with the adjacent Value plane. This wedge is the portion of GDP (0.31%) dedicated to commercial aircraft sales. We mark this market's demand for the light-shaded plane, with the bottom representing the lowest-priced vehicle in the market ($129,000 or $10^{5.11}$), while the upper limit is for the most expensive vehicle ($414 million, or $10^{8.62}$).

In contrast, the lateral extent of this plane describes yearly sales (5063, or $10^{3.7}$). We keep Value Planes with the same upper and lower limits, while the lateral extents of Value Planes 1 & 2 indicate the maximum number of seats (525 or $10^{2.72}$) and miles per hour (617 or $10^{2.79}$), respectively. The Angle between the aircraft value planes is 1.11° or 0.31% of the market. Stated another way, this market is a little more than 1/300th of GDP.

In Figure 9.29, we better understand how this system works. First, note that we find our familiar GDP core at the center of the diagram. Given

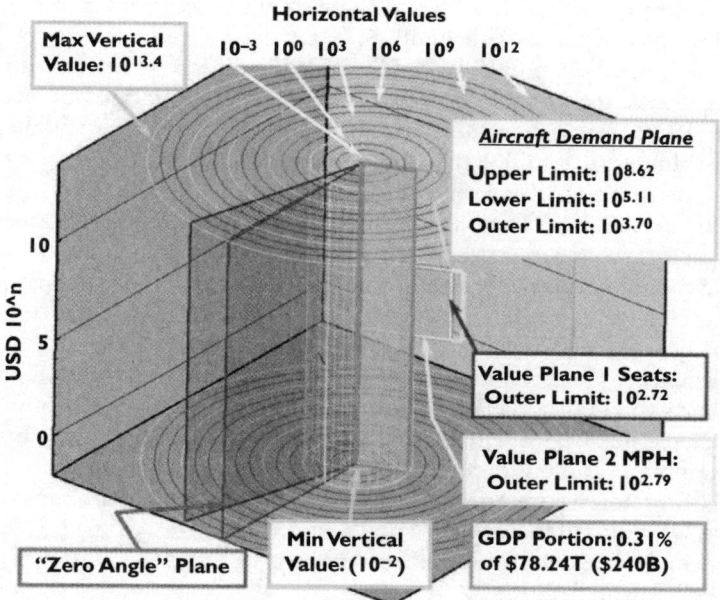

Horizontal Values

Max Vertical Value: $10^{13.4}$

10^{-3} 10^{0} 10^{3} 10^{6} 10^{9} 10^{12}

Aircraft Demand Plane
Upper Limit: $10^{8.62}$
Lower Limit: $10^{5.11}$
Outer Limit: $10^{3.70}$

USD $10^{\wedge}n$

10

5

0

Value Plane I Seats:
Outer Limit: $10^{2.72}$

Value Plane 2 MPH:
Outer Limit: $10^{2.79}$

"Zero Angle" Plane

Min Vertical Value: (10^{-2})

GDP Portion: 0.31% of $78.24T ($240B)

FIGURE 9.29 This is the framework for an N-dimensional system. Here, we've put one market (commercial aircraft) and four dimensions (Maximum Seats, Maximum Miles Per Hour, Price, Quantity Sold in a Year).[45–53]

the logarithmic scaling, we must start at a non-zero level, so we begin at one penny (10^{-2}), which we designate as the minimum vertical value. In contrast, our maximum vertical value remains $10^{13.4}$ ($24.9 trillion), as our diameter is still 1 (10^{0}), which we capture with the upright green cylinder. We have the minimum horizontal value set to 10^{4} (0.0001) to see the center pie easily. In Figure 9.2, the CIA divided world GDP into three broad portions, agriculture, services, and industry. Beginning from the starting "Zero Angle Plane," if we go clockwise 6.6% of the radius or 23.8°, we find another floor-to-ceiling plane, and wedge between the "Zero Angle Plane" and this plane, as limited by the dark central GDP core, defines the size of the agriculture market contribution to GDP. Another 62.4% of arc or 224.6° in the clockwise direction brings us to the base full-height plane, and the wedge between these final full-size planes inside the GDP core brings us to the service component of the economy. The remaining bit, 31% or 111.6° of arc, between the penultimate and the "Zero Angle Plane" dedicates itself to industry.

Our concentric circles come in handy here as we begin with a single vertical line serving as our axis, beginning at 10^{-2} ($0.01) and ending at $10^{13.4}$ ($29.4 trillion, GDP divided by π). We draw the innermost circle with a radius of 10^{-3} and keep increasing the circle diameter by factors of ten until we get to 10^0 or 1, which is our unit circle. The region contained by the green vertical cylinder is our GDP pie, and we have already accommodated the three sections that the CIA derived and extended the lines that cut the pie, as we did in Figure 9.18. To accept additional information, we continue in concentric circles to an arbitrary value of 1012 (1 trillion).

Suppose we want to characterize the contribution to GDP that the production of new civil aircraft offers. If we place it in Figure 9.29, we must first recognize that new aircraft fall into the industry segment. Then we need to determine this market's size; some research shows it was about $240 billion in 2015. We want to know something about demand as well. We find about 5,063 units delivered in 2015, with the lowest-priced model (the Champ by American Champion) coming in at $129,900 and the most expensive one selling for $414.4 million (the Airbus A380). We will find value parameters crucial, too, so we will find the models with the most seats (the Airbus A380, with 525 seats in a three-class arrangement) and the fastest (the Citation X, at 617 miles per hour).

Since we want the value and demand planes for this market to both mean something and stand out, we need a way of making each market unique. We know we can bind a rectangular plane on four sides. For our Demand Plane, we see that it is horizontally bounded inside by the axis, which has a lateral value of zero (in this picture, it is 10^{-4}, which we will treat as 0 for convenience). Let us suppose then that the vertical outer boundary of the Demand Plane is its yearly total, which is 5063, or $10^{3.7}$. Using this convention, we could suppose that the lower horizontal limit of the Demand Plane is the least expensive model, the American Champion Champ, at $129,000, or $10^{5.11}$. In contrast, the upper limit parallel to it is $414.4 million, or $10^{8.62}$, for the Airbus A380.

Continuing in this fashion, we shall suppose that each Value Plan has the same upper and lower limits as the Demand Plane. For the Valued Feature speed, the lateral limit is 617 miles per hour, or $10^{2.79}$, while that for maximum passengers is 525, or $10^{2.72}$. With the Demand Plane lying flat against one of the planes for the Value Features, the Angle between the Valued Features, at 1.1° or 0.031%, represents this market's share of GDP, just as it did in Figure 9.19. The difference here is that the Angle is more diminutive in representing the real world. We need more markets to get a complete view of the world economy.

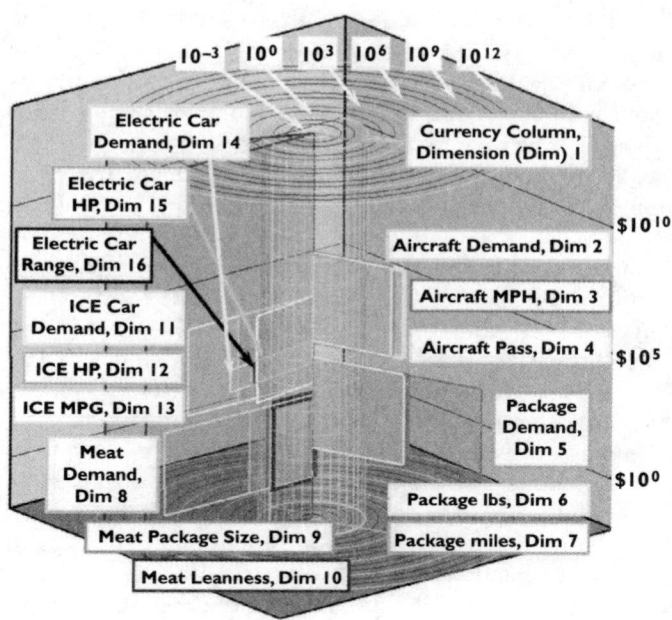

FIGURE 9.30 Using some of the recent techniques we learned, we swing the Demand Planes onto compressed Value Spaces for five markets and employ 16 mathematical dimensions. This view consists of two Valued Feature axes for each market, one Quantity axis for each market, and a single currency axis common to all markets. In theory, there is no limit to the number of markets we characterize in this fashion. Note that cars with Internal Combustion Engines (ICE) form the largest market in this study, with 2.35% of world GDP, over 347 times that of electric cars.[54–74]

Figure 9.30 provides us with that kind of view.

We begin with the market we analyzed in Figure 9.29 for civil aircraft and discover that it is still in the same position. Much space remains, so we add the Package Delivery market on the other side of the plane that separates industry from services as delivering packages belongs to the latter. The sector delivered roughly 23.5 billion packages in 2014, with prices demonstrated to be as low as $7.00 and as high as $30,000, and these points form the outer, lower, and upper bounds of the Demand Plane for this market, with the core axis, limiting the inner limit. The value planes for this market abide by the lower and upper limits, while we suppose that the Package Pounds (package weights) Value Plane weight limit is 6,000 pounds and the Package Miles Value Plane limit is 12,000 miles. This market uses the common currency axis and adds three dimensions, as shown in Figures 9.21 and 9.22.

The U.S. meat market, our third market, distributed approximately 49.4 billion packages, with the cheapest at roughly $0.52 and the most expensive at $968.72. This market's value plane also abides by these upper and lower price limits. In contrast, the Package Size Value Plane extends to 100 pounds, and leanness reaches 97%. As with the package delivery market, the market for meat in the United States adds three dimensions.

The internal combustion engines (ICE) car market is extensive, with about 89.7 million units sold in 2014. The Tata Gen X Nano appears to be the cheapest in the market, at $2,919 for the base model, while the most expensive model goes to the Maybach Exelero for $8 million. If you need it, along the Horsepower Value Plane, you can get an SSC Ultimate Aero with 1,500 horsepower, or if you would prefer gas mileage, the best model is the hybrid BMW i3, which, with 137 miles per gallon, defines the lateral extent of the Miles Per Gallon Value Plane. This market adds three more dimensions to the mix combined with the others.

Last, in the case at hand, we come to the market for electric cars, which sold approximately 119,000 units in 2013. The Chevrolet Spark was the least expensive at $18,495, while you could spend as much as $141,695 for a BMW i8. The Tesla P85D held the title for the car with the most horsepower, 691, and the most extended range, at 270 miles, thereby setting the horizontal limits for the Horsepower and Range Valued Feature axes.

We summarize our dimensions in Figure 9.31, showing that we studied five markets with one common axis, two Value axes for each market, and one Demand axis for each market for 16.

Collectively, these markets add up to about 3.1% of the total GDP, so we have more work to get a clearer picture of the world economy. We should understand now, however, that the split between what had been called microeconomics and macroeconomics can be seen anew with but a few added dimensions that show how the pieces add up to the total.

Market(s)	Dimension Name	Units	Dimension Type Common	Value	Demand	Markets	Number of Dimensions
All	Currency	Dollars	X				1
Civil Aircraft	Aircraft Demand	Units per year			X	1	2
	Maximum Speed	Miles per hour		X			3
	Passengers	Seats		X			4
Package Delivery	Package Delivery Demand	Parcels per year			X	2	5
	Package Size	Pounds/package		X			6
	Distance to Destination	Miles to delivery		X			7
United States Red Meat	Meat Demand	Pounds/year			X	3	8
	Package Size	Pounds/package		X			9
	Leanness	Percentage		X			10
Internal Combustion Engine Car	ICE Car Demand	Units per year			X	4	11
	HP	Horsepower		X			12
	MPG	Miles per gallon		X			13
Electric Car	Electric Car Demand	Units per year			X	5	14
	HP	Horsepower		X			15
	Range	Miles		X			16
All	Dimension Count		1	10	5		16

FIGURE 9.31 We can see how the market pattern works with this figure.[75]

SUMMARY

Adding new mathematical dimensions requires only a few everyday items or concepts: 1) pie, 2) logarithmic scaling, 3) Rolodexes, 4) concentric circles, and 5) parallelograms as in extendable mirrors. Pies have slices, which we can relate to world GDP. The log scaling we use to measure decibels and earthquakes allows us to compress our data into accessible pieces. Rolodexes provide evidence that their cards carry information with a certain height or lateral distance but are unrelated to other planes attached to the same axis, meaning they can lay flat on other surfaces without losing information. Concentric rings, like those for latitude, allow us to account for the distance from a common central core. Extendable mirrors have links that maintain their lengths but can change their angles to one another, forming a series of parallelograms known as pantographs.

Using these concepts, we can "swing the Demand Plane" for any given market flat against its corresponding Value Space and retain all of the information the Demand Plane provides. We can also compress Value Space and account for a position within it using a Polar Parallel Coordinate System. With each market compressed such that its Demand Plane lies against its Value Space and that the Angle between the Value Planes matches that market's contribution to world GDP, we can simultaneously account for any number of markets.

CHAPTER 10

An Amazon Mining Expedition

"Exploring the unknown requires tolerating uncertainty."

Brian Greene

By now, we understand that to make sense of a part of the financial world, we need to gather as much helpful information about that market as possible. We will always want to know what customers value, so we must find information about useful features for any product or service realm we wish to examine. As always, markets will limit their purchases, so we need data about quantities sold. Occasionally, there are constraints that some markets face, and if they exist, we need to be aware of them. In essence, we know what we need. Now, where do we find it?

While a wide variety of data services describe many markets for one-time or annual fees, we may often find ourselves interested in a particular part of the economy but have yet to receive data instantly retrievable about it. If we have no available market data to buy, we could throw our hands up and come up empty or get to work. Since we are interested in the knowledge that such work will bring us, we decide to dig in and get the information and insight we need. In those cases, we must mine, organize, and analyze our information. This is data mining.

As of this writing, in the early 21st century, we have a large retailer, Amazon,[1,2] that sells all manner of products via their website and then ships to its customers. While Amazon does not put up large data sets in the formats we know we have to create, it offers a fantastic amount of product detail if only we dig hard enough.

We could consider hundreds, if not thousands, of markets, all available on Amazon, but to resolve a single set of answers, we must settle on a single market. For our expedition, we will study the market for automobile manuals, and at Amazon, we will find them under the heading of books.

Unfortunately, the company does not simply list the copies sold for any of its books. Instead, it offers what it calls Amazon Best Sellers Rank, which characterizes the book's popularity, as shown in Table 10.1.

TABLE 10.1   Amazon Best Sellers Rank.[3, 4]

Rank	Copies Sold/day
1	3,000
10	650
100	100
1,000	13
10,000	2.2 (11 copies every 5 days)
100,000	0.2 (1 copy every 5 days)
1,000,000	0.006 (3 copies every 500 days)
2,000,000	0.0001 (1 copy every 1,000 days)

High ranks have more extensive sales and vice versa. Specifically, Amazon sales ranks and quantities sold have a mathematical relationship that a few people have attempted to characterize. We will use one of those relationships to gain sales data.[5]

Having derived the sales quantities, we need to consider what people deem valuable when they buy books, and in this case, specific kinds of volumes, automobile manuals. Since readers of auto manuals are trying to gather information from them, we might assume that the longer the book, the more data it would contain. Since mechanics will likely use this particular type of book in challenging conditions, such as a working garage, its durability will likely be crucial. Unlike a paperback, whose smallness may be an attractive feature, as that characteristic lends itself to portability, larger page sizes and print sizes will probably appeal to auto-manual customers. Finally, while it is clear that demand will increase for the entire market as prices fall, we may consider that proposition for each book for sale. We have witnessed that markets with only a few entrants sometimes demonstrate Product Demand Curves. We will always be uncertain of that potential relationship going into our data mining, but we should at least entertain it. In practice, we will usually have more variables as possible contributors to the analysis than we will use. It is better to have too many and only use some than to come to the end of the study without all the facts.

When we consider these factors and go off to the Amazon site, we derive Table 10.2, a portion of the more extensive database for automobile repair manuals. Note in this small set that we sell different prices and quantities. This bodes well for our upcoming demand analysis. There is also a sufficiently wide range of pages in each manual, while the page sizes, at least here, seem tightly grouped, except for the one Volvo manual listed. If we think about it, this list is probably not exhaustive—we do not address paper

TABLE 10.2   Here is a subset of 15 observations in our database of 50 automobile manuals.[6, 7]

Title (15 Samples from a Database with 51 Titles)	Hard Back Yes /no	Pages	Page Sqr In	Copies per Year	Price
VW Beetle & Karmann Ghia 1954 through 1979 All Models	No	240	88.0	248	$ 14.40
Chilton's Mini Cooper Mk 1 & Mk II 2002-11 Repair Manual	No	448	88.0	20	$ 19.88
Toyota Camry: 2007 Through 2011 (Chilton's Total Car Care Repair Manuals)	No	384	88.0	38	$ 17.95
Volvo, 1970-89 (Chilton's Repair Manual (Model Specific))	No	502	65.0	20	$ 6.26
Nissan Maxima 1985 thru 1992 (Haynes Repair Manuals)	No	303	86.3	17	$ 2.16
Saab 900 (October 1993-98) Service and Repair Manual	Yes	300	91.6	22	$ 96.69
Audi A4 (B6, B7) Service Manual: 2002-2008	Yes	1430	91.3	81	$ 95.95
Volvo S40 & V40 1996 to 1999 (N to T Reg)	Yes	350	91.6	20	$ 60.68
VW Polo Hatchback (1994-99) Service and Repair Manual	Yes	320	90.5	6	$ 24.50
Citroen Xantia (1993-98) Service and Repair Manual	Yes	300	92.4	3	$ 33.00
Toyota Prius Repair and Maintenance Manual: 2004-2008	Yes	648	95.7	53	$ 42.13
Triumph Herald Owner's Workshop Manual	Yes	203	88.0	7	$114.03
Mercedes-Benz 190, 190E and 190D (83-93) Service and Repair Manual	Yes	300	93.5	35	$ 25.98
Seat Ibiza and Cordoba (1993-99) Service and Repair Manual	Yes	300	93.5	4	$ 24.78
Renault 25 Service Repair Manual	Yes	344	86.1	2	$120.94

quality, whether the manuals were in color, or if the books can be made to lie flat on any page within them. We may need to address those features to get a complete market picture. In all likelihood, however, we probably have enough to find some relationships in the data, which is our charge. We will start with demand.

When we select the last two columns of Table 10.2, quantity and price, we have the data that populates the Demand Plane, as Figure 10.1 shows. We can already spot some trends in it, but we offer some characterization of the data in Figure 10.2, where we take the total sales quantity in each bin and then work out the average price, which appears as a series of dark triangles. When we run a line of best fit through these triangles, we describe Aggregate

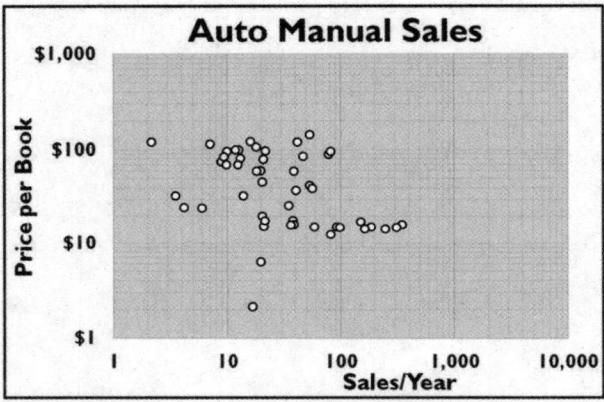

FIGURE 10.1 Quantities and prices for auto manuals on Amazon.[8]

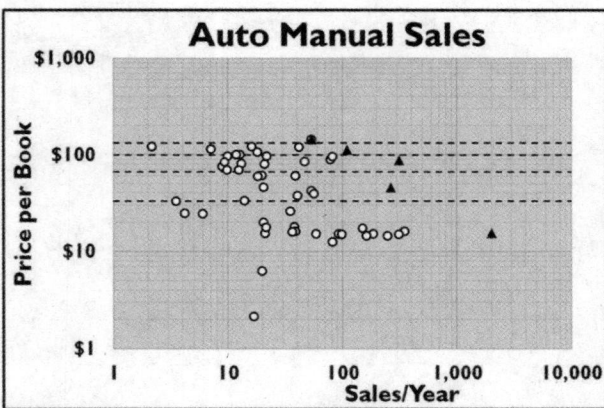

FIGURE 10.2 Create five bins with four lines and find the total quantity and average price in each.[9]

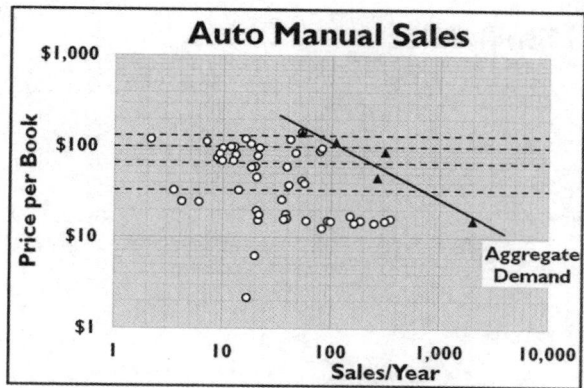

FIGURE 10.3   Find Aggregate Market Demand.[10]

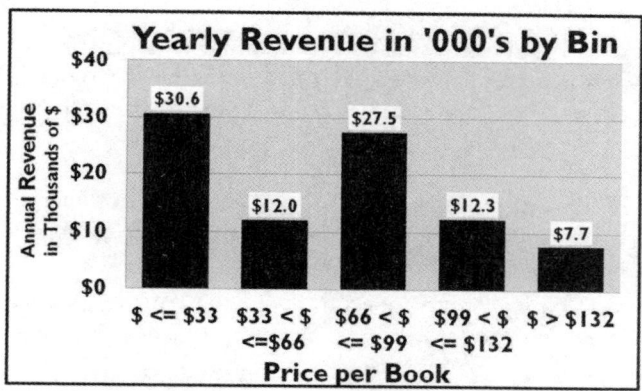

FIGURE 10.4   More money is at the bottom of the automobile manual market than at the top.[11]

Demand in Figure 10.3 with a slope slightly below –1.0, indicating that there is a little more money at the bottom of this market than at its top.

We can verify how the market spreads its money in Figure 10.4.

Figure 10.4 confirms our finding in Figure 10.3, though the money differences between the bins are less significant than others.

As we view Figure 10.5, we find a series of plus signs marking the outermost reaches of the database. We can draw a statistically significant yellow line as the Demand Frontier when we analyze them.

We will also want to understand how the market supports these automobile manual prices, which calls for value analysis, which we will do offline and bring the results into our present discussion.[12]

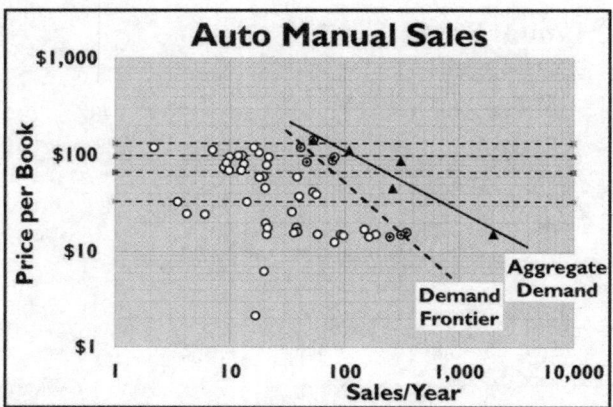

FIGURE 10.5   Demand Frontier.[13]

When we do, we find that the value of any manual is a function of the number of pages, the square inches on each page, whether it comes in paperback or hardback, and how many copies sell in a year. Specifically, we discover that:

> *For Page Count:* With a page range of 203 to 2,132, the data indicates that doubling the page count (from, for instance, 500 to 1,000) increases value by 52.3%.

> *For Square Inches:* For a page range of 65 to 99.2 square inches, adding 30% more area per page (from 70 to 91 square inches) increases value by 242%.

> *For Paperback or Hardback:* Moving from paperback to hardback increases value by 49.2%.

> *For Copies (Sales) per Year:* Doubling sales (from 100 to 200 as a potential case) decreases the value/unit sold by 10.6%.

Consider, if we are about to make a new automobile manual, the implications of parameters so seemingly straightforward as the page count and page size. Someone in a company might propose a paperback manual with 500 pages at 65 square inches per page. That works out to 32,500 square inches of page space, which we will call Case 1.[14] Suppose we made the manual with sheets 99.2 square inches each. If we need 32,500 square inches of page space, we would need a book of 328 pages, known as Case 2.[15] We might further assume, to make the problem more accessible, that the cost of producing a book of 32,500 square inches is the same regardless of page size, just as long as it is paperback. Since our equation for value considers the number of copies sold per year, we will premise that we will sell 100 copies of the manual sometime in the future.

Now we have all of the variables populated. So, we need to know: If the cost is the same for the 328-page book with 99.2 square inches per page as it is for the 500-page, at 65 square-inch models, what can we say about the value of two potential volumes? Losing page count drops value but gaining page size increases it. How do the two forces work together in this instance?

When we work out equations, we discover that reducing the page count drops the value by 22.6%, but increasing page size increases the value by 415%, such that the value of the *Case 1 book* is $9.45, while that of the *Case 2 book* is $30.33.[16]

We can only uncover this tremendous difference in value for differently configured books with the same amount of content if we do the analysis we just did. This is why we did all of this work. It enables us to reach a point where we can make more highly informed decisions about our products in a market. Having found that we can configure a product two different ways and get entirely different predicted values, we might want to experiment with the demand. In our current case, we have discovered that increasing the production of manuals drops the sustainable price statistically, but only a little bit. What does that mean for us?

One of the benefits of mining a site such as Amazon is that it constantly refreshes, providing us with updated market changes in a week or less. Contrast that with reports for military aircraft, where we find new forecasts yearly. When we need it, Amazon will let us define a narrow market (as, in the case at hand, we'll examine the subset of auto manuals from all books carried by the retailer). Amazon's rapid information turnover and ability to neck down searches lets us test markets and our hypotheses about them more rapidly, in the same way that geneticists often prefer fruit flies for research rather than other animals because of their small genome and that their generations turn over so quickly.[17]

When we do a little more work with our data, we find that we have what appears to be an overpriced manual for the BMW 5-Series according to our Value Equation, as shown in Figure 10.6. The actual price, at $121.31, is high above our prediction, at $42.07, through which we draw our Product Demand Curve using its slope and the predicted manual price.

As we see in Figure 10.7, we can draw the same Product Demand Slope through our actual number and realize that we do not know why the actual price is higher than our prediction, as we indicate with a note that there are some "effects not yet known" to us. It could be that other features we have not entertained are at work, the seller made a mistake, or both.

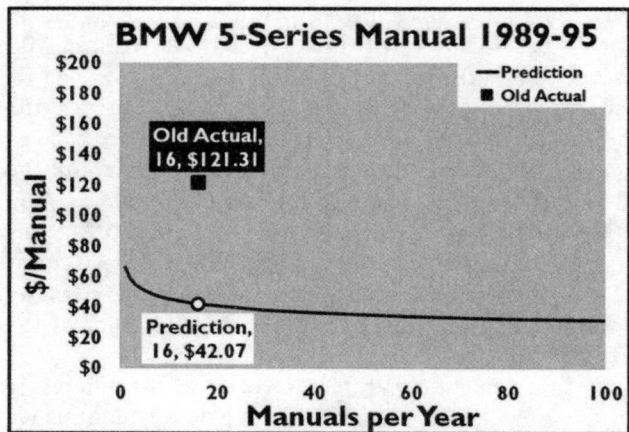

FIGURE 10.6 The BMW 5-Series Manual for 1989 to 1995 appears overpriced in this analysis.[18]

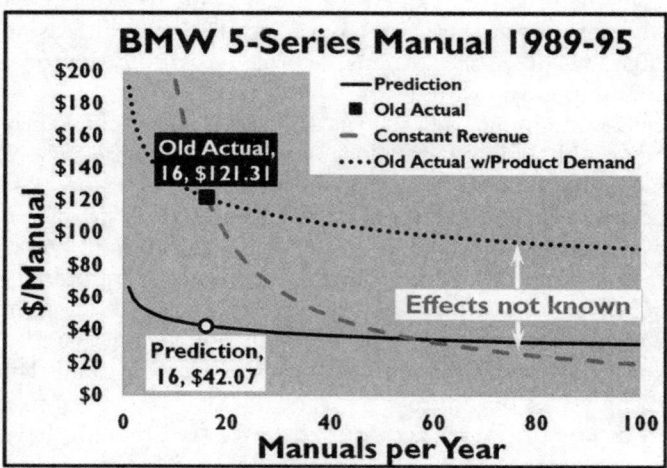

FIGURE 10.7 There may be some unknown effects accounting for the BMW 5-Series Manual being priced as high as it is. The dotted line through it, again, our Product Demand Slope, hints at how the market will respond to changes in its price.[19]

Amazon, ever-changing as always, provided a swift resolution to this case. We might have suggested a slight price decrease, as indicated by the dotted line in Figure 10.4, owing to the flat demand slope and the fact that we are still baffled about why the price was so high in the first place. As it happened, two weeks after the seller posted the initial price for the manual, that seller dropped the price by nearly $6 to $115.32 (Figure 10.8).

That resulted in manual revenue going up by over 4.5 (from $1,941 to $8,897), as Figure 10.9 reveals.

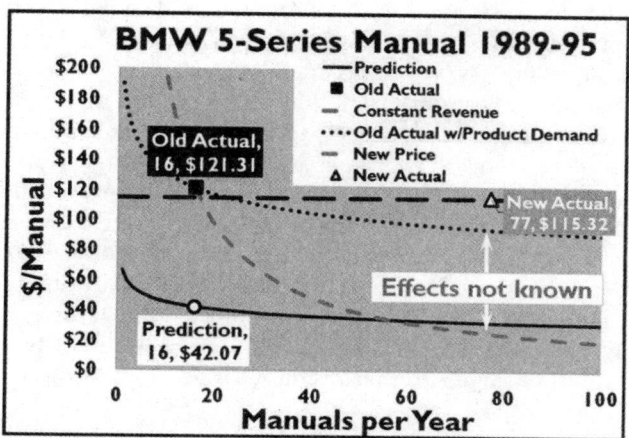

FIGURE 10.8 A slight price drop increased BMW-5 Manual sales dramatically.[20]

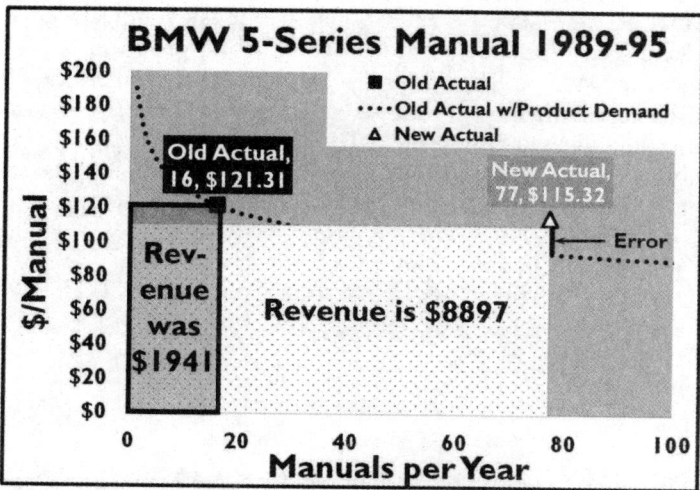

FIGURE 10.9 We can quantify the increase in revenue in the BMW-5 Series Manual. Note that the new sustainable price is above the dotted Product Demand Curve Slope, revealing the error in that term of the equation.[21]

Will this process always happen? Is this a typical example? Would a price drop result in massively increased revenue for every over-priced book, manual, or other good or service we could name? Certainly not—*all of the time*. As *we just witnessed, a slight price drop sometimes* has vast implications for revenue and profit. The trick, which is not a trick at all, is to study each market *exhaustively* to understand how it works, then decide how to work within it. The opinion is something we offer *after* we do the analysis.

Importantly, practitioners of Hypernomics are seldom going to be in the business of making absolute projections. There are "error bands" all about the equation, one for the equation in its entirety, one for the intercept, and others for the slopes of every term in every equation. These equations are derived from the actions of hundreds or thousands or even millions or billions of people, and their reactions to what producers place before them in a market can be as varied as they care to make it. In creating the analysis that describes market behavior, we are constantly dealing with the human element, and as such, there will always be some variability in our answers. As practitioners of Hypernomics, we will take that unpredictability down to its lowest practical limit. Once we do that, we move to the next project.

SUMMARY

This chapter is an exercise in applying what we already know: that Value Spaces and Demand Planes oppose each other in opposing but attached realms. As we have seen repeatedly, and here once again, producers make goods and services for sale and assign prices to them. If consumers judge prices too high based on their value assessments, sales will fall, and vice versa. In this instance, we randomly picked a market and got significant results. Unlike a few commodities with fixed prices worldwide, Hypernomics works for every market studied, provided we can find enough data to populate our studies correctly.

CHAPTER **11**

More

> *"You can never solve a problem on the level on which it was created."*
>
> Albert Einstein

> *"Is that all there is?"*
>
> Peggy Lee

No, Virginia, there may not be a Santa Claus, but there is much more to Hypernomics than has already met the eye. Given the mathematically unlimited scenarios we discovered using Hypernomics, we should leave well enough alone. We have plenty to digest, and are stuffed with knowledge. Should we all stop before we run out of the collective antacid?

Not at all.

Things are not quite as simple as this book might have made them out to be.

Why is that?

Once again, this gets back to something that you already know. It happens that *many markets are related to one another*. For example, jet aircraft need jet engines to fly. The engines' prices amount to about 20% to 40% of the aircraft's total cost, depending on the makes and models of each. As noted earlier, we need to build a seven-dimensional environment when considering two markets simultaneously as shown in Figure 11.1. If we add time, we have to have eight dimensions. Work has already been done on this problem.[1]

As Figure 11.1 demonstrates, ignoring those markets that supply you or you supply could lead to unexpected consequences. The world is full of markets that work hand in hand with others.

There are markets for electric cars, which use motors, tires, and batteries; smartphone markets rely on smartphone cases, wireless carriers, and mobile applications; the market for hens includes eggs, omelets, and diners.

Batteries have a particular value for them and their measures of demand. Making good batteries is complicated—clients constantly demand more

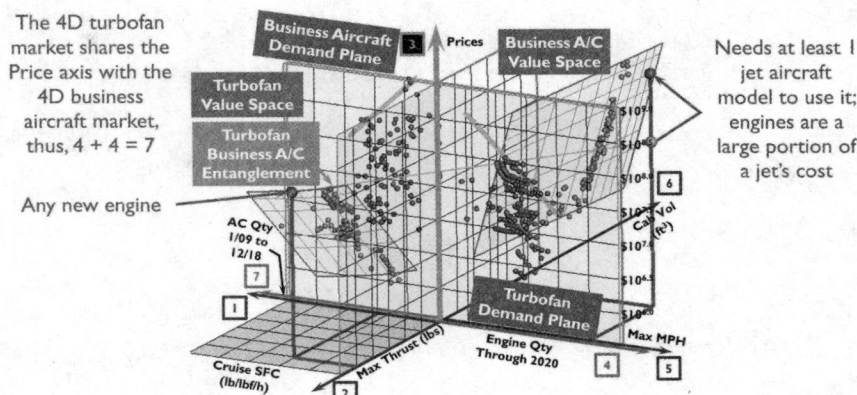

FIGURE 11.1 Adding one 4D market to another yields a 7D arrangement, as shown here. Jet aircraft work in concert with their jet engines. All engine manufacturers need one or more aircraft manufacturers to buy and install their jets on jet airliners.

power and energy densities, better temperature characteristics, and lower self-discharge rates.[2] Keeping the neighborhoods around the plants that make the batteries free of contamination can be expensive.[3]

Making a sizeable manufacturing plant for these devices also takes a significant investment. If you are a battery company, you might think this would scare off potential competitors, which it often does. But suppose you cannot work out ways to make your products sufficiently viable for a specific electric car manufacturer, one of your significant buyers. In that case, you risk having that buying group decide to use other suppliers[4] or go into business to make their batteries.[5] If you spend the time to figure out your buyers' markets, you may gain a larger market share by analyzing where their markets are headed.

If you make electric cars, you have a variety of tire manufacturers from which to choose, and you may not entertain going into that business. In the middle of the decade, the 2010s, the electric car market produced only a tiny portion of the total automobile market. There is little to be gained from building tires for these cars. However, experience shows that tires on heavier electric cars typically wear out more quickly than on their internal combustion engine (ICE) counterparts.

But you may find some potential benefits from making motors. Using alternative processes, you could add some performance and take some weight and costs out of those devices. In that case, you can make up your investment in that market.

The point is that you will only know if you take the time to do the work.

Suppose your company already has several different product lines, and you are thinking of your next good or service. In that case, you should study two or more of them simultaneously to decide which offers the best possibility of success or consider an adjacent market.

Decision-makers for the government have to allocate limited resources to various projects. Choosing the best options requires using Hypernomics to find the maximum benefits possible from a long list of choices. Hypernomics will let such analysts rank projects according to their potential advantages.

We finally realize now that markets, when properly diagrammed and analyzed, appear to us as a series of maps, with varying regions of congestion and open space, with mathematical relationships that we, the consumers, form. Understanding what it takes to fill those empty spaces is one of the features of Hypernomics. With enough work, we can figure out what to build now and what to make in the future and characterize our abilities to make profits in our endeavors. It will help any branch of the economy that cares to embrace it.

This work dramatically increases our understanding of how markets work.

However, this book is a primer, a first grab latching onto a new branch of thought. There is more to come from the author and scores of other budding Hypernomics researchers bent on finding discoveries in their fields of interest. There is much to gain from a wide range of analysts seeking out the best options in every market that they can imagine, constantly improving their chances for success. They will regale you with stories, not about what you can do for Hypernomics, but about what Hypernomics can do for you.

As the following vignette reveals, Hypernomics does not find itself limited to financial arenas. Many other uses for the discipline will undoubtedly be discovered and implemented.

Thus, dear reader, this is not the last time you will hear about Hypernomics.

VIGNETTE: WHAT DO MARKETS LOOK LIKE TO VIRUSES?

Many variables were at work in the COVID-19 pandemic. Hypernomics help visualize them. In markets, such structures use prices as objective functions. As the virus seeks to replicate, its goal is to infect hosts. We see each infection as a case.

In Figure 11.2, we plot countries' populations against their COVID-19 cases on April 28, 2020. Each dot signifies one of the 163 nations in the study. Unchecked, only the size of the global community caps the number of cases. However, we observe an upper line marking the disease's infection

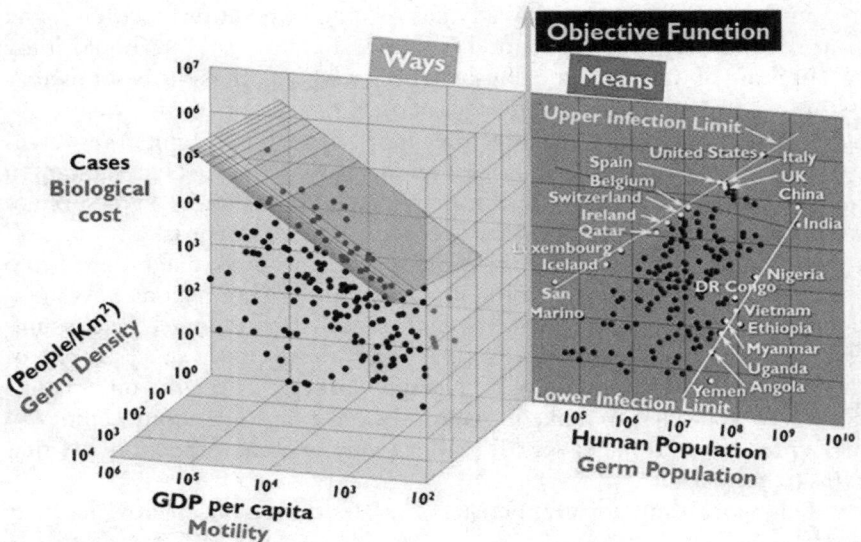

FIGURE 11.2   While the goal of a business is to make money, the objective function of a germ is to spread its DNA. In a four-dimensional Hypernomics snapshot of the COVID-19 pandemic from April 28, 2020, the virus satisfies its objective function by creating cases in humans.

limit on that date. That line is well correlated (98.6% R^2); there is little chance it came about accidentally (p-value of 8.21E-10). Countries on or near that frontier are worse off than those far away.

The left side plane represents an equation derived from the population (set to 720,000,000), density, and gross domestic product (GDP) per capita (p-values in turn of 3.13E-35, 0.68%, and 5.90E-35). While we would expect infection rates to go up with density and population, its strong relationship to GDP is unexpected. Wealthier nations have more resources to fight such outbreaks, but it appears their travel patterns more than offset that.

At that point in time, COVID-19 has a lower infection limit at work, too. Shown as the lower line, that threshold at the bottom has an adjusted R^2 of 93.5% and a p-value of 3.05E-06, reflecting that it, too, did not come about by chance. The difference in the countries that form each line is just as significant. Excepting Qatar and the United States, all the countries along the upper curve are European, and their southernmost extent is 37°55' N (the southern tip of Italy). The nations forming the lower infection limit are Asian or African, and if we remove India and China, their northernmost point is 28°32'N (Myanmar), with most of their landmasses in the tropics.

At left, the motility of the virus gets a boost from travel, driven by GDP per capita, as wealthier people tend to travel more, which enables it to move. It performs better (i.e., it creates more cases) when its density is higher, along with that of its hosts, the people it infects. Motility and density are the ways COVID creates cases, which exact a biological cost. If the biological cost is low enough and the pool of uninfected potential hosts is big enough, it can continue to make cases. COVID-19's population uses humanity as the means to extend its DNA.

Given the relative success of the tropical countries in ducking COVID near the beginning of the outbreak, we might wonder if people should increase sun exposure in northern climes. We might also want to model how sun angles to the ground regulate Vitamin D uptake and coronavirus infection rates.

CHAPTER 12

Appendix: Using Hypernomics on Your Own

"The tantalizing discomfort of perplexity is what inspires other-wise ordinary men and women to extraordinary feats of ingenuity and creativity; nothing quite focuses the mind like dissonant details awaiting harmonious resolution."

Brian Greene

"The details are not the details. They make the design."

Charles Eames

Many managers and executives will read this book knowing they will never become experts in the field of Hypernomics. They may read it, then likely put it aside. Still, hopefully, they will glean that the domain is an essential instrument in the toolbox when determining whether to enter new markets or improve products in the markets in which they already compete. However, when it comes to Hypernomics' theories and applications, for a large portion of upper management, there is too much there. Those employees schooled in Hypernomics will help decision-makers make more money than those not so trained. And that makes them valuable. For the implementation of the processes, for all those dreaded details, management needs people. They need *those* people.

People who need people are the luckiest people in the world. Just ask Barbra Streisand.[1]

Perhaps you are one of those people whom decision-makers need. If so, this chapter is for you.

You know who you are.

You do not satisfy yourself by just getting a new topic's gist. You do not fancy leaving the heavy lifting of weighty facts to somebody else. Yes, it will involve pulling in lots of data and making sense of the larger picture, but that is what you've come to love about Hypernomics. You want to know and use it; this is your opportunity. Now you get to go on a voyage of discovery of your own.

Sometimes, you will be the first to survey a longstanding market with these new tools. Other times, someone may ask you to figure out the market for what may seem to be an entirely new type of product. In either event, Hypernomics gives you ways to characterize the market in a statistically meaningful way.

In your position, the chances are that you will have to analyze markets to figure out 1) what to buy, 2) how to sell better, or 3) sell something new. By now, you know all the theories. Now comes applying your new-found knowledge. How do you go about implementing what you have just learned? Which tools should you use?

The research will show you that it is possible to do the math for Multi-dimensional Economic analyses in dozens of statistical programs, including Microsoft Excel. Furthermore, you can do the market visualizations for your work in software packages for Computer-Aided Design (CAD) or Computational Fluid Dynamics (CFD). If you want or need to do your job quickly, you may want an integrated program that does both. As of this writing, just one program is purpose-built for this work: MEE4D.[2] Designed for users with at least one semester of statistics, MEE4D works for all markets. Some markets are easy to analyze; others are not. The key is the *availability of information*.

Open governments like the United States often offer enough data to analyze many markets through their transparency requirements. Want to model the electricity or natural gas markets? Start with the U.S. Department of Energy; it has ample data for both.[3] Interested in the Value of Housing and Urban Development (HUD)-financed homes compared to the local Gross Domestic Product (GDP)? If so, go to the HUD[4] and Department of Commerce[5] websites, which will provide the data you need. Would you like to prove that the Law of Value and Demand applies to the U.S. military? If so, you would find that a pair of Department of Defense (DOD) sites are all you need.[6, 7]

Securities are particularly fertile fields for Hypernomics as each stock exchange contains a great deal of financial information about the companies that comprise them. The most significant entity of its type is the New York Stock Exchange (NYSE), with 2,400 listings.[8] The NYSE includes those companies that make up the Standard & Poor's 500 (S&P 500). As Figure 12.1 shows us, the S&P 500 behaves as we would expect from any other market concerning Demand.

You might expect, given that the S&P 500 demonstrates Demand characteristics consistent with those we find in other markets, the prices for the

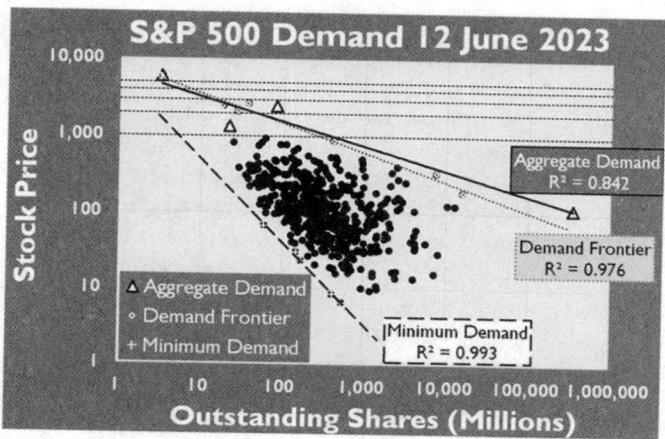

FIGURE 12.1 The S&P 500 has Demand Curves.[9]

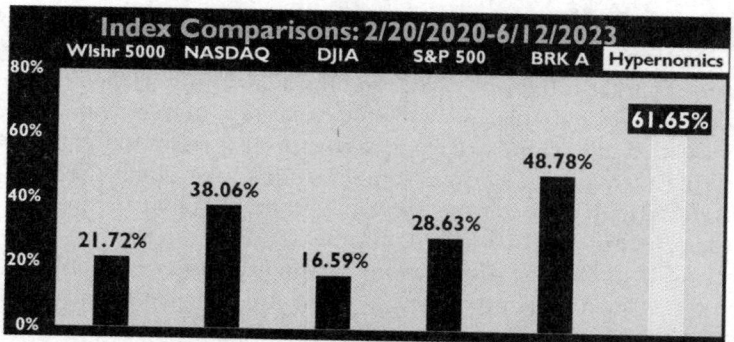

FIGURE 12.2 Value analysis of stocks within the S&P 500 allowed the author to exceed it for 40 months.[10]

stocks within it will likely have Valued Features that will draw investors to them. In support of that hypothesis, the author created his fund, Hypernomics, in February 2020. Using only stocks drawn from the S&P 500, no short positions and no options, as Figure 12.2 reveals, the fund has outperformed other large indices, Berkshire and its S&P 500 over 40 months.

If we were to perform Value Analysis of the securities that make up each group, we would find that for equity holdings, stockholders' value parameters such as dividends, earnings per share, and book value go up, all of which support higher prices. We would also discover that volume increases as prices fall (meaning that there are statistically significant Product Demand

Curves for Stocks, with individual stocks being those products). Hypernomics analysis shows how stocks measure up to competing financial products such as bonds, Treasury notes, or savings accounts before deciding to invest.

Other industries that Hypernomics handles easily include consumer electronics (consumers determine the Value of televisions, e.g., from features including, but not limited to, screen size, resolution, and refresh rates) and appliances (customers evaluate refrigerators by volume and energy efficiency). It also works for package delivery (time to destination, distance traveled, weight), train travel (volume per seat, speed, distance, number of stops), and food (size of a box of cereal, grams of protein, grams of fiber, grams of sugar), to name just a few. While the value variables in these product classes are typically easy to find, companies in several industries do not provide information on their sales quantities. If you were working for, say, a grocery chain, you would find that while you would not have all of the worldwide sales data for your various breakfast foods, you would have your own company's data on the number of cereal boxes sold. For many studies, that is sufficient to create all the required company demand curves, enough for a complete understanding of your market.

In other cases where companies do not publish their sales data directly, some associations gather it industry-wide, and the availability of their work makes complete studies possible. We will study one case of supplementing suppliers' data with a sales summary from an organization representing that industry. Walking through the various steps we must take along the way, we will find how MEE4D can get the answers you need. While anyone can manipulate the program once instructed, in practice, users with at least one course in statistics will find the results more meaningful, as users should be familiar with terms such as R^2, p-values, F-Stats, and Mean Absolute Percentage Error (MAPE).

STATING THE PROBLEM

People use Hypernomics to solve problems. You will, too. In theory, it sounds easy to describe an issue to work out, but sometimes it is time-consuming. If you were a regional manager of a retail electronics chain and your boss told you to increase sales, given that you have dozens of product categories, it may not be obvious where to start. In such cases, you may find that you will get the most significant improvements from your expensive product lines. Perhaps you could perk up profitability by doing a complete analysis of your televisions since their prices are higher than your earbuds. If you carry them, maybe refrigerators offer the most significant potential profit improvements. But, who knows, it may be the earbuds. The critical point is that you must start somewhere, and once you create an analysis, you will always be able to add to and update it.

To narrow down our general problem, we will produce a case study for a specific corporate aircraft market. We choose this market as we can gather virtually all the information we need about such conveyances from a series of open websites. We'll see how the same data set, reduced to its practical details through analysis, can support:

1. Buyers (discovering which of the models that they like are underpriced and therefore relatively good deals).
2. Sellers (intent on determining if value or demand considerations suggest price changes to increase profitability).
3. New market entrants (eager to see where gaps in the market lie).

For fun, we will provide three different possibility sets for the three preceding groups, all using the same data and tools each time, to demonstrate the methodology's flexibility.

DATA COLLECTION

Our boss told us to analyze the business jet market, so we must gather data. An excellent first step is to get a listing of all the manufacturers of the products in the market, and if possible, a complete accounting of all current models. Several sources suit this, and a Wikipedia site will often yield excellent results. Usually, it will provide you with all the known manufacturers and their offerings. You can visit each manufacturer's website for more information using these lists. Your primary source of data should always be from the producers themselves. Invariably, these firms will want you to know how great their products are; they will list features at great length to help convince you to buy.

However, you may find that new corporate jet prices are hard to find. Happily, there are consumer magazines for this sector of the economy. You will discover some[11–13] that routinely research and post the prices of the current business jets on offer. However, these magazines may not have all the sales data so you may need other information sources. Many industries have associations or research firms that work with manufacturers to compile yearly snapshots of the collective deliveries,[14, 15] and often, we can return to open governments for registration histories of some types of products.[16]

After our research, we will have a table like in Figure 12.3, which contains columns describing the market, its values and limits, and the manufacturers (the model makers).

Manufacturer	Model	$2019M	Maximum Miles per Hour (MPH)	Maximum Passengers	Cabin Volume Cubic Feet	Volume (Cubic Feet)/ Passenger	Range in Statute Miles	Quantity 1/1/09 to 12/31/18
Airbus	ACJ318 Elite	$61.88	541	8	5390	284	4830	8
Airbus	ACJ319	$74.43	541	8	5843	316	7763	26
Airbus	ACJ320 Prestige	$81.12	541	25	6968	367	6900	10
Airbus	ACJ321	$95.33	541	8	8547	450	4830	1
Airbus	ACJ330	$191.50	567	25	17235	907	11558	5
Airbus	ACJ340	$277.82	567	25	20503	820	11385	1
Avcraft	Envoy 3	$14.39	460	12	1183	99	1896	0
Boeing	Boeing Business Jet	$65.23	541	8	5396	656	8050	29
Boeing	Boeing Business Jet 2	$77.77	541	8	6525	837	7636	8
Boeing	Boeing Business Jet 3	$82.79	541	8	7290	911	7492	7
Boeing	737-800	$98.93	541	8	6525	837	7636	2
Boeing	Boeing Business Jet 747	$307.74	595	19	24955	1313	10206	9
Boeing	Boeing Business Jet 777	$275.96	608	19	20456	1077	13402	8
Boeing	Boeing Business Jet 787	$214.92	628	19	16501	868	11437	12
Bombardier	Global 7500	$72.00	611	19	2637	139	8855	1
Bombardier	Global 6000	$62.31	582	13	1997	154	6900	355
Bombardier	Global 5000	$50.44	582	13	1882	145	5984	153
Bombardier	CL 890	$47.50	542	14	2821	202	2719	8
Bombardier	CL 870	$40.53	542	14	2860	204	2878	1
Bombardier	CL 850	$30.99	528	14	1990	142	2824	12

FIGURE 12.3 Here is a partial list of the new business jets sold from January 1, 2009, to December 31, 2018.[17]

Where:

1. Model (the designation for the plane in each row).
2. Qty (the Quantity sold over a period, here, ten years): What can the market absorb?
3. Price M (in millions of dollars): What are buyers paying?
4. Max MPH (the maximum cruise speed, in miles per hour): Speed value.
5. Pass (the typical number of passenger seats in the business jet): Capacity.
6. Cab Vol (the Cabin Volume in cubic feet without the cockpit): More on capacity.
7. Vol Pass (The Cabin Volume per person Cabin Volume divided by seats): Comfort.
8. Range M (the range in statute miles, with normal reserves): Flexibility, Endurance.
9. Quantity sold from January 1, 2009, to December 31, 2018.

DATA ENTRY

Now that we have built our database, we can load it into the MEE4D template, as we do in Figure 12.4, where we observe that we see the top of the file. Note that this file looks much like what you see in Microsoft Excel.

Check Data	ShortNames LongNames Descriptions Units	Manufacturer	Model	$2019M	MxMPH	Pass	Cab Vol	VolPss	Range M	Qty0918	T1J2	Engs
	Data Types	Char	Char	Float	Float	ntege	Float	Float	Float	Float	Integer	Integer
Data Row 1		Airbus	ACJ318 Elite	61.88	541	25	5,390	283.7	4830	8	2	2
Data Row 2		Airbus	ACJ319	74.43	541	25	5,843	316.0	7763	26	2	2
Data Row 3		Airbus	ACJ320 Prestige	81.12	541	25	6,968	366.7	6900	10	2	2
Data Row 4		Airbus	ACJ321	95.33	541	25	8,547	449.8	4830	1	2	2
Data Row 5		Airbus	ACJ330	191.50	567	50	17,235	907.1	11558	5	2	2
Data Row 6		Airbus	ACJ340	277.82	567	50	20,503	820.1	11385	1	2	4
Data Row 7		Avcraft	Envoy 3	14.39	460	12	1,183	98.6	1896	0	2	2
Data Row 8		Boeing	Boeing Business Jet	65.23	541	25	5,396	656.3	8050	29	2	2
Data Row 9		Boeing	Boeing Business Jet 2	77.77	541	25	6,525	836.8	7636	8	2	2
Data Row 10		Boeing	Boeing Business Jet 3	82.79	541	25	7,290	911.3	7492	7	2	2
Data Row 11		Boeing	737-800	98.93	541	25	6,525	836.8	7636	2	2	2
Data Row 12		Boeing	Boeing Business Jet 747	307.74	595	50	24,955	1313.4	10206	9	2	4
Data Row 13		Boeing	Boeing Business Jet 777	275.96	588	50	20,456	1076.6	13402	8	2	2
Data Row 14		Boeing	Boeing Business Jet 787	214.92	595	50	16,501	868.5	11437	12	2	2
Data Row 15		Bombardier	Global 7500	72.00	611	19	2,637	138.8	8855	1	2	2
Data Row 16		Bombardier	Global 6000	62.31	582	13	1,997	153.7	6900	355	2	2
Data Row 17		Bombardier	Global 5000	50.44	582	13	1,882	144.8	5984	153	2	2
Data Row 18		Bombardier	CL 890	47.50	542	14	2,821	201.5	2719	8	2	2
Data Row 19		Bombardier	CL 870	40.53	542	14	2,860	204.3	2878	1	2	2
Data Row 20		Bombardier	CL 850	30.99	528	14	1,990	142.1	2824	12	2	2

FIGURE 12.4 The MEE4D template is the path from Microsoft Excel to MEE4D. It checks that each piece of data matches its specified type.[18]

With the data loaded, we can move to the MEE4D Model Tab, as shown in Figure 12.5.

This tab permits you to temporarily remove one or more pieces of data from consideration by using the filters near the bottom of the page. For example, you could pull an entire supplier—noting that Boeing Business Jets are converted commercial airliners—simply by enabling a filter and asking for all manufacturers that are not Boeing. If you decide to keep some converted planes but remove others, you might exclude any model costing more than $200 million. If one model were a noticeable outlier, asking for every model except that one would remove it from the analysis (or find out what makes it different).

In this case, we want to look at the most recent market, so we have filtered the data such that all models in the data from 2009 to 2018 must have had sales. Note the checked box in the first row of the "Filtering Enabled" section and how we selected that the Quantity sold from 2009 to 2018 must be greater than zero. The program allows us to highlight some data, too,

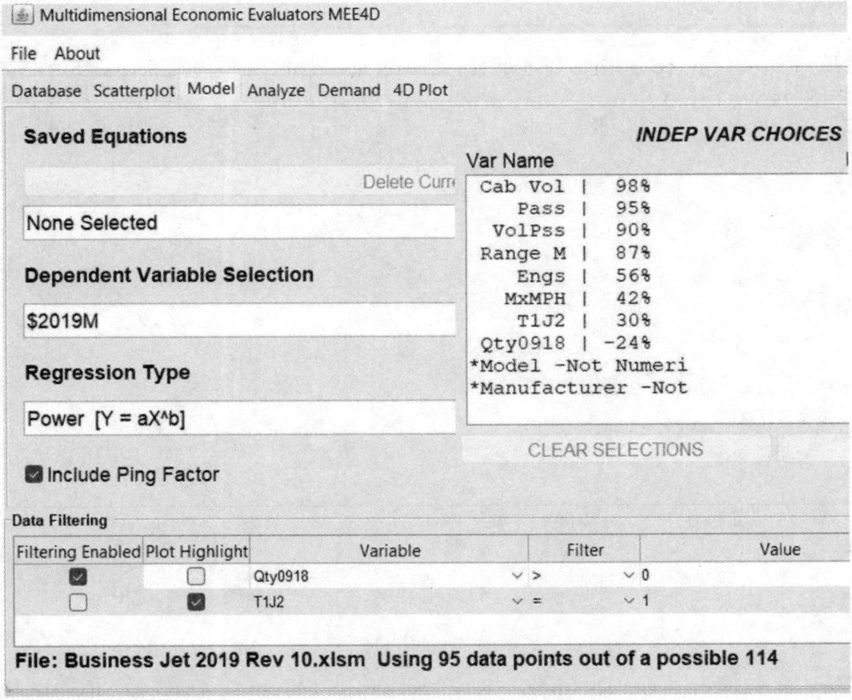

FIGURE 12.5 Hypernomics Inc. MEE4D software Model Tab lets users select the dependent variable, and filter the data.[19]

which we did when highlighting the variable "T1J2," indicating we want to know when "T" or "Turboprops" are selected.

Now we are beginning to take full advantage of the market data, and we can describe this market with a high degree of accuracy and precision very quickly. Recall that we are always trying to predict a dependent variable, and in Hypernomics, often that is Price. We can select "Price M" from the drop-down box in Figure 12.5, and this instantly provides us with a list of independent (Indep) variable (var) choices and characteristics that can affect the Price. Note that they are listed in correlation order, with the highest correlation (positive or negative) at the top, going down to those with the lowest at the bottom.

DATA MANIPULATION

Figure 12.5 shows that Cabin Volume correlates very well with Price (98%) and Max MPH. We wonder what we might see if we used them to predict Price; the results are shown in Figure 12.6.

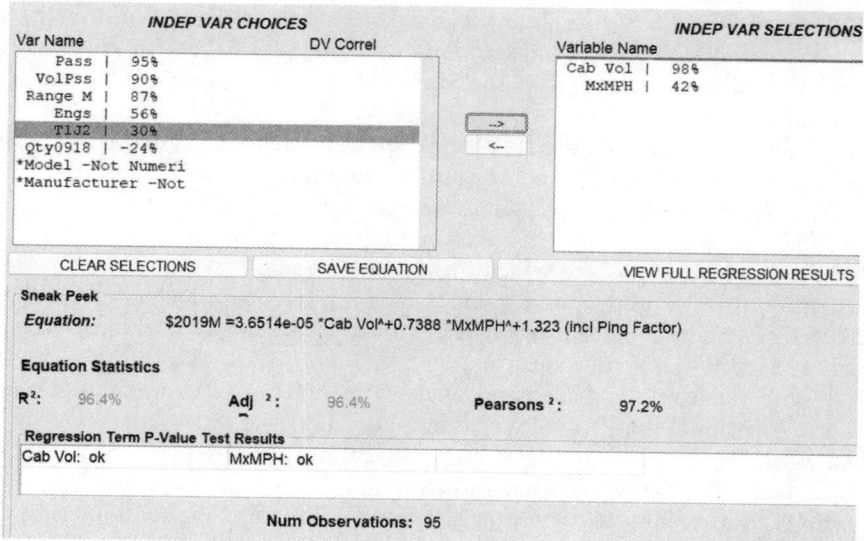

FIGURE 12.6 The MEE4D Model Tab does a great deal of work for the program. Here, we've picked $2019 million as our dependent variable and asked the independent variables, Cabin Volume (Cab Vol) and Maximum Miles per Hour (MxMPH), to predict that Price. We get the resulting equation and statistics immediately. We can save this equation or view full regression results to get the details.[20-28]

⊜ MEE, Inc   **FULL REGRESSION RESULTS REPORT**

Name Unsaved Model
Date: 15-Jun-2023   **Time** 08:10
Data File: Business Jet 2019 Rev 10.xlsm Ver: 1.00
Data Filtering: Qty0918>0

EQUATION & STATISTICS

EQUATION $2019M =3.6514e-05 *Cab Vol*+0.7388 *MxMPH*+1.323 (incl Ping Factor) (incl Ping Factor)
:
R 96.4%   Ac96.4%   Pea 97.2%   CV: 25.8%   MA 19.3%   F-Stat+1249 p-value=2.07e-67   StdEr +9.719
   Number of Observations: 95   Residual Degrees of 92
Regression Term P-Value Test Results
Cab Vol p-val = 3.72e-53   MxMPH p-val = 1.19e-22

FIGURE 12.7   The Full Regression Report from MEE4D
shows user crucial statistics resulting from their models.[29]

Just under the "Sneak Peek," near the center of the screen in Figure 12.6,
we see a power form equation from the analysis. Below the "Sneak Peek,"
we find the equation statistics for R^2, the adjusted R^2, and Pearson's[2].

If we need more information about the model, we can click the button
entitled "View Full Regression Results" below "Indep[endent] Var[iable]
Selections," and we get the view that we see in Figure 12.7. Here, we
get some more essential statistics, the CV or Coefficient of Variation, the
MAPE, or Mean Absolute Percentage Error, and the F-Test, F-Stat including the p-value for each independent variable (note that for this case,
we have only one), as well as the Standard Deviation, as represented by
"Std. Err."

Please note that our Standard Deviation using this equation is $15.4 mil-
lion. It is a critical figure that we want to minimize. We will want to work
to improve this figure. Note that we've adjusted the equation by the "Ping-
Factor," which is an adjustment factor that recognizes power form curves
have a downward bias, for which this factor corrects.[30]

Now that we understand Value, we can move on to Demand. On the
MEE4D Demand tab, we can pick a Quantity Variable (our horizontal axis)
and a Value Variable (our vertical axis). See Figure 12.8.

With the Value and Demand analysis complete, we can examine our
four-dimensional plot, which we do in Figure 12.9.

With Figure 12.9 plotted in linear space, we can appreciate how costs
rise concerning Cabin Volume and Maximum miles per hour while comparing those results to the reactions on the Demand Plane. Sometimes,
we may want to see how this chart looks in log space, which we do in
Figure 12.10.

Figure 12.11 reminds us that every point in the left-hand Value Space
has a matching partner on the right-hand Demand Plane.

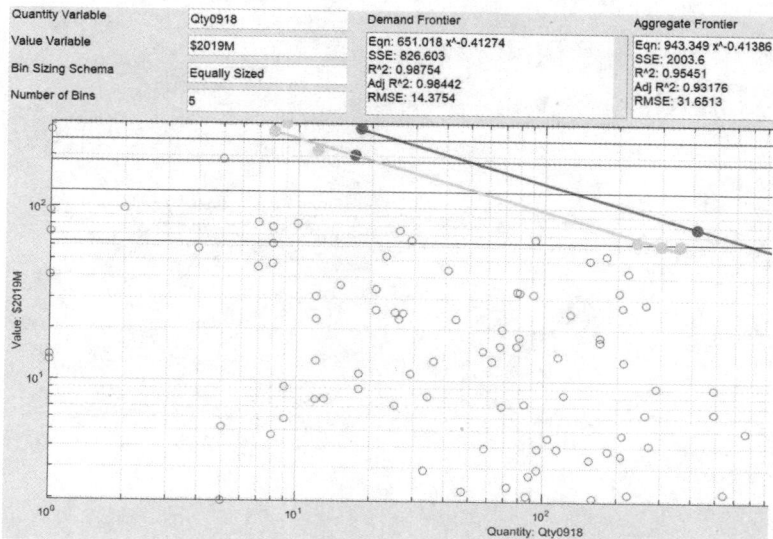

Quantity Variable	Qty0918	Demand Frontier	Aggregate Frontier
Value Variable	$2019M	Eqn: 651.018 x^-0.41274	Eqn: 943.349 x^-0.41386
Bin Sizing Schema	Equally Sized	SSE: 826.603 / R^2: 0.98754	SSE: 2003.6 / R^2: 0.95451
Number of Bins	5	Adj R^2: 0.98442 / RMSE: 14.3754	Adj R^2: 0.93176 / RMSE: 31.6513

FIGURE 12.8 We calculate Aggregate Demand using a series of bins. Here, we chose five, and the slope of its curve is –0.414 (note that the rightmost Aggregate Demand Point is "off the chart" to the right, which we truncated for display reasons). We discover the Upper Demand Frontier by picking the uppermost points in the range and highlighting them, forming the innermost line. Its slope is –0.413, almost identical to the Aggregate Market Demand.[31]

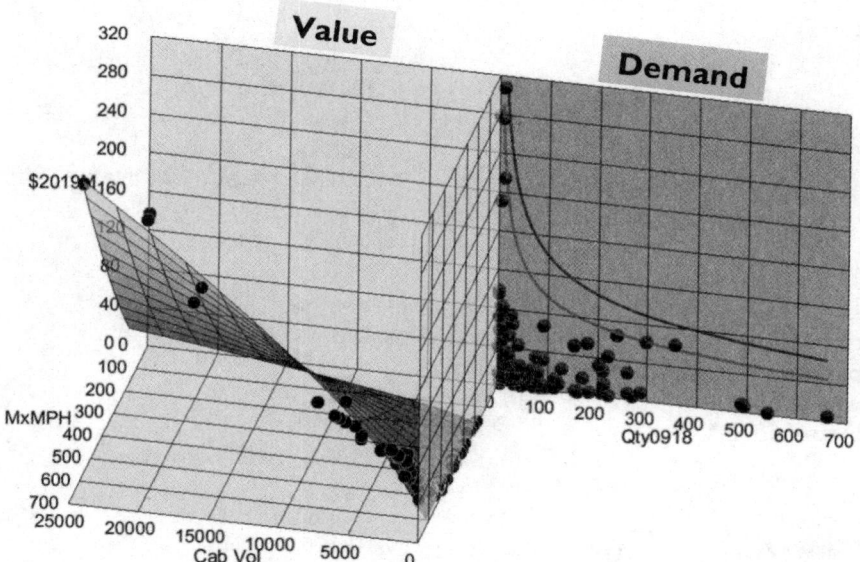

FIGURE 12.9 Linear four-dimensional display of Value and Demand for 2009–2018 business aircraft.[32]

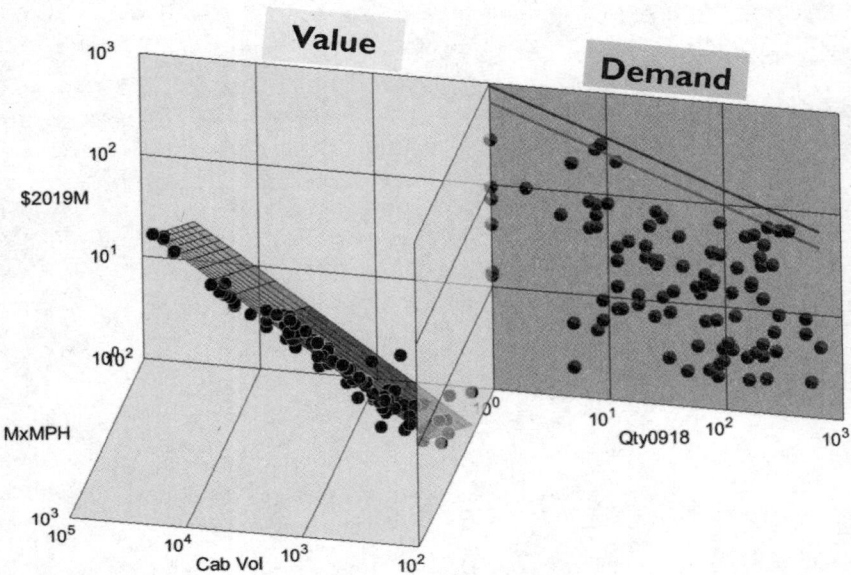

FIGURE 12.10 Log-Log-Log-Log four-dimensional display of Value and Demand for 2009–2018 business aircraft.[33]

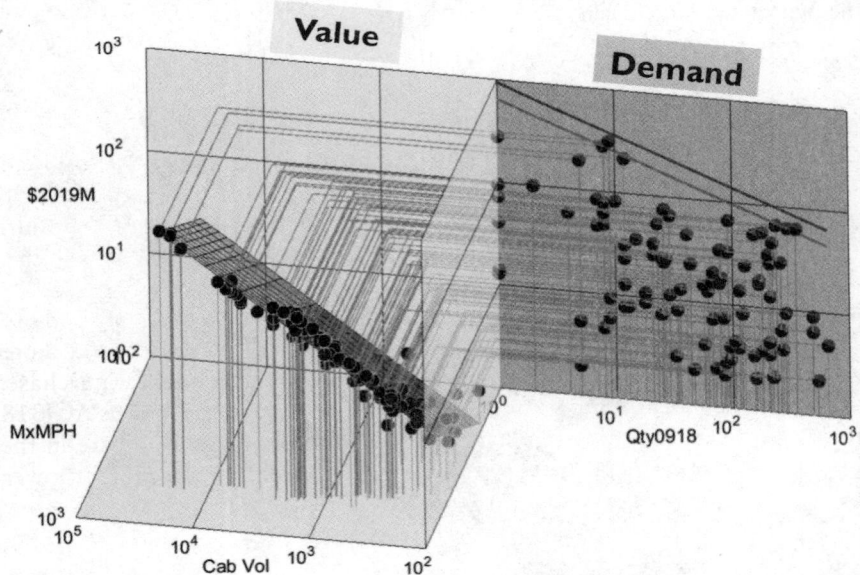

FIGURE 12.11 Demand and Value are always linked, as shown by these "Point-Lines" between each side.[34]

DATA INTERPRETATION

There are many uses for Hypernomics and the MEE4D software that supports it. Recall that we decided to see how three disparate groups might use the exact data for their purposes. One faction was that of the buyers, people looking to buy a new business jet. These could be individuals or people representing a corporation. Another was the manufacturers of the models, which also act as the sellers, including every one of the manufacturers we identified in this study and any that we may have left out. Finally, we wanted to see what the data revealed about openings in this market, which might provide a new opportunity for existing members of the manufacturing community or for companies new to the market that would like to enter it. The analysis could reveal something a potential new entrant would want to know. The point is that each group singled out has a different plan than the others. All of them could get the same answers we just did, using the data and software we just showed, but their interpretations are bound to differ. Let's see how each one of them could work with the analyses.

How Buyers Use MEE4D

Buyers want deals. They spend a lot of time figuring out how to save money, especially on large quantities of big-ticket items or products they need. Often purchased by a business group or leasing company, a business jet counts as a sizeable purchase. They want to get it right with millions of dollars at stake. After they have done all their work with the MEE4D and derived the same equation we did, they will now want to study the residuals (errors) and determine where the best Value lies.

Figure 12.12 shows that of all the planes considered, the HondaJet had the lowest actual Price compared to its predicted Value. While this vehicle may be an excellent choice for many buyers, we must temper that enthusiasm because we have not yet examined its other factors, such as range, customer service, or safety record. Also, given that it is new to the market, no one knows how it will fare later in its product life cycle. That uncertainty will dampen its sustainable Price, and we should factor that into a more detailed study to give us more insight if we consider this model for purchase.

Regarding airliners converted into business aircraft, the Airbus ACJ318 Elite offers excellent speed and tremendous cabin volume. If we are in the market for a larger plane, this may be very attractive, as its Price is far lower than our equation suggested it ought to be. We may need to extend our limited data analysis, but given what our equation tells us, the ACJ318 Elite looks like a good deal for buyers.

In any event, we may want to recheck the data and rerun our analysis if we find any changes in prices, specifications, or new models that have

Model	Actual Value	Predicted Value	Residual	Actual/ Predicted
Honda HA-420 HondaJet	$4.50	$9.48	–$4.98	47.5%
Textron CE-208B	$2.20	$3.57	–$1.37	61.6%
Embraer Phenom 100	$4.10	$6.40	–$2.30	64.0%
Pilatus PC-24	$8.93	$13.70	–$4.79	65.2%
Extra EA500	$1.95	$2.83	–$0.88	68.9%
Cessna 510 Citation Mustang	$3.57	$5.09	–$1.52	70.1%
Cessna CE-680A Citation Latitude	$17.00	$24.10	–$7.08	70.5%
Cirrus SF-50	$2.75	$3.87	–$1.12	71.1%
Airbus ACJ318 Elite	$61.90	$85.90	–$24.00	72.1%
Bombardier CL 870	$40.50	$53.90	–$13.40	75.1%

FIGURE 12.12 The difference between the actual Price and the one we predicted is an error term (or residual). Since we are comparing a wide range of prices simultaneously, instead of using Standard Deviation, which the pricier models highly influence, it makes sense to use a different measure of errors. Here, we define that relative sense as the Actual Value divided by the Predicted Value, where lower is better, which is a percentage error. Taking the mean absolute percentage error of all items in the data set gives us the Mean Absolute Percentage Error or MAPE.[35]

popped up since we began the process. We may begin to believe in that result when multiple analysts use Hypernomics techniques and converge on the same answer.

How Manufacturers Use MEE4D

Not surprisingly, manufacturers can also use analysis from the same database. Many sellers have high prices and are rightfully proud of them, as they accurately reflect their products' values. But what if they are *too* high? Before this analysis, we could not know which prices were low, just right, or too high. Now we know. What do we do? Let's look at another cut of our errors in Figure 12.13.

We can use the residual table to find out, according to our equation of two variables (recall those features were cabin volume and maximum cruise speed in miles per hour), which of the models we've studied appear to be overpriced. A glance suggests that the Pilatus PC-6, displayed in Figure 12.14, could be too expensive.

Model	Actual Value	Predicted Value	Residual	Actual/ Predicted
Gulfstream Gulfstream 650	$65.00	$51.10	$13.94	127.2%
Gulfstream Gulfstream 650ER	$66.50	$51.10	$15.44	130.1%
Bombardier Global 6000	$62.30	$45.50	$16.85	136.9%
Dassault Falcon 900LX	$44.00	$31.90	$12.07	137.9%
Dassault Falcon 7X	$53.80	$38.90	$14.94	138.3%
Dassault Falcon 8X	$58.00	$41.50	$16.52	139.8%
Pacific PAC 750XL	$2.36	$1.63	$0.74	145.2%
Gulfstream Gulfstream 550	$62.00	$40.60	$21.36	152.7%
Viking Twin Otter	$5.90	$3.48	$2.42	169.6%
Pilatus PC-6	$2.22	$1.06	$1.16	210.0%

FIGURE 12.13 The other end of the residual table shows us planes that may be priced too high.[36]

FIGURE 12.14 The Pilatus PC-6 specializes in taking off and landing in small spaces—there is Value in that.[37, 38]

Studying Figure 12.14, we notice this plane doesn't look like many others in our collection. Built as a utility aircraft and first flown in 1959, Pilatus designed it to operate in short and often unimproved airfields. Our simple equation doesn't take that into account. It turns out that there are operators who need a plane that does just that, and for hundreds of them, the Pilatus PC-6 was the answer. If we wanted to see the Value of aircraft working in tight quarters, we should probably add helicopters to the data and rerun our analysis.

Going back to Figure 12.13, note that it indicates that the Gulfstream G650 could be priced too high. We remembered our work with Demand Curves and decided to zoom in on the G650 on our Demand Plane in Figure 12.15.

Note that while the G650 approaches the Upper Demand Frontier, it has not yet reached it. That makes us wonder if we knew Product Demand for all business aircraft considered and the Learning Curve for the G650 specifically. We do not have such estimates, but we can lay in some hypothetical guesses as to what they might be in Figure 12.16.

In our imagined scenario in Figure 12.16, we have a relatively flat Product Demand Curve running through the "G650 was" point (the dotted line with tiny dots, indicating where the sales of the G650 were), showing how we believe Demand for the G650 will fall as Gulfstream sells more units. Below that, we have an assumed Learning Curve for the G650, one that might approximate how costs fell for the vehicle as the company built more units of it. Observe that the Learning Curve is steeper than the Product Demand Curve. That means that if they go on at the same rate, they will not

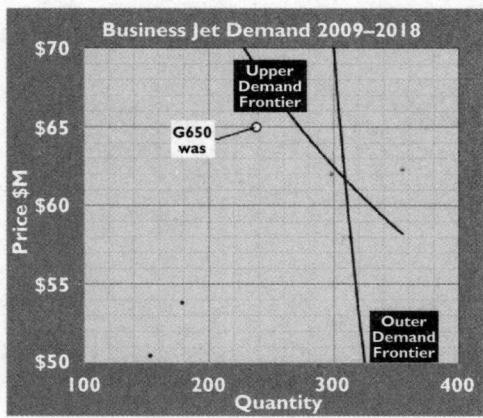

FIGURE 12.15 Here, we focus on the G650 (observe that we have changed to linear scaling).[39]

intersect. On the other hand, as drawn, the Product Demand Curve intersects both the Upper and Outer Demand Frontiers. What happens if we drop the Price from $65 million to $63.4 million? We find out in Figure 12.17.

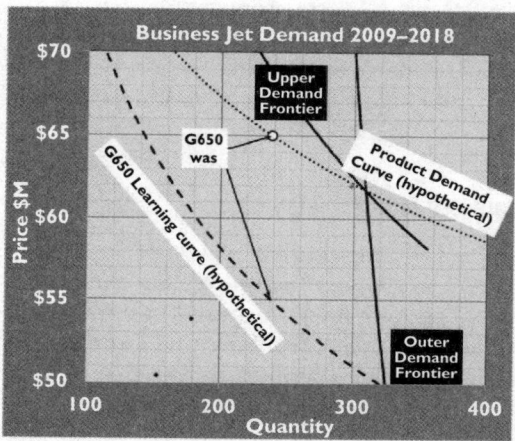

FIGURE 12.16 Producers will want to know their Product Demand and Learning Curves for all the items they make. Here, we imagine some hypothetical constructs for both for illustration purposes.[40]

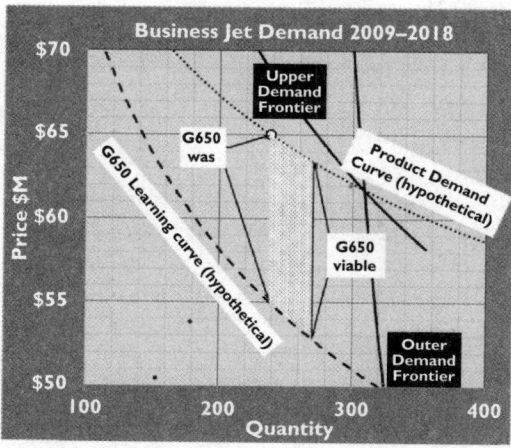

FIGURE 12.17 In this case, lowering the Price creates more sales, and the production line continues to build the plane for less than its Price.[41]

With Figure 12.17, we propose a new, lower, viable price. That drives us closer to the Demand Frontiers but does not project us past them. Costs fall more than proportionally, and the cross-hatched area represents the new projected profits the price drop will generate.

If analysis revealed an underpriced product, producers could run the process in reverse and see if it made sense to raise the Price and suffer fewer sales. You'll only get the answers when you do the work.

This exercise, while fictional, offers the approach all producers should employ for ongoing products.

How Potential New Market Entrants Use MEE4D

In any market, be it recently invented or longstanding, new entrants should strive to build products their market wants, does not have, and can afford. That means finding market gaps concerning prices, features, or both. In the long run, some companies eventually fill such gaps. We should aim to find them before our competitors, then design and build products that aim for these open spaces. We can see how this happened using our data.

In Figure 12.18, we plot the cabin volume of our business jets against the prices these planes fetch.

A standard practice new market entrants ought to adopt is to characterize the gaps in a market concerning features and prices. We do that for volume and prices in Figure 12.19.

Figure 12.19 shows us three significant gaps in the cabin volume of business aircraft. Airbus recognized the possibilities and developed a five-abreast airliner called the A220-100. In 2020, the company announced its first business jet based on this model. We can see how it filled the market in Figure 12.20.

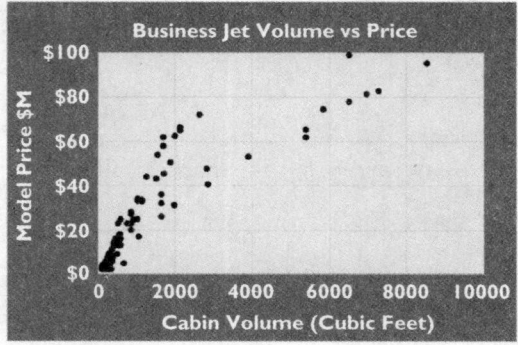

FIGURE 12.18 In business jets, Price partially depends on the volume of a plane's cabin.[42]

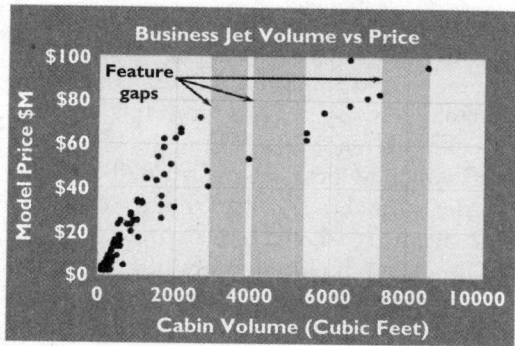

FIGURE 12.19 Through 2018, at least three sizeable gaps existed in the market relative to cabin volume.[43]

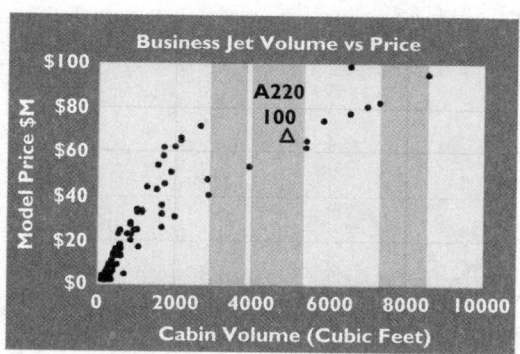

FIGURE 12.20 The Airbus Corporate Jet (ACJ) variant of the A220-100 found a large opening in the market, and the company designed the plane to fill it.[44–46]

We can also search for feature gaps regarding the range variable, a part of the equation we used for our study, and other variables that come to mind. The key is to stay within the open spaces that the market will absorb while giving it something different.

SUMMARY

This chapter addresses the practical matters relating to a market in four dimensions. A great deal of the effort in working through these analyses involves retrieving and verifying data used to build files that go into MEE4D.

MEE4D is already quite powerful. Once the analyst completes a comprehensive database, he or she can quickly analyze that data in minutes. It took the author less than five minutes to find equations that explained over 96% of the variation from the mean. Knowing there is room for improvement in the cases examined in this chapter reminds us of the importance of exhausting the data sources. With many new products worth millions over time, including the ones in this market, it makes excellent financial sense to dive deeply into the data and find all the market forces that affect Value, Demand, and cost. It takes time. But a few hundred hours of effort spent before product launch can prevent product failure and help you make a few extra million dollars. That must be worth your time.

VIGNETTE: THE IMPORTANCE OF GOING DEEP INTO THE DATA

"Everything counts in large amounts."

Depeche Mode

After focusing on two hugely essential features that explain over 96% of the variation in the data in business aircraft, we might consider our work done. With that same equation having a *p*-value of 2.07E-67 (again, recall the *p*-value is the probability the equation came about due to chance), anyone who studies statistics would tell you that is a highly significant result. And it is.

But consider a couple of airliners from different manufacturers. One of these manufacturers, Boeing, had its planes in our previous data set.

Figure 12.21 shows a Boeing Model 737 plane taking off. It is one of their −800 series (the series preceding the current 737 Max line). It is an exemplary model, and it and its variants can carry up to 177 passengers at cruise speeds of over 520 miles per hour for ranges of just over 3,000 miles. It lists for $63 to $106 million, but is often discounted to $30 to $50 million.

Boeing 737 Next Generation

Passengers: 108–177 Cruise MPH: 521
Range m: 2,935–3,010

FIGURE 12.21   The Boeing 737-800 is one of the company's most successful models.[47]

Production: 1997—now
Units sold: 7,077
List Price: $63M–$106M
Discount: $30M–$50M

We can contrast the Boeing plane with the Tupolev Tu-204 in Figure 12.22.

Tupolev Tu-204

Passengers: 142–215 Cruise MPH: 529
Range m: 2,500–3,600
Production: 1990–now
Units sold: 89
List Price: $43M–$48M
Discount: $20M–$23M

The Tupolev goes faster and farther than its Western Bloc counterpart and can carry more people. Yet, the Boeing models sell for more money and had over 7,000 units sold at the time of this writing, compared to less than 100 for the Russian plane. Why is that?

FIGURE 12.22 The Tupolev Tu-204 is a design from the Russian design bureau of the same name.[48]

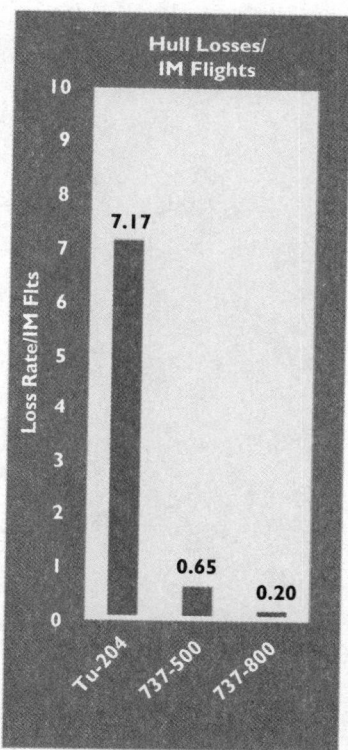

FIGURE 12.23 The Tupolev Tu-204 is incredibly safe, but its Boeing 737 equivalents are over 10X safer.[49]

We get a bit of insight with Figure 12.23.

In 2019, the National Safety Council (NSC) found the lifetime odds of dying was 1 in 543 as a pedestrian and 1 in 107 in a car crash. Meanwhile, Western aviation has gotten so safe that there have been years in which no fatalities were reported. In 2019, the NSC found the chances of dying in a plane crash too low to calculate. The Boeing 737 series was a big part of that. Tupolev did excellent work in enhancing safety but didn't approach what the Boeing Company did. Ultimately, that is one of several factors working on behalf of the Boeing 737 sales price and their extraordinary volume.

The lesson here is that many features must be considered when considering product valuation. Don't let great answers using part of the picture prevent you from depicting the economic forces at play as broadly as you can. You'll never attain perfection, but it pays to try.

CHAPTER 13

Neoclassical Economics and Hypernomics Differences

Hypernomics varies from Neoclassical Economics in many ways. Figure 13.1 lists some of the most important distinctions.

Column1	Neoclassical Economics	Hypernomics
Fundamental Theorem	Law of Supply and Demand	Law of Value and Demand
Default State and the reason for it	Equilibrium: Where upward-sloping product supply curve intersects downward-sloping demand curve	Sustainable disequilibrium: Where the Value (as a sustainable Price) of a product exceeds it Cost
Supply Curves	Hypothesized, upward-sloping	Observed: Upward-sloping for single-feature commodities; Downward-sloping for manufactured products
Demand Curves	Hypothesized	Observed
Types of Demand Curves	1	8 or more
Learning Curves	Not mentioned	Observed
Number of static analysis dimensions	2	4, or 3n+1, where n = the number of markets considered
Prices set by	Producers	Buyers
Profit Determination	What the market will bear	Financial Cat Scans
Inspiring field(s)	Thermodynamics	Biology, Geography, Math

FIGURE 13.1   Distinctions between Neoclassical Economics and Hypernomics.

Glossary

Aggregate Demand (of a market)   a measure of the price responsiveness of the market concerning price, in which we find the line of best fit between several vertically oriented bins that gather total quantities and average prices

Area of Interest   a region in which producers believe customers might want products

Average Demand (of a market)   a measure of the average sales in a market regarding price in which we find the line of best fit between several vertically oriented bins that gather average quantities and average prices

Battlefield Maps   akin to Market Maps and show the opponent's positions during a skirmish

Breakeven Equilibrium, Hypernomics   the point at which costs fall to meet value beyond which suppliers can make a product at a profit

Buyers' limits   limits regarding the maximum quantities they will purchase or maximum prices they will accommodate

Cartesian Coordinate Systems   two-dimensional and three-dimensional constructs that relate to points in physical space

Common Axis   the currency axis where all Value Spaces and Demand Planes meet

Demand Error Triangle   the triangle traced out horizontally (as quantity) and vertically (as sustainable price) between a target (as a quantity and price desired) and the product result (as the quantity and price attained)

Demand Frontier   the outer or rightmost limit on a market, concerning quantities on a horizontal axis, with prices on the vertical axis

Demand Plane   a two-dimensional plane with a horizontal quantity axis and a vertical currency axis

Demand Shifts   changes in the Demand Curve over time; a curve moving rightward indicates a growing market, and one moving inward or left depicts a shrinking market

Dot Plot   a method by which to plot one or more attributes of a product or multiple products in a market

Dual States   recognition that in each market, each buyer must value a product on the one hand and decide how many to buy of it on the other, meaning that value and demand are always connected in dual states with a standard vertical component measured in currency

Economic Trajectory Analysis (ETA)   the tracking of Financial Opportunity Space over time

Egg of Columbus   a likely apocryphal story about the explorer that shows when someone first figures out a new way of doing things, anyone can do it

End of Product Equilibrium, Hypernomics the point at which value falls to meet costs, which signals the end of a product, as beyond this point, the products suffer losses

Equilibrium, Neoclassical where upward-sloping Supply and downward-sloping Demand Curves intersect at a single point

Error Tetrahedron the tetrahedron traced out as miss distances north and south (as latitude), east and west (as longitude), and up and down (as elevation) between a target (as an artillery target) and the volley landing site (as from an artillery piece)

Error Triangle the triangle traced out horizontally (as elevation) and vertically (as azimuth or windage) between a target (as the center of a bullseye) and the shot entry (as from an arrow or bullet)

Feature Gaps market zones in which no competitors have offerings relative to a pair of valued features

Financial Cat Scans methods by which analysts start with four active dimensions, Valued Feature 1, Valued Feature 2, Price, and Quantity, and reduce problems to one dimension, a price difference between value and cost, performed by section cuts that mimic CT scans

Financial Opportunity Space (FOS) the region bounded by the lower value or demand on the upper side, cost on the lower side, and inner and outer feature constraints in which it is possible to make a profit

Five-Dimensional Coordinate System consists of axes for Valued Feature 1, Valued Feature 2, Currency, Quantity, and Time; eventually applies to all markets

Four-Dimensional Coordinate System consists of axes for Valued Feature 1, Valued Feature 2, Currency, and Quantity; applies to all markets

Hypernomics the study of markets in four or more dimensions; it is the same as Multidimensional Economics (ME)

Immediate Aiming the product configuration for an immediate need, designed to hit a specific price and composition with features proven to support that price

Invisible Hand Adam Smith's idea that individuals' efforts to pursue their interests may frequently benefit society more than if their actions were directly intended to help the community by attaining free market equilibrium

ISO-Value Line another name for a production possibility curve, which is a line providing the identical predicted value for different combinations of features

Law of Supply and Demand a neoclassical economic notion that a downward-sloping demand curve intersects an upward-sloping supply curve at a single equilibrium point

Learning Curve a line that represents that the time required to do a repetitive task falls the more times workers repeat that task

Market a collection of like products; it divides into smaller segments, also called submarkets or sub-submarkets

Market Constraints limits placed on markets, either by customers, as minimum or maximum requirements, or by regulation, technical limitations, physical boundaries, or other forces

Market Maps two-dimensional maps of markets relating quantity and price, or a pair of features, that demonstrate boundaries and openings to prices or features

Minimum Demand (of a market) a measure of the minimum sales in a market concerning price in which we find the line of best fit between several vertically oriented bins that gather the minimum quantities and average prices

Mission Market one of one or more market groups that fall within a more extensive classification as a sub-submarket

Multidimensional Economics (ME) the study of markets in four or more dimensions; it is the same as Hypernomics

N-Dimensional Coordinate System a series of four-dimensional markets connected to a common central axis; there are $3n+1$ dimensions for n number of markets considered

Neoclassical Aiming typically directed at a single price point in the future, which is one-dimensional aiming

Nonnegative Dimensions all dimensions in Hypernomics are nonnegative; negative values are displayed through the comparison of one nonnegative value to another

Ordered Quad Origin (0,0,0,0) with each position representing Valued Feature 1, Valued Feature 2, Currency, and Quantity, respectively

Ordered Quads the ways we designate a four-dimensional position in ME systems as Valued Feature 1, Valued Feature 2, Currency and Quantity

Pantograph a series of linked parallelograms like those found on extendable mirrors and used extensively for N-dimensional systems

Price Gaps market regions in which no competitors have offerings concerning prices

Prime Meridian a line dividing east and west, in which positive movement in either direction is not an adverse movement in the other, often used as a standard dividing line between Value Space and Demand Planes

Producers' Limits limits regarding the minimum quantities they can make or minimum prices they can offer and still make a profit

Product Demand Curve the responsiveness of a given product in units sold relative to changes in price given all of its features

Production Possibility Curve another name for an Iso-value curve, which is a line providing the identical predicted value for different combinations of features

Profit Line a line from the intersection of a value surface and demand limit reaching down vertically to the cost for a product, representing the per-unit profit available from a given product configuration, which is a result of Financial Cat Scanning

Residuals the errors between the actual and predicted values for an estimate

South Pole Model a technique used in Hypernomics to take all of the analysis to a single location with a standard pole; at the actual South Pole, several countries have territorial claims that meet there; in Hypernomics, it is a handy place to envision many markets at the same time

Submarket one of one or more market groups that fall within a more extensive classification as a market

Sub-submarket one of one or more market groups that fall within a more significant classification as a submarket

Supply Curve, Hypernomics   a cost curve sloping downward from left to right on a two-dimensional chart with quantity on the horizontal axis and price on the vertical axis, reflecting costs fall with quantity due to learning

Supply Curve, Neoclassical   a cost curve sloping upward from left to right on a two-dimensional chart with quantity on the horizontal axis and price on the vertical axis, reflecting costs rise with quantity as it is harder to retrieve less accessible raw materials like iron ore

The Law of Value and Demand   1) features determine value, 2) value determines the price, 3) price determines quantity sold, and 4) quantity sold is a feature

The Scientific Method   a repeatable course of action in which people define a question, gather information about it, form a hypothesis, test it, collect results, analyze, and retest it until they have results to publish

Ultimate Aiming   product configuration for an eventual need, designed to hit a specific price and composition with features proven to support that price in the future

Upper Right-Hand Quadrant   a two-dimensional Cartesian Coordinate System, the region in which neoclassical economists perform analysis

Value   the sustainable price a product will fetch based on its features

Value Error Tetrahedron   the tetrahedron traced out as miss distances; it is a line drawn from one feature (as Valued Feature 1) to another (as Valued Feature 2) and another (as Valued Feature 3, in another elevation); it depicts the miss between a targeted configuration (a configuration with a specified set of features) and the actual configuration (as the actual configuration)

Value Estimating Relationship   a collective estimate made by buyers in a market about the sustainable price or value of a product based on its features

Value-Price Threshold   the point at which the value of the product meets or exceeds its price of it, as evidenced by a purchase; this varies from buyer to buyer

Value Space   a three-dimensional space consisting of two horizontal Valued Feature Axes and a single vertical currency axis

Visible Hand   the theory from Hypernomics that every good or service offered in a market creates part of its collective map, and as such, may be guided to places within that market best suited for it

References

INTRODUCTION

1. Grimm, Brothers, *Grimm's Fairy Tales: Hansel and Gretel*, George H. Doran Company, 1930.
2. Grimm, Jacob, and Wilhelm, *Little Red Cap*, retrieved July 8, 2016, from https://en.wikipedia.org/wiki/Little_Red_Riding_Hood#cite_note-20
3. hyper-, https://www.thefreedictionary.com/hyper-,thefreedictionary.com, retrieved March 27, 2023, from thefreedictionary.com
4. https://www.thefreedictionary.com/-nomics, thefreedictionary.com, retrieved March 27, 2023, from thefreedictionary.com

CHAPTER 1

1. Meece, Stephanie, A bird's eye view—of a leopard's spots. The Çatalhöyük 'map' and the development of cartographic representation in prehistory, *Anatolian Studies,* vol. 56 2006, p. 2.
2. Jacobs, Joseph, *The Story of Geographical Discovery: How the World Became Known*, E-Book 14291, 2004, retrieved April 26, 2009, from www.gutenberg.org. *Anaximander also invented the gnomon.*
3. Stamatellos, Giannis, Anaximander of Miletus, Figures 1.1 and 1.2, retrieved April 26, 2009, from http://www.philosophy.gr/presocratics/anaximander.htm. *The author permitted their use in this book.*
4. History of Cartography, retrieved April 26, 2009, from http://en.wikipedia.org/wiki/History_of_cartography
5. Dawkins, Richard, *The Blind Watchmaker,* W.W. Norton and Company, Inc., 1996 Edition, p. 113.
6. Eratosthenes (2010). Eratosthenes' "Geography," retrieved January 3, 2019, from https://commons.wikimedia.org/wiki/File:Mappa_di_Eratostene.jpg; this work is in the public domain.
7. Figure 1.5 is original artwork by the author, based on the work of René Descartes.
8. Figure 1.6 is original artwork by the author, based on the work of René Descartes.
9. von Neumann, John, "The Mathematician," in Heywood, R. B., ed., *The Works of the Mind*, University of Chicago Press, 1947, pp. 180–196. Reprinted in Bródy, F., Vámos, T., eds., *The Neumann Compendium*, World Scientific Publishing Co. Pte. Ltd., 1995, ISBN 981-02-2201-7, pp. 618–626.

10. Smith, Adam, *An Inquiry into the Nature and Causes of the Wealth of Nations*, An Electronic Classics Series Publication, 1776, pp. 364–365, italics added, as retrieved August 11, 2013, from www2.hn.psu.edu/faculty/jmanis/adam-smith/wealth-nations.pdf

11. Smith, op. cit., *The Glasgow edition*, vol. 2a, pp. 145, 158, retrieved August 11, 2013, from http://en.wikipedia.org/wiki/Adam_Smith

12. Bishop, Sereno E. (May 1884), "The equatorial smoke-stream from Krakatoa," *The Hawaiian Monthly*, vol. 1, no. 5, pp. 106–110.

13. Figure 1-7 is from NASA/Goddard Space Flight Center, 24 January 2012. This file is in the public domain in the United States because it was solely created by NASA. Retrieved September 29, 2023, from https://en.wikipedia.org/wiki/File:Aerial_Superhighway.ogv

14. Smith, Adam, *An Inquiry into the Nature and Causes of the Wealth of Nations*, An Electronic Classics Series Publication, 1776, pp. 364–365, italics added.

15. Legendre, Adrien-Marie, "Nouvelles méthodes pour la détermination des orbites des comètes (New methods for the determination of the orbits of comets)," Firmin Didot, Paris, 1805. "Sur la Méthode des moindres quarrés (On the method of least squares)," appears as an appendix to the main article, retrieved August 13, 2013, from http://en.wikipedia.org/wiki/Regression_analysis

16. Gauss, Carl Fredrich, "Theoria Motus Corporum Coelestium in Sectionibus Conicis Solem Ambientum (Rotational motion of celestial bodies in a conic section surrounding the sun)," 1809, ibid.

17. Gauss, Carl Fredrich, "Theoria combinationis observationum erroribus minimis obnoxiae (Theory of combination of observations least subject to errors)," 1821, ibid.

18. There are many types of regression analysis. We will use what mathematicians call the ordinary least squares method. Figure 1.8 shows that we will use this in single-variable linear equations and then move to single-variable power equations. Later, we will add other independent variables for broader analysis in a process denoted by multiple regression.

19. In power form regressions, these lines curve in unit space. Later, we will discover surfaces that describe regression outputs.

20. There are many figures of merit in statistics. For our purpose here, we shall use the "p-value," which represents the chance that the equation (or, as we will use it later, an independent variable in an equation) affected the outcome due to chance. Typically, if the p-value is less than 0.05, we say that the equation is statistically significant. For Figure 1.7, the p-value is 1.68E-14, meaning that the equation passes the p-value test and is statistically significant.

21. Marshall, Alfred, *Principles of Economics*, MacMillan and Company, 1890, p. iv.

22. Ibid., p. 423.

23. Ibid.

24. Jespersen, Hal, Battlefield map of Gettysburg, undated, retrieved February 2, 2016, from http://commons.wikimedia.org/wiki/File:Gettysburg_Day1_1600.png. This is free to copy, transmit and distribute the work.

25. Figure 1.10 is the original artwork from the author, based on an ATV database he created.

26. All products have at least one feature that customers find important. Most have more than one. In the market for ATVs, up to nine independent variables simultaneously determine the sustainable price.
27. Figure 1.12 is original artwork by the author.
28. NPD, "Solo Diners Represent the Largest Share of U.S. Restaurant Visits among Party Sizes," March 3, 2020, retrieved March 26, 2023, from https://www.npd .com/news/press-releases/2020/solo-diners-represent-the-largest-share-of-u-s-restaurant-visits-among-party-sizes/
29. Figure 1.13 is original artwork by the author.

CHAPTER 2

1. Snow, John, *On the Mode of Communication of Cholera, 2nd Ed*, John Churchill, New Burlington Street, London, England, 1855, retrieved September 12, 2015, from http://matrix.msu.edu/~johnsnow/images/online_companion/ chapter_images/fig12-5.jpg. This image is in the public domain due to its age, as the author died in 1858. In the same source, Snow notes:

   > There is no doubt that the mortality was much diminished, as I said before, by the flight of the population, which commenced soon after the outbreak, but the attacks had so far diminished before the use of the water was stopped, that it is impossible to decide whether the well still contained the cholera poison in an active state, or whether, from some cause, the water had become free from it.

2. Snow, John, Letter to the Editor concerning "The Cholera Near Golden Square, and at Deptford," *Medical Times and Gazette*, 9: 321–22, September 23, 1854, Figure 2.1 retrieved September 29, 2023 from https://www.wired. com/2009/09/0908london-cholera-pump/
3. Samuelson, Paul A., *Economics*, 9th Ed., McGraw Hill, 1971, p. 63.
4. Figure 2.2 comes from the Reserve Bank of Australia and through ResearchGate. It is the latter site to which the author has access and permissions, retrieved April 29, 2023, from https://www.rba.gov.au/publications/smp/2015/ feb/graphs/graph-a2.html. The artwork for the supply and demand lines and the resulting equilibrium point was overlaid by the author.
5. Wikipedia, list of production battery electric vehicles, retrieved September 5, 2013, from http://en.wikipedia.org/wiki/List_of_production_battery_electric_ vehicles
6. Wikipedia, Commuter Cars Tango, retrieved September 5, 2013, from http:// en.wikipedia.org/wiki/Commuter_Cars_Tango
7. Wikipedia, Tesla Roadster, retrieved September 5, 2013, from http://en.wikipedia .org/wiki/Tesla_Roadster
8. Wikipedia, Think City, retrieved September 5, 2013, from http://en.wikipedia .org/wiki/Think_City

9. Wikipedia, Mitsubishi i-MiEV, retrieved September 5, 2013, from http://en.wikipedia.org/wiki/Mitsubishi_i-MiEV

10. Wikipedia, Smart Electric Drive, retrieved September 5, 2013, from http://en.wikipedia.org/wiki/Smart_electric_drive

11. Wikipedia, Nissan Leaf, retrieved September 5, 2013, from http://en.wikipedia.org/wiki/Nissan_Leaf

12. Wikipedia, Chevrolet Spark, retrieved September 5, 2013, from http://www.youtube.com/watch?v=QfZISH7NHBg

13. Wikipedia, Ford Focus Electric, retrieved September 5, 2013, from http://en.wikipedia.org/wiki/Ford_Focus_Electric

14. Wikipedia, Honda Fit, retrieved September 5, 2013, from http://en.wikipedia.org/wiki/Honda_Fit

15. Wikipedia, Wheego Whip, retrieved September 5, 2013, from http://en.wikipedia.org/wiki/Wheego_Whip

16. Wikipedia, Bolloré Bluecar, retrieved September 5, 2013, from http://en.wikipedia.org/wiki/Bollor%C3%A9_Bluecar

17. Wikipedia, BYD e6, retrieved September 5, 2013, from http://en.wikipedia.org/wiki/BYD_e6

18. Wikipedia, Renault Fluence Z.E., retrieved September 5, 2013, from http://en.wikipedia.org/wiki/Renault_Fluence_Z.E.

19. The author estimated sales quantities and five-year prices based on the preceding websites associated with their manufacturers.

20. Table 2.1 is original artwork by the author.

21. Roth, Hans (2011-03), *Das erste vierrädrige Elektroauto der Welt* [*The first four-wheeled electric car in the world*] (in German), pp. 2–3, retrieved September 5, 2013, from http://en.wikipedia.org/wiki/Electric_car

22. http://oica.net/category/production-statistics/, retrieved September 5, 2013, from http://en.wikipedia.org/wiki/Automotive_industry

23. Table 2.1 is original artwork by the author.

24. Figure 2.3 is original artwork by the author

25. Figure 2.4 is original artwork by the author.

26. Figure 2.5 is original artwork by the author.

27. Table 2.2 is original artwork by the author.

28. Figure 2.6 is original artwork by the author.

29. Figure 2.7 is original artwork by the author.

30. Figure 2.8 depicts the territorial claims in Antarctica. This file is licensed under the Creative Commons Attribution—Share Alike 2.5 Generic license, retrieved April 27, 2023, from https://en.wikipedia.org/wiki/Territorial_claims_in_Antarctica

31. Figure 2.9, Spindler, Bill, U.S. Antarctic Program, National Science Foundation. This image is a work of a National Science Foundation employee, taken or made as part of that person's official duties. As a work of the U.S. federal government, the image is in the public domain, retrieved April 27, 2023, from https://commons.wikimedia.org/wiki/File:Amundsen-scott-south_pole_station_2007.jpg

32. Figure 2.10, McCranie, Judson Photograph of Elvis Presley's birth house in Tupelo, Mississippi, October 25, 2018. This file is licensed under the Creative Commons Attribution—Share Alike 3.0 Unported license, retrieved April 27, 2023, from

https://commons.wikimedia.org/wiki/File:Elvis_Presley_Birthplace,_Tupelo,_MS,_US_(04).jpg

33. Figure 2.11 is Meagan Swanson, the author's daughter. This picture is used with her permission.
34. Figure 2.12 is Meagan Swanson, the author's daughter. This picture is used with her permission.
35. Figure 2.13 is original artwork by the author.
36. Figure 2.14 is from Zasadni, Jerzy, Hand-made raised-relief map of the High Tatras, November 27, 2007. Permission is granted to copy, distribute and/or modify this document under the terms of the GNU Free Documentation License, Version 1.2, or any later version published by the Free Software Foundation, retrieved April 28, 2023, from https://en.wikipedia.org/wiki/Raised-relief_map#/media/File:Tatry_Mapa_Plastyczna.JPG
37. Figure 2.15 is from NordNordWest, July 4, 2008. Permission is granted to copy, distribute and/or modify this document under the terms of the GNU Free Documentation License, Version 1.2, or any later version published by the Free Software Foundation, retrieved April 28, 2023, from https://commons.wikimedia.org/wiki/File:100_montaditos_footprint_in_Spain_and_Andorra.png
38. Figure 2.16 is original artwork by the author, overlaid on the material from Figure 2.14 and Figure 2.15.
39. Figure 2.17 is original artwork by the author.
40. Figure 2.18 is a picture of the author's daughter, Meagan Swanson, with his artwork overlaid on a photograph from Amble, The South Pole geographic marker in January 2010, with the elevated station "beer can" and galley. Power plant and satellite communications facility in the background, January 18, 2010, retrieved April 29, 2023, from https://commons.wikimedia.org/wiki/File:South_pole_geographic_el_station.jpg. Figure 2.17 to Figure 2.20 all use this picture in the background.
41. Figure 2.19 is a picture of the author's daughter, Meagan Swanson, with his artwork overlaid.
42. Figure 2.20 is original artwork by the author.
43. Figure 2.21 is original artwork by the author.
44. Figure 2.22 is original artwork by the author.
45. Figure 2.23 is original artwork by the author.
46. Figure 2.24 is original artwork by the author.
47. Table 2.3 is original artwork by the author.
48. Figure 2.25 is original artwork by the author.
49. *Figure 2.26 is from Hill, John, a photo of an ancient ruler from Shaanxi History Museum*, Xi'an, June 29, 2011, retrieved April 29, 2023, from https://commons.wikimedia.org/wiki/File:Gilded_Bronze_Ruler_-_1_chi_%3D_231_cm._Western_Han_(206_BCE_-_CE_8)._Hanzhong_City.jpg
50. Figure 2.27, ibid.
51. This is the first definition of the word "dimension" from thefreedictionary.com.
52. This is definition 4a of "dimension" from thefreedictionary.com.
53. Figure 2.28, 4D model from Hypernomics, Inc., retrieved April 29, 2023.
54. Figure 2.29, ibid.
55. Figure 2.30 is a picture of the Prime Meridian at the Naval Observatory in Greenwich, UK, overlaid with a photograph of his daughter, Meagan Swanson.

CHAPTER 3

1. NASA/JPL CNEOS. January 6, 2019, discovery statistics, retrieved May 4, 2023, from https://en.wikipedia.org/wiki/Near-Earth_object
2. Yeung, Bill, and Denny, Bob, J002E3 discovery images taken by Bill Yeung on September 3, 2002. J002E3 is in the circle, retrieved May 4, 2023, from https://cneos.jpl.nasa.gov/images/j002e3/yeung.gif
3. Information on J002E3 retrieved May 4, 2023, from https://en.wikipedia.org/wiki/J002E3
4. NASA Press Release 22-105, "NASA Confirms DART Mission Impact Changed Asteroid's Motion in Space," October 11, 2022, retrieved May 4, 2023, from https://www.nasa.gov/press-release/nasa-confirms-dart-mission-impact-changed-asteroid-s-motion-in-space
5. Jespersen, Hal, Figure 3.2 Battlefield map of Gettysburg Day 1, undated, www.posix.com/CW, retrieved May 4, 2023, from https://commons.wikimedia.org/wiki/File:Gettysburg_Day1_1600.png
6. Jespersen, Hal, Figure 3.3 Battlefield map of Gettysburg Day 2, 10 July 2010, www.posix.com/CW, retrieved May 4, 2023, from https://en.wikipedia.org/wiki/Battle_of_Gettysburg,_second_day#/media/File:Gettysburg_Battle_Map_Day2.png
7. Jespersen, Hal, Figure 3.4 Battlefield map of Gettysburg Day 3, 29 March 2006, retrieved May 4, 2023, from www.posix.com/CW
8. Table 3.1 uses the data from notes 5–19 in Chapter 2.
9. Figure 3.5 is original artwork by the author, based on the data in Table 3.1.
10. Figure 3.6 is original artwork by the author, based on the data in Table 3.1.
11. Figure 3.7 is original artwork by the author, based on the data in Table 3.1.
12. For more on Think Global, see http://en.wikipedia.org/wiki/Think_Global
13. Figure 3.8 is original artwork by the author, based on the data in Table 3.1.
14. Figure 3.9 is original artwork by the author, based on the data in Table 3.1.
15. Figure 3.10 is original artwork by the author, based on the data in Table 3.1.
16. Figure 3.11 is original artwork by the author, based on the data in Table 3.1.
17. The p-values, or likelihood that the curves shown are due to chance, is 0.0195 for 2012 and 0.00746 for 2013. The typical threshold for the p-value is 0.05; if a p-value is above that level, we should accept the null hypothesis, below that threshold, we do not accept it. Thus, we reject the null hypothesis and may accept the proposition that both lines represent aggregate demand for their respective years.
18. Plutarch (trans. John Dryden), *Pyrrhus*, hosted on The Internet Classics Archive, retrieved October 13, 2013, from http://en.wikipedia.org/wiki/Pyrrhic_victory
19. Figure 3.12 is original artwork by the author, based on Table 3.1.

CHAPTER 4

1. Heights displayed for random males and females come from Schilling, Mark F., Watkins, Ann E., and Watkins, William, "Is Human Height Bimodal?" *The American Statistician*, vol. 56, no. 3 (August 2002), pp. 223–229, retrieved September 28, 2015, from http://faculty.washington.edu/tamre/IsHumanHeightBimodal.pdf.

This paper cited this data as its source: U.S. Census Bureau (1999), Statistical Abstract of the United States: 1999. Table #243, p. 155. The source of the table: U.S. National Center for Health Statistics, unpublished data. Data reorganized from U.S. Department of Health and Human Services (DHHS), National Center for Health Statistics, Third National Health, and Nutrition Examination Survey, 1988–1994, NHANES III Laboratory Data File. Public Use Data File Documentation Number 76200. Hyattsville, MD: Centers for Disease Control and Prevention, 1996. Wand. M. P. (1997), "Data-Based Choice of Histogram Bin Width," The U.S. Census Bureau (1999), Statistical Abstract of the United States: 1999. Table #243, p. 155.

2. Figure 4.1 is original artwork by the author, based on the data from preceding note 1.
3. Watkins and Watkins, op. cit.
4. Figure 4.2 is original artwork by the author, based on the data from preceding note 1.
5. NBA All-Star player heights retrieved September 28, 2015, from http://www.nba-allstar.com/players/lists/players-by-height.htm
6. Figure 4.3 is original artwork by the author, based on the data offered from preceding notes 1 through 3.
7. Schilling, et al., op. cit.
8. Figure 4.4 is original artwork by the author, based on the data offered from preceding note 1.
9. Figure 4.5 is original artwork by the author, based on the data offered from preceding note 1.
10. Bentham, Jeremy, "On the Greatest Good for the Greatest Number," from an unpublished article, as found in *The Classical Utilitarians: Bentham and Mill*, edited by John Troyer, Hackett Publishing Company, 2003, p. 92.
11. On the other hand, if you are manic-depressive and are in the high phase, any amount of utils may make you positively ecstatic.
12. Jagger, Mick and Richards, Keith, "(I Can't Get No) Satisfaction," from the album *Out of Our Heads,* Decca Records, 1965.
13. The story of Mick Jagger's purchase and subsequent crash of his Aston Martin DB6 may be found here at this site, retrieved May 9, 2023, from https://www.hotcars.com/the-true-story-of-mick-jagger-crashing-his-db6-in-london/
14. According to the University of British Columbia, in 1966, 1 British Pound equaled \$2.80 U.S. Dollars, according to this website retrieved September 23, 2015, from http://fx.sauder.ubc.ca/etc/GBPpages.pdf
15. The U.S. Bureau of Labor Statistics indicates that \$1.00 in July 1966 (Consumer Price Index [CPI] value of 32.7) is worth \$9.23 as of March 2023 (301.836; $301.836/32.7 = 9.23. 9.23 * \$2.80/\pounds * \pounds25,000 = \$646,132$, which rounds to \$646K). Retrieved May 11, 2023, from https://www.bls.gov/cpi/tables/supplemental-files/historical-cpi-u-202303.pdf
16. Figure 4.6 is original artwork by the author.
17. Figure 4.7 is original artwork by the author.

18. There are many important exceptions to freedom of supplier choice relative to product features. Producers of automobiles, for example, cannot sell a family car that takes up the equivalent of two lanes of traffic, nor can train manufacturers sell locomotives that require a type of track that no one uses.

19. Independent variables are values that determine the value of other dependent variables.

20. Dependent variables are changeable amounts determined by one or more other inputs, known as independent variables, for their value.

21. The Dark Heart of the Milky Way, a press release from The Royal Swedish Academy of the Sciences, retrieved October 28, 2012, from http://www.kva.se/Documents/Priser/Crafoord/2012/pop_crafoord_astro_en_2012.pdf

22. Descriptions of the scientific method abound. This Wikipedia article, retrieved October 28, 2012, provides a good introduction, http://en.wikipedia.org/wiki/Scientific_method#cite_note-46

23. List of production battery electric vehicles, retrieved September 5, 2013, from http://en.wikipedia.org/wiki/List_of_production_battery_electric_vehicles

24. Commuter Cars Tango, retrieved September 5, 2013, from http://en.wikipedia.org/wiki/Commuter_Cars_Tango

25. Mitsubishi i-MiEV, retrieved September 5, 2013, from http://en.wikipedia.org/wiki/Mitsubishi_i-MiEV

26. Smart Electric Drive, retrieved September 5, 2013, from http://en.wikipedia.org/wiki/Smart_electric_drive

27. Nissan Leaf, Retrieved September 5, 2013, from http://en.wikipedia.org/wiki/Nissan_Leaf

28. Chevrolet Spark, retrieved September 5, 2013, from http://www.youtube.com/watch?v=QfZISH7NHBg

29. Ford Focus Electric, retrieved September 5, 2013, from http://en.wikipedia.org/wiki/Ford_Focus_Electric

30. Honda Fit, retrieved September 5, 2013, from http://en.wikipedia.org/wiki/Honda_Fit

31. Wheego Whip, retrieved September 5, 2013, from http://en.wikipedia.org/wiki/Wheego_Whip

32. Bolloré Bluecar, retrieved September 5, 2013, from http://en.wikipedia.org/wiki/Bollor%C3%A9_Bluecar

33. BYD e6, retrieved September 5, 2013, from http://en.wikipedia.org/wiki/BYD_e6

34. Renault Fluence Z.E., retrieved September 5, 2013, from http://en.wikipedia.org/wiki/Renault_Fluence_Z.E.

35. Renault Zoe, retrieved September 24, 2015, from https://en.wikipedia.org/wiki/Renault_Zoe

36. Tesla Model S, Model S Signature, *Model S Signature Performance*, retrieved September 24, 2015, from https://en.wikipedia.org/wiki/Tesla_Model_S

37. Toyota RAV 4EV, retrieved September 24, 2015, from https://en.wikipedia.org/wiki/Toyota_RAV4_EV

38. Roewe E50, retrieved September 24, 2015, from https://en.wikipedia.org/wiki/Roewe_E50

39. Fiat 500e, retrieved September 24, 2015, from https://en.wikipedia.org/wiki/Fiat_500_(2007)#Fiat_500e_.282013-.29

40. Table 4.1 is original artwork by the author, based on preceding notes 23–39. The author estimates sales quantities and five-year prices based on the websites associated with their manufacturers, which then included replacement battery costs.

41. Figure 4.8 is original artwork by the author, based on the data from preceding notes 3 to 39. We find this "line of best fit" using *linear regression*. Several textbooks and websites address this process in detail.

42. Figure 4.9 is original artwork by the author, based on the data from preceding notes 23 to 39. This line is statistically significant. It has a "p-value" of 6.1E-07. (The p-value tests an independent variable's impact upon a dependent variable. A p-value less than 0.05 indicates strong evidence against the null hypothesis. Since that applies here, we reject the null hypothesis and accept the hypothesis that horsepower influences price.)

43. Figure 4.10 is original artwork by the author, based on the data from preceding notes 23 to 39. This is original artwork by the author, based on the analysis. This equation has an adjusted R^2 of 50.8% and a p-value of 0.0009.

44. Figure 4.11 is original artwork by the author, based on the data from preceding notes 23 to 39.

45. United Parcel Service (UPS) domestic rates for the United States, January 2010, as retrieved January 15, 2010, from http://www.ups.com/media/en/af_zones_rates_upc.pdf

46. UPS Zone list for the U.S. Zip Codes 910XX, Retrieved January 15, 2010, from http://www.ups.com/content/us/en/shipping/cost/zones/continental_us.html

47. Air miles from Los Angeles International Airport (LAX) to cities in different UPS zones retrieved January 15, 2010, from http://www.travelmath.com/flight-distance/from/LAX/to/

48. Figure 4.12 is original artwork from the author, based on preceding notes 45 to 47.

49. Figure 4.13 is original artwork from the author.

50. "Standard deviation is a number used to tell how measurements for a group are spread out from the average (mean) or expected value. A low standard deviation means that most of the numbers are very close to the average. A high standard deviation means that the numbers are spread out," retrieved September 25, 2015, from https://simple.wikipedia.org/wiki/Standard_deviation

51. Hypernomics, Inc. (previously, MEE Inc.), "2014–2015 Civil Helicopter Report," 2014, page 16, permitted the author to use this report, found here http://www.meevaluators.com/Store/MarketReportsAndDatabases/CivilHelicopters/CivilHelicopterComplete/index.html

52. Top five rows are wholesale ground beef prices retrieved January 8, 2012, from http://www.beefretail.org/CMDocs/BeefRetail/WholesalePrice/Wholesale%20Pricing%20Chart%20123011.pdf

53. Bottom 15 rows are retail prices for ground beef, retrieved January 8, 2013, *from Walmart Supercenter 3523, 26471 Carl Boyer Drive*, Santa Clarita, CA 91350.

54. Table 4.2 is original artwork by the author, based on data from preceding notes 52 and 53.
55. Figure 4.15 is original artwork by the author, based on data from preceding notes 52 and 53.
56. Figure 4.16 is original artwork by the author.
57. Howarth, Douglas K., "Business Model for Successful Commercialization of Aircraft Designs," *presented at the 2011 SAE Aerotech Congress and Exhibition*, Toulouse, France, October 18, 2011, doi:10.4271/2011-01-2502, 16 pages, http://papers.sae.org/2011-01-2502
58. Aboulafia, Richard, "Eclipse Aviation Eclipse Series," October 2008, published by The Teal Group, retrieved September 26, 2015, from http://download.aopa.org/epilot/2008/eclipse1008.pdf
59. George, Fred, "Pilot Report: Eclipse 550," *Aviation Week online*, August 1, 2014, retrieved September 26, 2015, from http://aviationweek.com/business-aviation/pilot-report-eclipse-550
60. Haines, Thomas B., "Turbine Pilot: Eclipse 500: Typed and Tried," Aircraft Owners and Pilots Association (AOPA) online, *August* 1, 2008, retrieved September 26, 2015, from http://www.aopa.org/News-and-Video/All-News/2008/August/1/Turbine-Pilot-Eclipse-500-Typed-and-Tried
61. Ibid.
62. Customers care instead for the product's features and make their decisions based on them. Producer costs do not influence them.
63. Greenhill, Jim, Sgt. 1st Class, 21 March 2017, took this photograph of Rocky Bleier.
64. Details about Rocky Bleier's story come from https://en.wikipedia.org/wiki/Rocky_Bleier, retrieved June 22, 2023.
65. Ibid.
66. The story about Rocky Bleier's 40-yard dash improvement retrieved June 22, 2023, from https://www.steelernation.com/rocky-bleier-was-told-hed-never-play-football-again-he-thought-otherwise
67. Data forming the equations used for Figures 4.18 and 4.19 retrieved July 20, 2020, from https://www.pro-football-reference.com/years/2019/receiving.htm
68. Figures 4.18 and 4.19 use the same equation. It has p-values of 6.43E-07, 0.41%, and 3.6% for catches/game, age, and 40-yard times, in that order, and 2.32E-06 for the entire equation.
69. Figure 4.18 is original artwork by the author.
70. Figure 4.19 is original artwork by the author.

CHAPTER 5

1. Map of Melbourne, Florida, retrieved October 3, 2015, from https://www.google.com/maps/place/Melbourne,+FL/@28.1174805,-80.6552775,12z/data=!3m1!4b1!4m2!3m1!1s0x88de0e2c4771994d:0x8bcdb254a90cd2a8
2. From J. Reynolds, Allen L. Churchill, Francis Trevelyan Miller (eds.), *The Story of the Great War, Volume V*. New York. The specified year is 1916, more likely 1917 or 1918. Map of the 2016 Western Front, retrieved October 3, 2015, from

https://upload.wikimedia.org/wikipedia/commons/thumb/9/97/Western_front_August_1916.jpg/441px-Western_front_August_1916.jpg

3. Boeing B-52H data retrieved December 31, 2021, from http://en.wikipedia.org/wiki/Boeing_B-52_Stratofortress

4. Rockwell (now Boeing) B-1B data retrieved December 31, 2021, from https://en.wikipedia.org/wiki/Rockwell_B-1_Lancer#B-1B_program

5. McDonnell Douglas (now Boeing) AV-8B data retrieved December 31, 2021, from http://en.wikipedia.org/wiki/AV-8#cite_note-Remanufacture_scrapping-5

6. McDonnell Douglas (now Boeing), F/A-18A-D data retrieved December 31, 2021, from http://en.wikipedia.org/wiki/McDonnell_Douglas_F/A-18_Hornet

7. McDonnell Douglas (now Boeing), F/A-18E/F data retrieved December 31, 2021, from http://www.boeing.com/defense-space/military/fa18ef/docs/EF_overview.pdf

8. F/A-18A-D production delivery data from *Jane's All the World's Aircraft Development and Production 2013–2014*, p. 720, retrieved December 31, 2021.

9. McDonnell Douglas (now Boeing) F-15E data retrieved December 31, 2021, from http://www.fas.org/man/dod-101/sys/ac/f-15.htm

10. F-15E production delivery data from 1996 and 2006 retrieved December 31, 2021, from http://tealgroup.com/images/TGCTOC/sample-wmcab2.pdf.

11. Lockheed (now Lockheed Martin) F-117A data retrieved December 31, 2021, from http://en.wikipedia.org/wiki/F-117_Nighthawk

12. General Dynamics (now Lockheed Martin), F-16A/D data retrieved December 31, 2021, from http://en.wikipedia.org/wiki/F-16

13. General Dynamics (now Lockheed Martin), F-16A/D 1996 delivery data extrapolated from https://www.codeonemagazine.com/article.html?item_id=141, which stated that the 1572nd delivery was made by July 11, 1986, the 2500th unit was delivered December 7, 1989, and the 3500th unit delivered April 27, 1995. *The author extrapolated to the year-end* 1996.

14. Lockheed Martin F-22 data retrieved December 31, 2021, from http://en.wikipedia.org/wiki/F-22

15. Northrop Grumman B-2 data retrieved December 31, 2021, from http://en.wikipedia.org/wiki/B-2

16. Northrop Grumman B-2 1996 delivery data retrieved December 31, 2021, from https://www.globalsecurity.org/wmd/systems/b-2-production.htm

17. Grumman (now Northrop Grumman) A-6 data retrieved December 31, 2021, from http://en.wikipedia.org/wiki/A-6_Intruder

18. Fairchild Republic A-10 data retrieved December 31, 2021, from https://en.wikipedia.org/wiki/Fairchild_Republic_A-10_Thunderbolt_II

19. Grumman (now Northrop Grumman) F-14 data retrieved December 31, 2021, from http://en.wikipedia.org/wiki/F-14

20. General Dynamics (now Lockheed Martin) F-111 data retrieved December 31, 2021, from http://en.wikipedia.org/wiki/F-111

21. McDonnell Douglas (now Boeing) F-4 data retrieved December 31, 2021, from http://en.wikipedia.org/wiki/F-4

22. Ling-Temco-Vought (LTV) A-7 data retrieved December 31, 2021, from http://en.wikipedia.org/wiki/A-7_Corsair_II

23. Vought F-8 data retrieved December 31, 2021, from http://en.wikipedia.org/wiki/F-8

24. Douglas (later McDonnell Douglas) A-4 8 data retrieved December 31, 2021, from http://en.wikipedia.org/wiki/Douglas_A-4_Skyhawk

25. Northrop F-5 data retrieved December 31, 2021, from http://en.wikipedia.org/wiki/Northrop_F-5

26. Lockheed Martin F-35A data retrieved December 31, 2021, from https://en.wikipedia.org/wiki/Lockheed_Martin_F-35_Lightning_II

27. Ibid.

28. Ibid.

29. General Atomics MQ-9 data retrieved December 31, 2021, from https://en.wikipedia.org/wiki/General_Atomics_MQ-9_Reaper

30. General Atomics MQ-1 data retrieved December 31, 2021, from https://en.wikipedia.org/wiki/General_Atomics_MQ-1_Predator

31. Table 5.1 is original artwork by the author, based on the data from preceding notes 3–30.

32. Figure 5.3 is original artwork by the author, based on the data from preceding notes 3–30.

33. Figure 5.4 is original artwork by the author, based on the data from preceding notes 3–30.

34. The 2021 Demand Frontier equation has an adjusted R^2 of 98.7% and a p-value of 5.30E-08, while the one for 1996 had an adjusted R^2 of 97.7% and a p-value of 2.38E-06. These lines are "log-linear" curves, which appear straight in charts in which the axes are of the "log-log" type, meaning that the major divisions of its axes go up by powers of 10. If we instead plotted this data on a chart with linear scales on both axes, they would display as a curve.

35. Figure 5.5 is original artwork by the author, based on the data from preceding notes 3–30.

36. Figure 5.6 is original artwork by the author, based on the data from preceding notes 3–30.

37. U.S. Government Accounting Office (US GAO), "Strategic Bombers: B-2 Program Status and Current Issues," *GAO/NSIAD-90-120*, February 22, 1990.

38. Howarth, D., "What DAIV (Demand as an Independent Variable) Says about Your Market," *SAE Int. J. Aerosp.* vol. 6, no. 2, 616–625, 2013, doi:10.4271/2013-01-2239. Here, we show the Demand Frontier with the B-2 as a part of it. This begs the question of whether the Demand Frontier would be the same without it. The analysis indicates that removing the B-2 and the next most expensive model, the B-1B, has little effect on the slope of this curve.

39. US GAO, "Joint Strike Fighter: [Department of Defense] DOD Actions Needed to Further Enhance Restructuring and Address Affordability Risks," GAO-12-437, June 2012.

40. Howarth, op cit. The chance of Lockheed Martin selling 2457 F-35s to the U.S. government at $139 million (in 2013 currency) is much less than one in a thousand.

41. This curve has an R^2 of 99.4%.

42. Figure 5.7 is original artwork by the author, based on the data in preceding notes 3–30.

43. The data dictates the choice and placement of bins. While no one offers hard and fast binning rules, some guidelines exist. First, the number of bins should typically be a whole number between the fourth and square root of the number of observations. In this case, the fourth root of the number of observations (24) is 2.21 (which we could round to 2), while the square root is 4.89, which rounds to 5. You will notice here that we have three bins. Second, for binning to work (i.e., to generate a statistically valuable result), we need more observations in the lower than upper bins.

44. Nearly all the demand curves examined by the author have better correlations using power equations than linear ones. The exponent here is -0.59, greater than -1.0, meaning there is more money in the lower bins than the higher ones.

45. We will see some steeper demand curves later.

46. Figure 5.8 is original artwork by the author, based on the data from Table 5.1.

47. Figure 5.9 is original artwork by the author, based on the data from Table 5.1.

48. Figure 5.10 is original artwork by the author, based on the data from Table 5.1.

49. In 1991, the U.S. Secretary of Defense, Dick Cheney, canceled the A-12 Avenger II program for a breach of contract. For more information, see this site retrieved October 7, 2015, from https://en.wikipedia.org/wiki/McDonnell_Douglas_A-12_Avenger_II

50. Northrop funded the F-20 Tigershark itself, hoping to win domestic and foreign contracts. It won neither. You can find out more about this program from this site retrieved October 7, 2015, from https://en.wikipedia.org/wiki/Northrop_F-20_Tigershark

51. This model proved too expensive, and President Kennedy canceled it. For additional reading, see this site retrieved October 7, 2015, from https://en.wikipedia.org/wiki/North_American_XB-70_Valkyrie

52. Figure 5.11 is the original artwork by the author, based on the S&P 500 data on July 6, 2021.

53. Figure 5.12 is original artwork by the author.

54. Figure 5.13 is original artwork by the author.

55. Figure 5.14 is original artwork by the author.

56. Figure 5.15 is original artwork by the author.

57. Figure 5.16 is original artwork by the author.

58. Howarth, D., "What DAIV (Demand as an Independent Variable) Says about Your Market," *SAE Int. J. Aerosp.* 6(2): 616–625, 2013, doi:10.4271/2013-01-2239

59. U.S. currency sizes retrieved June 21, 2023, from https://www.thecoldwire.com/are-all-100-dollar-bills-the-same-size/

60. Currency sizes for the European Union retrieved June 21, 2023, from https://en.wikipedia.org/wiki/Euro_banknotes#:~:text=The%20euro%20banknotes%20are%20pure,a%20variety%20of%20color%20schemes

61. M-1 money supply definition retrieved on July 12, 2019, from https://simple.wikipedia.org/wiki/Money_supply

62. The exchange rate definition retrieved on July 12, 2019, from https://simple .wikipedia.org/wiki/Exchange_rate

63. Inflation rate definition retrieved on July 12, 2019, from https://simple.wikipedia .org/wiki/Inflation

64. Foreign Exchange Reserves definition retrieved on July 12, 2019, from https://www .thestreet.com/dictionary/f/foreign-exchange-reserves#:~:text=Foreign%20 exchange%20reserves%20are%20a,be%20easily%20turned%20into%20 cash

65. The M-1 money supply figures for Tables 5.2, 5.3, and 5.4 were retrieved on July 12, 2019, from https://tradingeconomics.com/country-list/money-supply-m1

66. Figures 5.17, 5.18, and 5.19 use each country's exchange rate against the U.S. Dollar (USD), which is information that changes constantly, data retrieved on July 12, 2019, from https://www.exchangerates.org.uk/US-Dollar-USD-currency-table.html

67. The foreign-exchange reserves are given in the equivalent Value in USD and were retrieved for Figures 5.17, 5.18, and 5.19 on July 12, 2019, from https:// en.wikipedia.org/wiki/List_of_countries_by_foreign-exchange_reserves

68. Inflation rates in Figures 5.17, 5.18, and 5.19 were retrieved on July 12, 2019, from https://tradingeconomics.com/country-list/inflation-rate?continent=world

69. Figure 5.17 is original artwork by the author, based on the data from References 61-64.

70. Figure 5.18 is original artwork by the author, based on the data from References 61-64. While the statistics for this analysis are significant (p-values of 3.30E-12 for the equation, 4.96% for Prime, 3.06E-12 for Volume, 0.01% for Foreign Exchange Reserves), the Mean Absolute Percentage Error (MAPE) is high, at 117.5%, meaning there is more work needed to decompose this market.

71. Figure 5.19 is original artwork by the author, based on the data from References 61-64.

72. Figure 5.20 is original artwork by the author, based on the data from Tables 5.2, 5.3, and 5.4, plus cryptocurrency data retrieved August 1, 2019, from https:// finance.yahoo.com/cryptocurrencies

73. Figure 5.21 is original artwork by the author, using the sources for Figures 5-17, 5-18, and 5-19.

74. Figure 5.22 is original artwork by the author, using the sources for Figures 5-17, 5-18, and 5-19.

75. Figure 5.23 is original artwork by the author. While the statistics for this analysis are significant (p-values of 3.30E-12 for the equation, 4.96% for Prime, 3.06E-12 for Volume, 0.01% for Foreign Exchange Reserves), the Mean Absolute Percentage Error (MAPE) is high, at 117.5%, meaning there is more work needed to decompose this market. Figure 5-23's analysis also applies to Figure 5-24. Note that the values in the tables above have changed since the analysis was performed, thus changing results.

76. Figure 5.24 is original artwork done by the author.

77. Figure 5.25 is original artwork done by the author.

CHAPTER 6

1. Historic beef prices from the U.S. Department of Agriculture retrieved December 6, 2015, from http://www.ers.usda.gov/data/foodconsumption/ FoodAvailSpreadsheets.htm#mtredsu

2. Figure 6.1 is original artwork by the author, based on the data from preceding note 1.

3. McConnell, Campbell R., and Brue, Samuel L, *Economics: Principles, Problems, and Policies,* Seventeenth Edition, McGraw-Hill/Irwin, 2008, p. 63.

4. Minkow, N. *Gregory,* Principles of Economics, Fourth Edition, Thomsen South-Western, 2007, p. 75.

5. Samuelson, Paul A., and Nordhaus, William D., *Economics,* Sixteenth Edition, Irwin McGraw-Hill, 1998, p. 52.

6. Original artwork by the author based on the data from preceding notes 3, 4, and 5. All three books in those references describe equilibrium in nearly identical ways.

7. Samuelson, Paul A., and Nordhaus, William D., op. cit., p. 48. The previously cited McConnell/Brue and Minkew books have essentially the same descriptions on p. 50 and p. 71, respectively.

8. Samuelson, Paul A., and Nordhaus, William D., op. cit., p. 27, with the italics offered in the citation. The previously cited McConnell/Brue and Minkew books have primarily the same descriptions on p. 53 and p. 75, respectively.

9. All textbooks for introductory market economics address some additional conditions about shifts in the supply and demand curves or both. We need not address these elements for our purposes, as we will find that the Law of Value and Demand can address all market conditions more thoroughly and precisely.

10. Figure 6.3's average price is drawn from the data in Table 4.2.

11. Figure 6.3 is original artwork by the author, based on the data from Table 4.2.

12. Data from Figure 4.12.

13. Figure 6.4 is original artwork by the author, based on the data from Figure 4.12.

14. A notable exception to this rule applies to government agencies. Many make it their business only to allow a sure profit (called a fee) above cost.

15. Retrieved May 27, 2023, from https://www.researchgate.net/figure/Cost-curve-for-global-iron-ore-mines-Cost-per-tonne-US-t-iron-ore-62-equivalent-CFR_fig15_260871377

16. Swanson's Law is named after Robert Swanson, the founder of SunPower, a solar power manufacturer. Here is a graph for solar photovoltaic modules' prices over nearly 40 years, retrieved December 9, 2015, from https://en.wikipedia.org/wiki/Swanson%27s_law

17. Wright, T.P. "Factors affecting the costs of airplanes." *Journal of the Aeronautical Sciences* 3: 122–128,193, doi:10.2514/8.155. Most experts attribute the initial discovery of the learning or experience curve to T. P. Wright. For a link to this work, see this one retrieved December 9, 2015, https://en.wikipedia.org/wiki/Swanson%27s_law

18. Abernathy, William, *Productivity Dilemma: Roadblock to Innovation in the Automobile,* The Johns Hopkins University Press, 1978, 279, ISBN-13: 978-0801820816.

19. Ford Model T history retrieved May 27, 2023, from https://en.wikipedia.org/wiki/Ford_Model_T
20. Table 6.1 is original artwork by the author.
21. As of this writing, and for roughly the past couple of decades, a popular expression states that an individual may be "facing a steep learning curve." The typical implication of this phrase is, in the speaker's mind, supposed to convey a huge task looming before the individual in question, one fraught with difficulty that could take much time to master. In reality, however, steep learning curves mean that people performing a task learn quickly and rapidly, reducing their time to perform the job in shorter order.
22. Howarth, D., "What DAIV (Demand as an Independent Variable) Says about Your Market," *SAE Int. J. Aerosp.* 6(2): 616–625, 2013, doi:10.4271/2013-01-2239
23. U.S. Government Accounting Office (USGAO), "Strategic Bombers: B-2 Program Status and Current Issues," February 1990. NSAID-90-120: Published: February 22, 1990. *Publicly Released: February* 22, 1990. Retrieved December 22, 2015, from http://www.gao.gov/products/NSIAD-90-120
24. Figure 6.8 is original artwork by the author.
25. Figure 6.9 is original artwork by the author.
26. Statistics on clothing price indices retrieved December 22, 2015, from the U.S. Bureau of Labor Statistics (USBLS), http://www.bls.gov/spotlight/2012/fashion/
27. Figure 6.10 is original artwork by the author based on the cited BLS data.
28. Ibid.
29. Figure 6.11 is original artwork by the author, based on the cited BLS data.
30. See this site retrieved May 29, 2023, from https://en.wikipedia.org/wiki/Aerion_AS2
31. https://en.wikipedia.org/wiki/Concorde
32. Figure 6.12 is original artwork by the author, based on data and analysis the author performed on the market for business aircraft in December 2015. Various sources are available on request.
33. Figure 6.13 is original artwork by the author.

CHAPTER 7

1. Benzoni, Girolamo (1565), *Historia del Mondo Nuovo;* Venice. English version *History of the New World* by Girolamo Benzoni, Hakluyt Society, London, 1857, retrieved December 28, 2015, from https://en.wikipedia.org/wiki/Egg_of_Columbus
2. *Columbus Breaking the Egg,* by William Hogarth, retrieved December 28, 2015, from https://en.wikipedia.org/wiki/Egg_of_Columbus
3. Columbus, Christopher, *Book of Prophecies*, retrieved December 28, 2015, from https://www.studentnewsdaily.com/daily-news-article/christopher-columbus-in-his-own-words1/
4. "Viajes de colon en" by Viajes_de_colon.svg: Phirosiberiaderivative work: Phirosiberia (talk)—Viajes_de_colon.svg. Retrieved December 29, 2015, and Licensed under CC BY-SA 3.0 via Commons, https://commons.wikimedia.org/wiki/File:Viajes_de_colon_en.svg#/media/File:Viajes_de_colon_en.svg

5. Johnson, George, "How Many People Ever Lived?" *Discover Magazine,* August 11, 2013, retrieved December 28, 2015, from http://blogs.discover-magazine.com/fire-in-the-mind/2013/08/11/how-many-people-ever-lived/#.VoICXPkrKUk

6. Haub, Carl, "How Many People Have Ever Lived on Earth?" *Population Reference Bureau,* October 2011, retrieved December 28, 2015, from http://www.prb.org/Publications/Articles/2002/HowManyPeopleHaveEverLivedonEarth.aspx

7. Roberts, Charles Henry, 1914, Map of the *Cherokee Outlet in Figure* 7.3 retrieved May 30, 2023, from https://upload.wikimedia.org/wikipedia/commons/thumb/1/12/Map_of_Cherokee_Outlet.pdf/page1-1280px-Map_of_Cherokee_Outlet.pdf.jpg

8. Figure 7.4, ibid.

9. Original artwork overlays in Figure 7.4 by the author.

10. "Rain Follows the Plow," an article retrieved December 31, 2015, from https://en.wikipedia.org/wiki/Rain_follows_the_plow#cite_note-1

11. Dust Bowl map in Figure 7.5 retrieved May 30, 2023, from https://upload.wikimedia.org/wikipedia/commons/thumb/e/ed/Map_of_states_and_counties_affected_by_the_Dust_Bowl%2C_sourced_from_US_federal_government_dept._%28NRCS_SSRA-RAD%29.svg/2236px-Map_of_states_and_counties_affected_by_the_Dust_Bowl%2C_sourced_from_US_federal_government_dept._%28NRCS_SSRA-RAD%29.svg.png

12. Dobrzański, Krzysztof, August 22, 2010, *Aviat Husky photograph in Figure* 7.6 retrieved May 30, 2023, from https://commons.wikimedia.org/wiki/File:Aviat_A-1_Husky_Turbia_(4956636425).jpg

13. Figure 7.7 is original artwork by the author, a sample database available on request.

14. Figure 7.8 is original artwork by the author; the sample database is available on request.

15. Figure 7.9 is original artwork by the author, a sample database available on request.

16. Figure 7.10 is original artwork by the author, a sample database available on request.

17. Definition of *tomography*, retrieved January 2, 2016, from http://www.thefreedictionary.com/tomography

18. Figure 7.11 is a CT scan of a human head, retrieved January 2, 2016, from Computed Tomography of the human brain—large" by the Department of Radiology, Uppsala University Hospital. *Uploaded by Mikael Häggström,* March 23, 2007. Licensed under CC0 via Common, https://commons.wikimedia.org/wiki/File:Computed_tomography_of_human_brain_-_large.png#/media/File:Computed_tomography_of_human_brain_-_large.png

19. Figure 7.12 is original artwork by the author.

20. Figure 7.13 is original artwork by the author.

21. Figure 7.14 is original artwork by the author.

22. Figure 7.15 is original artwork by the author.

23. Figure 7.16 is original artwork by the author.

24. Figure 7.17 is original artwork by the author.

25. Figure 7.18 is original artwork by the author.

26. Figure 7.19 is original artwork by the author.
27. Figure 7.20 is original artwork by the author.
28. Figure 7.21 is original artwork by the author.
29. Figure 7.22 is original artwork by the author.
30. Figure 7.23 is original artwork by the author. To derive the number of required combinations, we need to use the following formulation:

$$x = n!/(r!(n-r)!)$$

Where: x = number of combinations
n = no. of types from which to choose
r = number of variables chosen

For the cases at hand (1 engine and 2 engine configurations),

x = 4!/(2!(4-2)!) = 24/4 = 6 (for each configuration, or 12 for both configurations)

Since
4 = n (height, range, pass, MPH)
2 = r (two variables combined)

CHAPTER 8

1. Figure 8.1 is original artwork by the author.
2. Figure 8.2 picture of an archer retrieved June 2, 2023, from https://en.wikipedia.org/wiki/File:WA_target_shot_with_a_compound_bow_%28Devizes_Bowmen%29.jpg
3. Problems in external ballistics retrieved January 7, 2016, from https://en.wikipedia.org/wiki/External_ballistics#Gyroscopic_drift_.28Spin_drift.29
4. Bullseye in Figure 8.3 retrieved January 9, 2016, from Belk, Jim, July 27, 2007, https://en.wikipedia.org/wiki/File:Colored_Bullseye.png
5. Elevation, Azimuth, and error triangle artwork added to Figure 8.3 by the author.
6. Figure 8.4 Battlefield picture from Aitken, *Tom*, 1916, retrieved January 10, 2016, from http://rarehistoricalphotos.com/shells-creeping-bombardment-on-german-lines-1916
7. Curtis C-1 Canada Bomber, retrieved June 3, 2023, from https://commons.wikimedia.org/wiki/File:Curtiss_C-1_Canada_bomber_Aircraft_of_the_First_World_War_Q33818_%28cropped%29.jpg
8. Figure 8.5 is a photo of a pilot in an entirely intact Caudron G.3 retrieved January 10, 2016, from http://www.airminded.net/caug3/CaudronGIII.jpg
9. Figure 8.6 is a family photograph from the author's collection that shows his grandfather, Everett Howarth, a member of the US Expeditionary Force sent to France in World War I, sitting in the cockpit of his Caudron G.3 after a mission in which friendly fire hit and removed the aft section of the plane's fuselage.
10. From the front of the propeller to the back of the rear seat, the fuselage of the Caudron G.3 is about 8.2 feet, as calculated by this drawing retrieved January 10, 2016, from http://www.theaerodrome.com/forum/showthread.php?t=19783

11. Specifications for the Caudron G.3, retrieved January 10, 2016, from https://en.wikipedia.org/wiki/Caudron_G.3#Survivors

12. Caudron G.3 photograph, retrieved January 10, 2016, in Figure 8.7 from https://www.pinterest.com/ne912/aircraft-of-world-war-1/

13. Original artwork in Figure 8.7 from the author.

14. Database available by request from the author.

15. Figure 8.8 artwork originates from the author. Note that with more than three independent valued features considered, we express the miss as a Tailed Value Error Tetrahedron. Details about that will come in a follow-up book.

16. Original artwork in Figure 8.9 from the author based on the database mentioned in preceding note 14.

17. Original artwork in Figure 8.10 from the author based on the database mentioned in preceding note 14.

18. Figure 8.11 is a photo of Drew Brees and Larry Fitzgerald retrieved June 4, 2023, from https://commons.wikimedia.org/wiki/File:New_Orleans_Saints_quarterback_Drew_Brees,_left,_prepares_to_throw_the_ball_to_Arizona_Cardinals_wide_receiver_Larry_Fitzgerald_during_pregame_warm_up_for_the_National_Football_League%27s_2012_Pro_Bowl_game_120129-M-DX861-033.jpg

19. Ball sequence in Figure 8.12 retrieved June 4, 2023, from https://commons.wikimedia.org/wiki/File:Ball_in_and_out_of_play_2.svg

20. Figure 8.13 is original artwork by the author, based on the Electric Car Database previously mentioned.

21. In 2012, after an initial amount of $3,423, each added horsepower commanded $95 from the market, while each added mile of range fetched $218.

22. We did not know this surface at the time, and the depiction here is entirely notional and for instructional purposes only.

23. Figure 8.14 is original artwork by the author, based on the previously mentioned Electric Car Database. The producer cost surfaces are entirely notional.

24. In 2013, after an initial outlay of $6,488, each added horsepower retrieved $102 from the market, while each added mile of range garnered $172.

25. The 2013 Cost Response Surface, at the bottom of the 2013 Financial Opportunity Space, is entirely notional.

CHAPTER 9

1. Picture of Key Lime pie in Figure 9.1 retrieved June 5, 2023, from https://commons.wikimedia.org/wiki/File:Key_Lime_Pie_in_aluminum_pie_plate,_September_2008.jpg

2. For a cylinder, $V = \pi r^2 h$, where V = volume of the cylinder, r = radius of the cylinder, and h = height of the cylinder.

3. The unit of measure here is not critical; we use one foot as it will fit nicely into the House of Elvis later in the chapter.

4. Data from CIA World Fact Book, retrieved January 17, 2016, from https://www.cia.gov/library/publications/the-world-factbook/geos/xx.html.

5. The chart in Figure 9.2 drawn by the author, using the data in preceding note 4.

6. Map of Antarctica in Figure 9.3 retrieved January 17, 2016, from http://www.businessgreen.com/bg/news/2422000/planet-racking-up-climate-debt-after-earth-overshoot-day-is-reached

7. If GDP, and r = 1, then $r^2 = 1$, $\pi r^2 = \pi$, height = \$78.28 trillion/π = 249,173 miles.

8. The Moon's maximum distance from Earth is about 406,700 kilometers or 252,712 miles. The Moon never appears directly over either pole. For more Moon facts, see https://en.wikipedia.org/wiki/Moon

9. Figure 9.4 artwork is original and done by the author.

10. Description of logarithms taken from this article, retrieved January 18, 2016, https://en.wikipedia.org/wiki/Logarithm

11. \$78,280,000,000,000 / π = \$24,917,297,890,467; Log (24,917,297,890,467) = \$13.3965. Alternatively, in reverse, $10^{13.3965}$ = \$24,917,297,890,467 * π = \$78,280,000,000,000.

12. *Rolodex* definition retrieved January 19, 2016, from https://en.wikipedia.org/wiki/Rolodex

13. Rolodex picture in Figure 9.6 retrieved June 5 5, 2023, from https://commons.wikimedia.org/wiki/File:Rolodex%E2%84%A2_67236_Rotary_Business_Card_File.jpg

14. The picture in Figure 9.7 was one of the author's wife, Jackie, taken 16 October 2023, at the The Crazy Horse Memorial in the Black Hills, in Custer County, South Dakota, United States, and is used with her permission. The posters describe monument's progress.

15. Original artwork added to Figure 9.7 by the author.

16. Figure 9.8 map retrieved June 6, 2023, from https://commons.wikimedia.org/wiki/File:Antarctica_major_geographical_features.jpg, which came from this source file http://lima.nasa.gov/antarctica/

17. Original artwork added to Figure 9.8 map by the author.

18. Online program to compute the distance from latitude and longitude retrieved January 17, 2016, from http://www.stevemorse.org/nearest/distance.php

19. Extendable mirror pictures in Figure 9.9 retrieved January 20, 2016, from https://en.wikipedia.org/wiki/Pantograph#/media/File:Pantograph_Mirror.gif

20. Original artwork added to Figure 9.9 by the author.

21. Pantograph description retrieved January 20, 2016, from https://en.wikipedia.org/wiki/Pantograph

22. In 1965, Jackie DeShannon sang a song with Hal David lyrics and Burt Bacharach's music entitled "What the World Needs Now Is Love." *For more about this song, see this link* retrieved January 20, 2016, from https://en.wikipedia.org/wiki/What_the_World_Needs_Now_Is_Love

23. Original artwork in Figure 9.10 by the author.

24. Original artwork in Figure 9.11 by the author.

25. Original artwork in Figure 9.12 by the author.

26. Original artwork in Figure 9.13 by the author.

27. Original artwork in Figure 9.14 by the author.

28. Original artwork in Figure 9.15 by the author.

29. Original artwork in Figure 9.16 by the author.

30. Original artwork in Figure 9.17 by the author.

31. Original artwork in Figure 9.18 by the author. The formula for determining the number of dimensions required to display any number of markets is:

$$D = 3n+1$$

  Where: D = number of dimensions required to display the markets in consideration

      n = number of markets considered

32. Wireframe diagram for Figure 9.19 retrieved June 7, 2023, from https://commons.wikimedia.org/wiki/File:Latitude_and_Longitude_of_the_Earth.svg
33. Overlaid lines in Figure 9.19 by the author.
34. Figure 9.20 is original artwork by the author.
35. Figure 9.21 is original artwork by the author.
36. Figure 9.22 is original artwork by the author.
37. Figure 9.23 is original artwork by the author.
38. Figure 9.24 is original artwork by the author.
39. From the geometry that we have in Figure 9.21, if we zoom in, we see

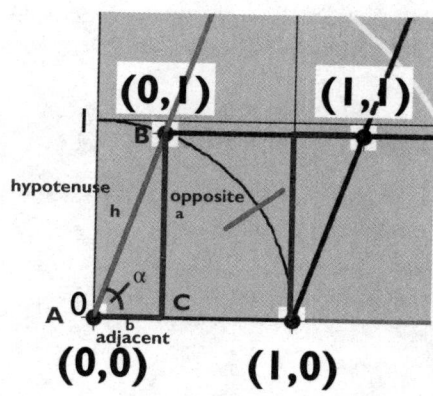

Sin (70°) = opposite/hypotenuse = 0.9397
For a right triangle, from the Pythagorean Theorem:

$$a^2 + b^2 = h^2;$$

thus for the case at hand, with h = 1:

$$0.9397^2 + b^2 = 1^2$$
$$b^2 = 0.117$$
$$b = 0.342$$

So, the new position for (0.1) at 70° is (0.342, 0.9397)

The same trigonometry can be applied to new point denoted (1,1), which, since it also has a "link" of 1 unit from (0,1), which, therefore means that (1,1) at 70° is (1.342. 0.9397)

In Microsoft Excel, if the origin is (0,0), then the values for (1,1) for a given angle are:

For x:	x = x value + y value * (COS (PI()/180 * Angle in Degrees)
For x=0, y=1, ∠ = 90°	x = 0 + 1*(COS (PI()/180 * 90) = 0 + 0 = 0
For y:	y = y value *(SIN (PI()/180 * Angle in Degrees)
For x=0, y=1, ∠ = 90°	y = 1 * ((SIN (PI()/180 * 90) = 1 * 1 = 1
For x:	x = x value + y value * (COS (PI()/180 * Angle in Degrees)
For x=0, y=1, ∠ = 70°	x = 0 + 1*(COS (PI()/180 * 70) = 0 + 0.342 = 0.342

For y: y = y value *(SIN (PI()/180 * Angle in Degrees)
For x=0, y=1, ∠ = 70°   y = 1 * ((SIN (PI()/180 * 70) = 0.940
For x: x = x value + y value * (COS (PI()/180 * Angle in
                     Degrees)
For x=1, y=1, ∠ = 70°   x = 1 + 1*(COS (PI()/180 * 70) = 1 + 0.342 = 1.342
For y: y = y value *(SIN (PI()/180 * Angle in Degrees)
For x=1, y=1, ∠ = 70°   y = 1 * ((SIN (PI()/180 * 70) = 0.940

In Cartesian space, with 90° angles between horizontal and vertical axes, the horizontal distance between (0,1) and (1,1) is 1 since the heights are unchanged. Previously, we discovered that with the Angle set to 70°, the "x" position of (0,1) was 0.342. Then, while the "y" position was 0.940, and for (1,1), the "x" position was 1.342, while the "y" was still 0.940, meaning the horizontal distance between (0,1) and (1,1) was unchanged.

40. Figure 9.25 is original artwork from the author.
41. Figure 9.26 is original artwork from the author.
42. Figure 9.27 is original artwork from the author.
43. Figure 9.28 is original artwork from the author.
44. We have some math to do to find the positions of all points, which we explain here:

What was once x is now y. As we go from Market 1 to Market 1, the y-axis from Market 1 (Y_{PP1} in green) forms the basis for the x-axis in Market 2 (X_{PP2} in white). Value axes abutting one another swap "x" and "y" values as we know them in the Cartesian sense. For example, the ordered pair in Market 1 denoted by (0,1) is immediately adjacent to the Market 2 ordered pair (1,0), just as the ordered pair (0,2) in Market 1 abuts the ordered pair (2,0) in Market 2, as shown in A.

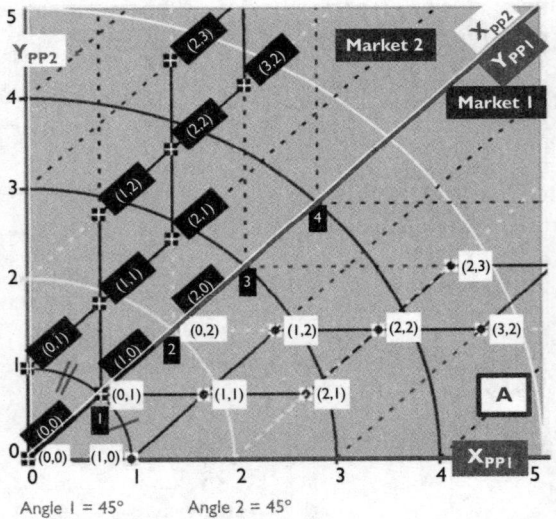

Angle 1 = 45°   Angle 2 = 45°

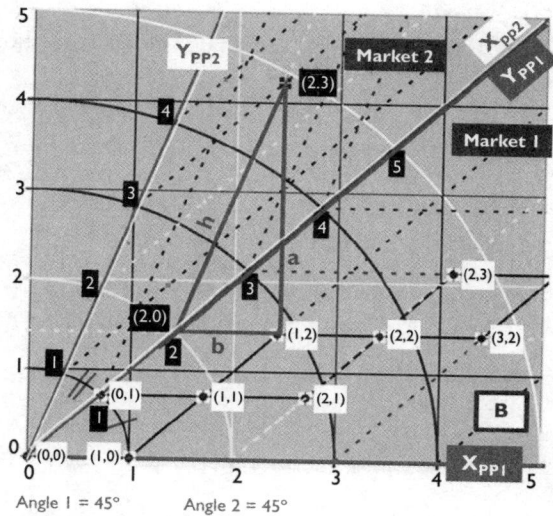

This pattern in A repeats for all markets adjacent to one another. Figuring out position with multiple instantiations of Polar Parallel Coordinates involves some analytic geometry and trigonometry, as shown in B.

Angle 1 = 45°   Angle 2 = 45°

To calculate the Cartesian position in Market 2, we need to begin with a point of reference. The Market 1 "y-axis," or the Market 2 "x-axis," the dividing line between Markets 1 and 2, the 45° line, is useful here. We call the first Angle (relating to Market 1), or Angle 1, θ_1, and the second Angle (relating to Market 2), or Angle 2, θ_2. We additionally call the Polar Parallel coordinates in Market 1 (x_{pp1}, y_{pp1}) and those in Market 2 (x_{pp1}, y_{pp1}). We can derive the Cartesian Coordinates for Polar Parallel values in Market 2, beginning with the values from this dividing line. If we call the Cartesian Coordinates relating to Market 1 (x_{c1}, y_{c1}) as well, recall that within Market 1

$$x_{c1} = x_{pp1} + y_{pp1} * Cos\theta_1$$
$$y_{c1} = y_{pp1} * Sin\theta_1$$

In Market 2, we use these equations to derive the Cartesian coordinates that we denote (x_{c2}, y_{c2})

$$x_{c2} = x_{c1} + y_{pp2} * Cos\ (\theta_1 + \theta_2)$$
$$y_{c2} = y_{c1} + y_{pp2} * sin\ (\theta_1 + \theta_2)$$

Consider point (2,3) in Market 2. We can observe that its "x" value in the Cartesian system lies between 2 and 3 while its "y" Cartesian value is between 4 and 5. These equations call for selecting x and y coordinates from Market 1. We start from (0,2) in Market 1 (which is (2,0) in Market 2) since these form a common point of reference between each zone and lie on the parallel gridline for the "x" term in Market 2. For (0,2) as our ordered pair in Market 1, with a Market 1 angle of 45°, using our Market 1 equations, we find that

$$x_{c1} = x_{pp1} + y_{pp1} * Cos\theta_1$$

$$x_{c1} = 0 + 2 * (Cos\ 45°) = 0 + 2 * 0.7071 = 1.4142$$

$$y_{c1} = y_{pp1} * Sin\theta_1$$

$$y_{c1} = 2 * (0.7071) = 1.4142$$

Now, with the Cartesian coordinates for Market 1 at (0,2) established as (1.4142,1.4142), we can find the values for (2,3) in Market 2 using these equations

$$x_{c2} = x_{c1} + y_{pp2} * Cos\ (\theta_1 + \theta_2)$$

$$x_{c2} = 1.4142 + 3 * Cos\ (45° + 25°)$$

$$x_{c2} = 1.4142 + 3 * 0.342 = 2.4402$$

$$y_{c2} = y_{c1} + y_{pp2} * sin\ (\theta_1 + \theta_2)$$

$$y_{c2} = 1.4142 * 3 * sin\ (45° + 25°)$$

$$y_{c2} = 1.4142 + 3 * 0.9397 = 4.2333$$

Thus, the Cartesian coordinates for (2,3) in Market 2 with an angle of 25°, given that the Angle in Market 1 is 45°, is (2.4402, 4.2333), and given that our Cartesian starting point is (0,0).

45. Figure 9.29 is original artwork from the author, using data retrieved from the later citations.
46. The Aerospace Industries Association, or AIA, estimated that in 2014, the civil market reached $240.4 billion, in a document retrieved January 30, 2016, from http://www.aia-aerospace.org/assets/2014_AIA_Annual_report_web.pdf
47. The total of 5,063 planes comes from Airbus (635 units), Boeing (762 units), and the General Aviation Manufacturers Association (3,666 units). Airbus, retrieved January 30, 2016, from http://www.airbus.com/company/market/orders-deliveries/
48. Boeing deliveries retrieved January 30, 2016, from http://atwonline.com/manufacturers/boeing-commercial-aircraft-deliveries-54-2015
49. General aviation deliveries retrieved from January 30, 2016, http://www.gama.aero/media-center/industry-facts-and-statistics/shipment-database?page=show_year&tab=year&type1=all&year=2014&quarter=1&type=all&comp_id=&submit=Go Note that this may exclude some regional jets
50. American Champion model Champ retrieved September 1, 2015, from http://www.americanchampionaircraft.com/champ.html
51. Airbus A380 price retrieved January 30, 2016, from http://www.aviationbusinessme.com/gallery/2014/jan/14/321080/#a380-800-new-price-us-4144-million-about-the-largest-commercial-airplane-in-operation-carries-525-passengers-in

52. Ibid.
53. The Citation X is the fastest plane, with speeds up to 617 miles per hour, as indicated by this article retrieved January 30, 2016, from http://www.paramount-businessjets.com/blog/2015/01/worlds-5-fastest-jets/
54. Figure 9.30 is original artwork from the author, using data retrieved from later citations.
55. Data retrieved January 31, 2016, from https://pressroom.ups.com/pressroom/ContentDetailsViewer.page?ConceptType=FactSheets&id=1426321563187-193
56. Data retrieved January 31, 2016, from http://cars.about.com/od/helpforcarbuyers/tp/Cheapest_09.htm
57. Data retrieved January 31, 2016, from http://www.thesupercars.org/top-cars/most-expensive-cars-in-the-world-top-10-list-2007-2008/
58. The exact weight limit would be the most significant number posted by the logistics company willing to take the most considerable load. This requires analysis of all shippers. The author did not do that but instead took a limit reflective of UPS and FedEx rate schedules.
59. In round numbers, halfway around the planet is 12,000 miles, which forms a theoretical limit on the distances that packages can travel.
60. Data retrieved January 31, 2016, from http://www.beefretail.org/CMDocs/BeefRetail2/Sales%20Data/Sales%20Featuring/nov-2015-retail-beef-performance.pdf
61. Data retrieved January 31, 2016, from http://www.wcpo.com/money/consumer/dont-waste-your-money/who-has-the-lowest-turkey-price-this-year
62. Data retrieved January 31, 2016, from http://www.rakuten.com/prod/wagyu-rib-eye-ms8-whole-cut-to-order/288875903.html?listingId=469068263&sclid=pla_google_GourmetFoodStore&adid=29963&rmatt=tsid:1012713%7ccid:247411609%7cagid:14868890329%7ctid:pla-125916169729%7ccrid:60879544129%7cnw:g%7crnd:5450091563032521415%7cdvc:c%7cadp:1o5&gclid=CjwKEAiAuKy1BRCY5bTuvPeopXcSJAAq4OVs0EIwurXSFzLhSInuroczPHnqFHrlZgftaD6lKi7jqhoCFDXw_wcB
63. Data retrieved January 31, 2016, from http://www.ams.usda.gov/mnreports/lm_xb403.txt
64. Data retrieved January 31, 2016, from http://www.sparkpeople.com/myspark/Calorie_Finder.asp?FoodID=5640907
65. Data retrieved January 31, 2016, from http://www.oica.net/category/production-statistics/
66. Data retrieved January 31, 2016, from http://auto.ndtv.com/news/2015-tata-genx-nano-launched-prices-start-at-rs-199-lakh-764296 using currency conversions retrieved January 29, 2016, from http://www.oanda.com/currency/converter/
67. Data retrieved January 31, 2016, from http://www.abcnewspoint.com/top-10-most-expensive-cars-in-the-world-2015/
68. Data retrieved January 31, 2016, from http://www.cheatsheet.com/automobiles/the-koenigsegg-regera-is-the-most-powerful-production-car-ever.html/?a=viewall

69. Data retrieved January 31, 2016, from http://www.forbes.com/pictures/ehmk45eegem/1-bmw-i3/
70. An estimate by the author, based on his data, available on request.
71. Data retrieved January 31, 2016, from http://www.chevrolet.com/spark-ev-electric-vehicle.html
72. Data retrieved January 31, 2016, from http://www.abcnewspoint.com/top-10-most-expensive-cars-in-the-world-2015/
73. Data retrieved January 31, 2016, from http://www.usatoday.com/story/money/cars/2014/10/11/tesla-p85d-price-performance/17098819/
74. Ibid.
75. Figure 9.31 is artwork created by the author.

CHAPTER 10

1. The Amazon home website, retrieved on February 3, 2016, is http://www.amazon.com/
2. For a description of Amazon, see this site retrieved February 3, 2016, https://en.wikipedia.org/wiki/Amazon.com
3. Sales rank data for Amazon Retrieved February 3, 2016, https://thewriteagenda.wordpress.com/2011/11/22/blogger-gets-it-wrong-amazon-sales-rankings-are-valuable-metrics-if-benchmarked-over-time/
4. Data retrieved on February 3, 2016, from www.Amazon.com
5. To convert to sales per week, we use this equation:

$$\text{Sales/week} = e^{\,(10.526-(.87*\text{Ln(sales rank)}))}$$

   The author retrieved the equation above on February 3, 2016, from The Write Agenda, op. cit.
6. Database in Table 10.2 derived by the author in June 2013 *from* www.Amazon.com
7. Detailed information about Table 10.2 data is available on request.
8. Figure 10.1 is original artwork by the author.
9. Figure 10.2 is original artwork by the author.
10. Figure 10.3 is original artwork by the author, and the equation is

$$\text{Aggregate Demand} = 56.5\,\text{Quantity}^{-0.623}$$

   This equation has an Adjusted R2 of 85.7%, a *p*-value of 0.02, and no bias.
11. Figure 10.4 is original artwork by the author.
12. When we do this analysis, we get an equation for value which is

$$\text{Price} = 3.06\text{E-07} * \text{Pages}^{0.607} * \text{Sqr. In.}^{3.37} * \text{Sales}^{-0.161} * (\text{P-back} =1, \text{H-back}=2)^{0.577}$$

   Where: Price = Sustainable price for the manual, in 2013 U.S. Dollars
           Pages = number of pages in the manual
           Sqr In. = Manual page height x page width in square inches

Sales = Estimated sales per year for manual
Paperback =1, Hardback = 2 = Step function for binding method

With the *p*-values for the independent variables = 2.27E-05, 2.35E-02, 3.21-E02, 4.31E-02, respectively, while the Adjusted R^2 for the equation is 64.5%, with F-Stat 1.31E-09, and the Mean Absolute Percentage Error (MAPE) is 43.1%.

13. Figure 10.5 is original artwork by the author. The equation for the Demand Frontier is

$$\text{Demand Frontier} = 6990 \text{Quantity}^{-1.06}$$

This equation has the bias removed and correlates to 90.8%.

14. 500 * 65 = 32,500.

15. 32,500 / 99.2 = 328.

16. In our first example, which we will call *Case 1*, we have 500 pages, 65 square inches per page, and a paperback with a target of 100 units sold yearly. This works out as follows:

$$\text{Price} = 3.06\text{E-}07 * \text{Pages}^{0.607} * \text{Sqr. In.}^{3.37} * \text{Sales}^{-0.161} * (\text{P-back} =1, \text{H-back=2})^{0.577}$$
$$= 3.06\text{E-}07 * 500^{0.607} * 65^{3.37} * 100^{-0.161} * 1^{0.577}$$
$$= \$9.45$$

In *Case 2*, we have 328 pages, 99.2 square inches per page, a paperback, and 100 copies:

$$\text{Price} = 3.06\text{E-}07 * \text{Pages}^{0.607} * \text{Sqr. In.}^{3.37} * \text{Sales}^{-0.161} * (\text{P-back} =1, \text{H-back=2})^{0.577}$$
$$= 3.06\text{E-}07 * 328^{0.607} * 99.2^{3.37} * 100^{-0.161} * 1^{0.577}$$
$$= \$30.33$$

17. Christmann, Bethany, "Why Fruit Flies Are a Good Model Organism for Research," *Brandeis University blog post, August* 1, 2014, retrieved February 6, 2016, from http://blogs.brandeis.edu/flyonthewall/fly-life-why-fruit-flies-are-a-good-model-organism-for-research/

18. Figure 10.6 is original artwork by the author.

19. Figure 10.7 is original artwork by the author.

20. Figure 10.8 is original artwork by the author.

21. Figure 10.9 is original artwork by the author.

CHAPTER 11

1. Figure 11-1 is original artwork done by the author, originally created for Howarth, Douglas K., "8D Cost Trades with Entanglement," *Journal of Cost Analysis and Parametrics*, vol. 11, no. 1, April 2023, pp. 70–88, ISSN: 2160-4746, retrieved June 12, 2023, from chrome-extension://efaidnbmnnnibpca-jpcglclefindmkaj/https://www.iceaaonline.com/wp-content/uploads/2023/04/JCAPv11i1042423.pdf

2. For more about battery characteristics, see this link retrieved August 26, 2016, from http://www.mpoweruk.com/performance.htm

3. Cleanup of the Exide lead contamination case in Southern California will likely take years and hundreds of millions of dollars. For more information, see this link retrieved August 26, 2016, from https://en.wikipedia.org/wiki/Exide_lead_contamination

4. Tesla used Panasonic to provide most of its batteries but used a couple of new suppliers, LG Chem and Samsung SDI, for its Roadster 3.0. See this link retrieved August 26, 2016, from https://electrek.co/2016/06/02/tesla-sourcing-battery-cells-samsung/

5. Tesla and Panasonic have partnered on the largest battery factory in the world. See this retrieved August 26, 2016, from http://www.nbcnews.com/tech/innovation/tesla-opens-gigafactory-expand-battery-production-sales-n617676

6. Figure 11-2 is original artwork done by the author, using data about the COVID-19 epidemic available at that time.

CHAPTER 12

1. Barbra Streisand had a hit record entitled "People" in 1964. See this link retrieved 19 October 2016, from https://en.wikipedia.org/wiki/Barbra_Streisand#Discography

2. Hypernomics, Inc. is the author's company, for which he is their Chief Executive Officer. MEE4D™ is its proprietary software, for which the United States Patent and Trademark Office (USPTO) issued Shad Torgerson, Kent Joris, and Doug Howarth U.S. Patent 10,402,378, chrome-extension://efaidnbmnnnibpcajpcgl-clefindmkaj/https://image-ppubs.uspto.gov/dirsearch-public/print/download-Pdf/10402838

3. If you want electricity or natural gas market information specifically, go to this link retrieved November 8, 2016, from http://www.eia.gov/electricity/wholesale/

4. You can find HUD homes for sale from this site, retrieved November 8, 2016, from http://www.hudhomestore.com/Home/Index.aspx

5. The U.S. Department of Commerce runs the Bureau of Economic Analysis (BEA), which puts out this site for local GDP, retrieved November 8, 2016, from http://www.bea.gov/newsreleases/regional/gdp_metro/gdp_metro_news-release.htm

6. The U.S. Army has payment information on this site, retrieved November 8, 2016, from http://www.goarmy.com/benefits/money/basic-pay-active-duty-soldiers.html

7. The Defense Manpower Data Center, an arm of the DOD, maintains personnel totals by rank and grade at this site, retrieved November 8, 2016, from https://www.dmdc.osd.mil/appj/dwp/dwp_reports.jsp

8. Data retrieved November 7, 2016, from https://en.wikipedia.org/wiki/New_York_Stock_Exchange

9. Figure 12.1 is original artwork by the author.

10. Figure 12.2 is original artwork by the author. This fund is not open to the public currently. Past results are no guarantee of future returns.

11. *Flying* magazine is a good source here; the link retrieved November 9, 2016 from http://www.flyingmag.com/

12. Another excellent resource is *Aviation Week*, a link retrieved November 9, 2016 from http://aviationweek.com/

13. Another site to consider when chasing information on business jets is the Robb Report, a link retrieved November 9, 2016 from http://robbreport.com/

14. The civil aviation community has an organization, the General Aviation Manufacturers Association (GAMA), which compiles most of the delivery dates for the industry for no cost to its users, as shown in this link retrieved November 10, 2016, from https://www.gama.aero/media-center/industry-facts-and-statistics

15. Jane's Information Group (commonly referred to as "Jane's") provides detailed accounts of aircraft model histories, including deliveries. Their services are fee-based, as shown in this link retrieved November 9, 2016, from http://www.janes.com/

16. As pointed out by this link retrieved November 9, 2016, from https://en.wikipedia.org/wiki/Aircraft_registration, "In accordance with the Convention on International Civil Aviation (also known as the Chicago Convention), all civil aircraft must be registered with a national aviation authority (NAA) using procedures set by each country." Governments provide online tools to track the numbers issued in their respective countries. Using these sources, one can trace how many planes of each type are registered worldwide over time.

17. Figure 12.3 is original artwork by the author. The numbers in Figure 12.3 could be entirely notional, and they would still suit our purpose for a case study. In this case, we used the suppliers' site for the specifications and various magazine articles to get prices. GAMA provided the quantities sold, though they provided information about the Gulfstream line as a group and not individually. The author prorated the Gulfstream sales by Price, which is a valid approximation. A more detailed examination would require studying tail number data recorded by the Federal Aviation Administration (FAA). The balance of Figure 12.3 database is on the author's website, along with the MEE4D software to run it. You can find it here: www.doughowarth.com

18. The author created Figure 12.4 with MEE4D, used with permission from Hypernomics, Inc. The MEE4D template conditions data from Excel into MEE4D. Primarily, it checks for two things. First, it checks to confirm that there is data in every cell. If data is missing, the program will flag it. Second, it verifies that the data types (the last row in blue in Figure 12.4) match every data element in the column below. If there is a mismatch, such as calling something a "float" variable, which deals with numbers, for one of the model names, which is a "char" (short for the character) variable (a common error in Excel), here, too, the template will call it out. The template lists the errors on a second sheet, showing the cell for each one, and describes each one separately, thus giving users a quick way to fix them.

19. The author created Figure 12.5 with MEE4D, used with permission from Hypernomics, Inc.

20. The author created Figure 12.6 with MEE4D, used with permission from Hypernomics, Inc.
21. R^2 is the coefficient of determination. It shows the portion of the variability in the model's data set. As the R^2 approaches 1, the correlation improves.
22. The Adjusted R^2 adjusts the R^2 to account for added explanatory variables added to a model. It is always less than or equal to the R^2. For more on this statistic, see https://en.wikipedia.org/wiki/Coefficient_of_determination
23. Pearson's[2] is an alternative measure of the coefficient of determination. For more, see https://en.wikipedia.org/wiki/Coefficient_of_determination
24. The Coefficient of Variation, or CV, is the standard deviation divided by the mean of the dataset, expressed as a ratio. The closer this ratio is to zero, the better the model's fit. For more, see https://en.wikipedia.org/wiki/Coefficient_of_variation
25. The Mean Average Percentage Error, or MAPE, may be considered the "average miss" of the model about the data. The closer the MAPE is to zero, the better the fit of its associated model. For more on this, see https://en.wikipedia.org/wiki/Mean_absolute_percentage_error
26. The F-Test, or F-Stat, is the explained variance ratio to the unexplained variance from the data model. For more, see https://en.wikipedia.org/wiki/F-test
27. The p-value is a number that reflects the chance that the independent variable affected the dependent variable due to chance. If the p-value is sufficiently low (a typical threshold might be 0.05 or less), the chances are high that this independent variable influenced the dependent variable. Therefore, we can reject the null hypothesis (the null hypothesis is that the independent variable did not affect the dependent variable). For more, see https://en.wikipedia.org/wiki/P-value
28. The Standard Deviation is a measure of the dispersion of a data set. Smaller is better here for modeling purposes. For more, see https://en.wikipedia.org/wiki/Standard_deviation
29. Figure 12.7 is a full regression result report created by the author using MEE4D.
30. Hu, Shu-Ping, "The Impact of Using Log-Error CERS Outside the Data Range and Ping Factor," International Society of Parametric Analysts (ISPA)/Society of Cost Estimating Analysts (SCEA) 2005 Joint Conference Technical Paper, https://www.aceit.com/Pages/Content/ContentPage.aspx?id=a85f2104-c734-4663-930f-def4597fe31f. Not using the Ping Factor here results in a constant value of 0.0805929, which is the Value that you would get if you used, say, Microsoft Excel to perform a linear analysis of the natural logs of the original values. The Ping Factor recognizes a downward bias in log form estimates and corrects it with that factor. In this instance, the Ping Factor is 1.029, which, when multiplied times the baseline constant of 3.54903e-05, yields an adjusted constant of 3.6514e-05. This factor falls as the baseline correlation improves.
31. The author created Figure 12.8 using MEE4D.
32. The author created Figure 12.9 using MEE4D.
33. The author created Figure 12.10 using MEE4D.

34. The author created Figure 12.11 using MEE4D.
35. The author created Figure 12.12 using MEE4D.
36. The author created Figure 12.13 using MEE4D.
37. Figure 12.14 is from Kambui, June 2004. retrieved June 17, 2023, from https://commons.wikimedia.org/wiki/File:Switzerland_-_Air_Force_Pilatus_PC-6-B2-H2M-1_Turbo_Porter_V-614_%2822721943198%29.jpg
38. Howarth, Douglas K., "VSTOL Market Analysis," February 1, 2009, *The Aeronautical Journal*, vol. 113, no. 1140, pp. 107–118.
39. The author created Figure 12.15 in Microsoft Excel using the statistical results from MEE4D.
40. The author created Figure 12.16 in Microsoft Excel using the statistical results from MEE4D.
41. The author created Figure 12.17 in Microsoft Excel using the statistical results from MEE4D.
42. The author created Figure 12.18 in Microsoft Excel using the statistical results from MEE4D.
43. The author created Figure 12.19 in Microsoft Excel using the statistical results from MEE4D.
44. The author created Figure 12.20 in Microsoft Excel using the statistical results from MEE4D.
45. Data on A220-100 business jet schedule retrieved June 19, 2023, from https://en.wikipedia.org/wiki/Airbus_A220
46. A220-100 list price data from https://infogram.com/bca-table-2023-jets-1ho16vorwrp8x4n, which, in turn, was retrieved June 18, 2023 from https://en.wikipedia.org/wiki/Airbus_Corporate_Jets#cite_note-BCA-PPH-2023-18
47. Salard, Eric, April 16, 2015, retrieved June 20, 2023, from https://commons.wikimedia.org/wiki/Category:Boeing_737-800#/media/File:American_Airlines,_Boeing_737-823(WL),_N969AN_-_LAX_(22300501588).jpg, which, in turn, was originally posted to Flickr by airlines470 at https://flickr.com/photos/16103393@N05/22300501588. It was reviewed on October 31, 2015 by FlickreviewR and was confirmed to be licensed under the terms of the cc-by-sa-2.0.
48. Terekhov, Dmitry, September 25, 2010. They were retrieved on June 20, 2023, from https://commons.wikimedia.org/wiki/File:Tupolev_Tu-204-300_(5041654601).jpg, which was originally posted to Flickr by Dmitry Terekhov at https://www.flickr.com/photos/44400809@N07/5041654601. It was reviewed on January 26, 2015 by FlickreviewR and was confirmed to be licensed under the terms of the cc-by-sa-2.0.
49. Figure 12.23 is artwork done by the author for Hypernomics, Inc., and used with its permission.

Index